J W Masters
Galesburg
Ill

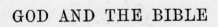

GOD AND THE BIBLE

GOD & THE BIBLE

A REVIEW OF
OBJECTIONS TO 'LITERATURE & DOGMA'

BY

MATTHEW ARNOLD

FORMERLY PROFESSOR OF POETRY IN THE UNIVERSITY OF OXFORD
AND FELLOW OF ORIEL COLLEGE

New York
MACMILLAN AND CO.
1883

"Im Princip, das Bestehende zu erhalten, Revolutionären vorzubeugen, stimme ich ganz mit den Monarchisten überein; nur nicht in den Mitteln dazu. Sie nämlich rufen die Dummheit und die Finsterniss zu Hülfe, ich den Verstand und das Licht." GOETHE.

("In the principle, to preserve what exists, to hinder revolutionists from having their way, I am quite at one with the monarchists; only not in the means thereto. That is to say, they call in stupidity and darkness to aid, I reason and light.")

Printed by R. & R. CLARK, *Edinburgh*.

PREFACE.

In reading through the following chapters, I see that the faults, as I think them, of German critics of the Bible are marked with an emphasis which renders necessary some acknowledgment of the other, the meritorious, side in those critics, and of the much gratitude due to them. Their criticism, both negative and constructive, appears to me to be often extremely fanciful and untrustworthy. But in collecting, editing, and illustrating the original documents for the history of Christianity, those critics now perform for the benefit of learning an honourable and extremely useful labour, once discharged by Paris, Oxford, and Cambridge, but discharged by them no longer;—perform it with modern resources, and for the most part admirably. Some of them are men of great ability. Ferdinand Christian Baur, whose theories respecting the Fourth Gospel are controverted in the following pages, was a man of pre-eminent ability. His exegesis is often full of instruction and of light. Whoever wishes to be convinced of it has only to turn to his remarks on the phrase *poor in spirit*,[1] or to his

---

[1] *Geschichte der christlichen Kirche*, vol. i. p. 26.

exposition of the parable of the unjust steward.[1]
Nevertheless Baur is, on the whole, an unsafe guide,
for a reason which makes the generality of critics of
the Bible, in the Protestant faculties of theology in
Germany, unsafe guides. These professors are under
strong temptations to produce new theories in Biblical
criticism, theories marked by vigour and rigour ; and
for this purpose to assume that things can be known
which cannot, to treat possibilities as if they were
certainties, to make symmetry where one does not
find it, and so to land both the teacher, and the
learner who trusts to him, in the most fanciful and
unsound conclusions. There are few who do not
succumb to their temptations, and Baur, I think, has
succumbed to them.

Even while acknowledging the learning, talents,
and services of these critics, I insist upon their radical
faults ; because, as our traditional theology breaks up,
German criticism of the Bible is likely to be studied
here more and more, and to the untrained reader its
vigorous and rigorous theories are, in my opinion, a
real danger. They impose upon him by their bold-
ness and novelty. To his practical hold on the Bible
they conduce nothing, but rather divert from it ; and
yet they are often really farther from the truth, all
the while, than even the traditional view which they
profess to annihilate.

The alleged bitter hatred of St. Peter and the
other *pillar*-apostles against St. Paul, and St. Paul's

---

[1] *Kritische Untersuchungen über die kanonischen Evangelien*,
p. 450.

reciprocation of it, is a case in point. This hatred is supposed to have filled the first years of the Christian Church, and to give the clue to its history. The invectives in the Apocalypse against Balaam and his followers are said to be aimed at Paul and Pauline Christianity. The Simon Magus of the pseudo-Clementine Homilies is taken to be Paul, and Peter's unwearying war against Simon Magus and his false doctrine represents Peter's war against Paul.[1] The Acts, finally, are a late work designed to wipe out the memory of this hatred, and to invent a harmony between Paul and the pillar-apostles which never existed. Now, it is easy to dress up this theory so as to make it look plausible, but I entirely disbelieve its truth. To its vigorous and rigorous inventors the consideration that the nearness of the pillar-apostles to Jesus, and that the religious greatness of St. Paul, were good for very little if they could not so much as prevent a hatred of this kind, will probably appear quite insignificant; with me it has, I confess, serious weight. It would need plain and strong facts to make me accept, in despite of this consideration, the Tübingen theory. But no such facts are forthcoming.

The identification of the Balaam of the Apocalypse with Paul requires us first to assume that the Tübingen theory is true. Now, the evidence of Paul's own letters is against the theory. True, there was dif-

---

[1] Paul is, in fact, "der Apostate, der Irrlehrer, dessen als samaritanisische Ketzerei bezeichnetes falsches Evangelium höchst wahrscheinlich die Entstehung der ganzen Sage von dem Magier Simon veranlasst hat."—Baur, *Lehrbuch der christlichen Dogmengeschichte*, p. 65.

ference between him and the older Apostles respecting the obligation of the Jewish law. They were
narrower and more timid than he was, and he tells
us of his having once at Antioch "withstood Peter
to the face because he was to be blamed." But he
tells us, also, of his having come to a satisfactory
arrangement with the pillar-apostles, and of their
having "extended to him the right hand of fellow-
ship." The hardest word he has for them is to call
them "apostles exceedingly."[1] On the other hand,
quite distinct from the pillar-apostles whose action
it sought to force, is the real Judaising party whom
Paul stigmatised as "false brethren," and to whom
he "will not give place by subjection, no, not for an
hour."

Again, of real antinomianism in morals among his
Gentile converts Paul clearly saw the danger and
vehemently rebuked the symptoms. He discounte-
nanced, even, all unnecessary displays of liberalism
and of superiority to prejudice, which might offend
and do harm. Now, the Peter of the pseudo-Clementine Homilies controverts nothing that can be said to
be Pauline. But he attacks either Gnostic heresies,
or else that antinomianism in morals which is well
known to have been rife in some of the Gnostic sects.
True, he represents his profane opponents as question-
ing his authority, and as *withstanding* him ; and the
language which he attributes to them is undoubtedly
an adaptation of Paul's language in the Epistle to
the Galatians. This is the whole and sole foundation

---

[1] τῶν ὑπερλίαν ἀποστόλων. 2 Cor. xi. 5, and xii. 11.

of positive proof for the alleged hatred between Peter and Paul. But what could be more natural, than that the antinomian enemies of strictness of every kind should have possessed themselves of phrases of Paul, the great liberal, and above all should have possessed themselves of his famous rebuke of the narrower and more timid Peter, and turned it against whoever blamed and restrained them; and that such an employment and such employers of Paul's language are what the Peter of the Homilies has in view? For my part, I feel convinced that this is the true explanation, and that the plausible theory of the bitter and persistent hatred between St. Peter and St. Paul is quite erroneous. But if erroneous it is, how grave is the error! and in how serious a misconception of the beginnings of Christianity does it involve us! This must be my defence, if I appear to have dwelt too much on the untrustworthiness of the authors of this and similar theories, not enough on their learning and acuteness.

In revising the present volume, the suspicion and alarm which its contents, like those of its predecessor, will in some quarters excite, could not but be present to my mind. I hope, however, that I have at last made my aim clear, even to the most suspicious. Some of the comments on *Literature and Dogma* did, I own, surprise me, in spite of a tolerably long experience of men's propensity to mistake things. Again and again I was reproached with having done, in that book, just what I had formerly blamed the

Bishop of Natal for doing. But *Literature and Dogma* had altogether for its object, and so too has the present work, to show the truth and necessity of Christianity, and its power and charm for the heart, mind, and imagination of man, even though the preternatural, which is now its popular sanction, should have to be given up. To show this, was the end for which both books were written.

For the power of Christianity has been in the immense emotion which it has excited; in its engaging, for the government of man's conduct, the mighty forces of love, reverence, gratitude, hope, pity, and awe,—all that host of allies which Wordsworth includes under the one name of *imagination*, when he says that in the uprooting of old thoughts and old rules we must still always ask :—

> " Survives *imagination*, to the change
>   Superior ?   Help to virtue does she give ?
>   If not, O mortals, better cease to live ! "

Popular Christianity, drenched in the preternatural, has enjoyed abundantly this help of the imagination to virtue and conduct.   I have always thought, therefore, that merely to destroy the illusions of popular Christianity was indefensible.   Time, besides, was sure to do it; but when it is done, the whole work of again cementing the alliance between the imagination and conduct remains to be effected.   To those who effect nothing for the new alliance but only dissolve the old, we take once more our text from Wordsworth, and we say :—

> " Why with such earnest pains dost thou provoke
> The years to bring on the inevitable yoke,
> Thus blindly with man's blessedness at strife ?
> Full soon his soul will have its earthly freight ;"—

soon enough will the illusions which charmed and
aided man's inexperience be gone; what have you
to give him in the place of them ?

Dr. Colenso had nothing, and hence our dissatis-
faction with his work. But undoubtedly it is not
easy to re-unite man's imagination with his virtue
and conduct, when the tie between them has been
once broken. And therefore there will always be
many well-meaning people who say : Why meddle
with religion at all ? why run the risk of breaking a
tie which it is so hard to join again ? And the risk
is not to be run lightly, and one is not always to
attack people's illusions about religion merely because
illusions they are. But at the present moment two
things about the Christian religion must surely be
clear to anybody with eyes in his head. One is, that
men cannot do without it ; the other, that they cannot
do with it as it is.

And first, that they cannot do without it is shown
by the certainty,—as Baur, with whom I am glad to
agree at last, well says,—by the certainty with which
"the predominance of an all-denying unbelief does
but call forth a keener craving for belief."[1] Nowhere did the old Christian belief seem to be so
reasoned down, laughed out of court, exploded and
extinct as in France ; and in no country do we

[1] " Die Herrschaft eines alles verneinenden Unglaubens ruft
nur ein um so heisseres Glaubensverlangen hervor."

witness such a recrudescence, as liberals would say, of superstition, so formidable a clerical reaction. In England the old Christian belief has never ceased to be a mighty power. Yet even here the voice of modern liberalism has of late more and more been raised to decry it and to foretell its speedy extinction; and the astonishing popularity of the American revivalists is the answer. Why is this so?

It is so, because throughout the world there is a growing feeling, that, whatever may have been amiss with the old religion, modern liberalism, though it confidently professed to have perfect and sufficient substitutes for it, has not; and though it promised to make the world get on without it, cannot. Even Frenchmen are losing their long cherished belief in the gospel of the rights of man and the ideas of 1789 as a substitute for it. Indeed, one has only to keep one's head clear and one's judgment impartial, to see that however poorly men may have got on when their governing idea was: *The fear of the Lord is the beginning of wisdom*, they can get on even less by the governing idea that *all men are born naturally free and equal*. The barrenness and insufficiency of the revolutionary formulas are visible to common sense as they lose the gloss of novelty. Either they are vague;— as when Michelet, for instance, talks of "my idea, and Proudhon's, of Justice, of Revolution, an idea the opposite of Christianity;" where the term *Christianity* has no doubt a plain enough meaning for us, but the terms *Justice* and *Revolution*, its supposed opposites, have not. Or if the formula is explained,

it turns out to be something jejune, after all, which
is meant;—as when Michelet tells us what Justice,
the *pensée du siècle*, the thought of the Age of
Revolution, the opposite of Christianity is, and it
is this : "Unity of administration, gradual suppres-
sion of privilege, equal taxation." But this is politics,
it is merely what we call *machinery ;* and the "thought
of the age," the idea of Justice and Revolution, the
idea which is the opposite of Christianity, must give
us something more than this, or to replace Christianity
it is quite ludicrously insufficient.

All this most people are now beginning to see
clearly enough; hence the reaction on which secularists
so little counted. But indeed it is much more surprising that they should ever have reckoned that
their ideas of revolution and liberty, and of the
spread of physical science dispelling a host of illusions, could at all do for the world what Christianity
had done for it and serve as a substitute for Christianity, than that they should now find themselves to
be out in their reckoning. For Christianity enabled,
or professed to enable, mankind to deal with personal
conduct,—with an immense matter, at least three-
fourths of human life. And it seems strange that
people should even imagine, either that men will not
demand something enabling them to do this, or that
revolution, and equality, and knowing that not the
sky moves but the earth, can in any way do it. And
so the revolutionists find themselves at fault in their
calculations ; and the best scientific specialists are
forward to confess, what is evident enough, both that

religion must and will have its claims attended to,
and that physics and religion have, as Joubert says,
absolutely nothing to do with one another. Charlatans may bluster; but, speaking in defence of the
genuine men of science, M. Réville declares of them
that "they willingly recognise the legitimateness of
the religious element in the human spirit, but they
say that to provide the satisfaction due to it is not a
business with which they are competent to deal." [1]

It is true, all specialists are not equally sober-
minded. Thus we find a brilliant mathematician,
Professor Clifford, launching invectives which, if they
are just, would prove either that no religion at all has
any right to mankind's regard, or that the Christian
religion, at all events, has none. He calls Christianity
"that awful plague which has destroyed two civilisa-
tions and but barely failed to slay such promise of
good as is now struggling to live amongst men." He
warns his fellow-men against showing any tenderness
to "the slender remnant of a system which has made
its red mark on history and still lives to threaten
mankind." "The grotesque forms of its intellectual
belief," he sternly adds, by way of finish, "have sur-
vived the discredit of its moral teaching."

But these are merely the crackling fireworks of
youthful paradox. One reads it all, half sighing,
half smiling, as the declamation of a clever and con-

[1] "Ils reconnaissent volontiers la légitimité de l'élément
religieux de l'esprit humain ; mais ils disent qu'il ne rentre pas
dans leur compétence de lui fournir les satisfactions qu'il
réclame."

fident youth, with the hopeless inexperience, irredeemable by any cleverness, of his age. Only when one is young and headstrong can one thus prefer bravado to experience, can one stand by the Sea of Time, and instead of listening to the solemn and rhythmical beat of its waves, choose to fill the air with one's own whoopings to start the echo. But the mass of plain people hear such talk with impatient indignation, and flock all the more eagerly to Messrs. Moody and Sankey. They feel that the brilliant freethinker and revolutionist talks about their religion and yet is all abroad in it, does not know either that or the great facts of human life ; and they go to those who know them better. And the plain people are not wrong. Compared with Professor Clifford, Messrs. Moody and Sankey are masters of the philosophy of history. Men are not mistaken in thinking that Christianity has done them good, in loving it, in wishing to listen to those who will talk to them about what they love, and will talk of it with admiration and gratitude, not contempt and hatred. Christianity is truly, as in *Literature and Dogma* I have called it, "the greatest and happiest stroke ever yet made for human perfection." Men do not err, they are on firm ground of experience, when they say that they have practically found Christianity to be something incomparably beneficent. Where they err, is in their way of accounting for this, and of assigning its causes.

And here we reach our second point : that men cannot do with Christianity as it is. Something true and beneficent they have got hold of in it, they

know; and they want to rely upon this, and to use
it. But what men rely upon and use, they seek to
give themselves account of, they seek to make clear
its right to be relied upon and used. Now, the old
ways of accounting for Christianity, of establishing
the ground of its claims upon us, no longer serve as
they once did. Men's experience widens, they get to
know the world better, to know the mental history
of mankind better; they distinguish more clearly
between history and legend, they grow more shy of
recourse to the preternatural. I have quoted in the
present volume the saying of Pascal: "In good truth,
the world is getting mistrustful, and does not believe
things unless they are evident to it." [1] But no one
can more set this consideration at defiance than does
Pascal himself in his account of Christianity. Gleams
of astonishing insight he has, as well as bursts of un-
surpassable eloquence; there is no writer on the
Christian religion who more than Pascal deserves a
close study. But the basis of his whole system is the
acceptance, as positive history and literal matter of
fact, of the story of Adam's fall. The historical difficulty of taking this legend seriously, for us so decisive,
Pascal hardly saw at all; but he saw plenty of other
difficulty. Nothing, he observes, can be "more contrary to the rules of our miserable justice than to
damn eternally a child born now for a crime committed six thousand years before he came into being."
Nevertheless Pascal accepts the story, because "with-

[1] "En vérité, le monde devient méfiant, et ne croit les choses
que quand il les voit."

out this mystery, the most incomprehensible of all mysteries, we are incomprehensible to ourselves." That is, he sees no other way of explaining the mixture of grandeur and infirmity which he finds in man,—of desire for happiness and of inability to reach it. So that, if we put ourselves under Pascal's guidance, the necessary approach to our use of the salvation offered by the Christian religion is to believe the story of Adam's fall to be historical, and literally true. And his famous figure of the wager is used by Pascal to reconcile us the better to this belief. The chances are such, he says, that we shall do well at all events to lay our stake in favour of the story's truth. If we say we *cannot* believe it, let us set to work to attain belief as others have attained it; and how was this? "By acting just as if they *did* believe it; by taking holy water, having masses said, etc.; *quite naturally that will make you believe, and render you stupid!* [1] —But that is just what I am afraid of.—And why; what have you to lose? What harm will come to you from taking this course? You will be faithful, honest, humble, grateful, charitable, sincere, a friend whom men can trust?"

[1] "*Naturellement même cela vous fera croire et vous abêtira.*" The Port Royal editors suppressed this wonderful sentence, and indeed the whole passage which follows the words *and how was this?* What Port Royal substituted was the following: "Imitez leurs actions extérieures, si vous ne pouvez encore entrer dans leurs dispositions intérieures ; quittez ces vains amusements qui vous occupent tout entier." Pascal's words were not restored until M. Cousin reverted to the original manuscript. See M. Havet's careful and valuable edition of Pascal's *Pensées*, vol. i. pp. 152, 158.

Did ever a great reasoner reason so madly? And this is the man who saw that the world no longer believes things unless it has evidence of them! In the first place, there is no evidence that man is only comprehensible on the assumption that the story of Adam's fall is true. But even if it were so, man must still ask himself: *Is* the story true? And if it is not true, then the conclusion must be simply that man is not comprehensible. Now, sooner or later, as our experience widens, we must see that the story is not true; we must inevitably come to say to ourselves: "It is all a legend! it never really happened, any of it!" It is no more real history than the Peruvian account of Manco Capac and Mama Ocollo, the children of the Sun, "who appeared on the banks of the Lake Titiaca, sent by their beneficent parent, who beheld with pity the miseries of the human race, to instruct and to reclaim them."[1] For a little while, even for a generation or two perhaps, man may, after he has begun to doubt the story's truth, still keep himself in the belief of it by "taking holy water, rendering himself stupid;" but the time comes when he cannot. That a story will account for certain facts, that we wish to think it true, nay, that many have formerly thought it true and have grown faithful, humble, charitable, and so on, by thus doing, does not make the story true if it is not, and cannot prevent men after a certain time from seeing that it is not.

And on such a time we are now entering. The

[1] Robertson's *History of America*, book vi.

more we may have been helped to be faithful, humble
and charitable by taking the truth of this story, and
others equally legendary, for granted, the greater is
our embarrassment, no doubt, at having to do without
them. But we have to do without them none the
less on that account. We may feel our hearts still
vibrate in answer to the Old Testament telling us
that "the fear of the Lord is the beginning of wisdom,"
and to the New telling us that Jesus Christ saves his
people from their sins. But this fear of the Lord,
and this safety through Jesus Christ, can have Adam's
fall for their fundamental basis and explanation no
longer.

Cardinal Manning narrates the miraculous resuscitation of the Virgin Mary, and his argument for
believing it is that the story is a beautiful one, and
that it is a comfort and help to pious souls to think
it true. Both may be freely conceded to him; but
really as much may be said for the miraculous apparition of Cinderella's fairy godmother. The story is
pathetic and beautiful, and it is a pleasure to kind
souls to see the tables turned by enchantment in
favour of the poor little good Cinderella. But this
does not make the story true. And if a story is
unsubstantial in its foundation and character, no connecting of it with our affections, or with what does
us good, can in the end prevent people from saying:
"But it is not true! it never really happened, any
of it!"

I heard Mr. Moody preach to one of his vast
audiences on a topic eternally attractive,—salvation

by Jesus Christ. Mr. Moody's account of that salvation was exactly the old story, to which I have often
adverted, of the contract in the Council of the Trinity.
Justice puts in her claim, said Mr. Moody, for the
punishment of guilty mankind; God admits it.
Jesus intercedes, undertakes to bear their punishment,
and signs an undertaking to that effect. Thousands
of years pass; Jesus is on the cross on Calvary.
Justice appears, and presents to him his signed
undertaking. Jesus accepts it, bows his head, and
expires. Christian salvation consists in the undoubt-
ing belief in the transaction here described, and in
the hearty acceptance of the release offered by it.

Never let us deny to this story power and pathos,
or treat with hostility ideas which have entered so
deep into the life of Christendom. But the story is
not true; it never really happened. These personages never did meet together, and speak, and act, in
the manner related. The personages of the Christian
Heaven and their conversations are no more matter
of fact than the personages of the Greek Olympus
and their conversations. Sir Robert Phillimore seeks
to tie up the Church of England to a belief in the
personality of Satan, and he might as well seek to tie
it up to a belief in the personality of Tisiphone.
Satan and Tisiphone are alike not real persons, but
shadows thrown by man's guilt and terrors. Mr.
Moody's audiences are the last people who will come
to perceive all this; they are chiefly made up from
the main body of lovers of our popular religion,—the
serious and steady middle class, with its bounded

horizons. To the more educated class above this, and to the more free class below it, the grave beliefs of the religious middle class in such stories as Mr. Moody's story of the Covenant of Redemption are impossible now; to the religious middle class itself they will be impossible soon. Salvation by Jesus Christ, therefore, if it has any reality, must be placed somewhere else than in a hearty consent to Mr. Moody's story. Something Mr. Moody and his hearers have experienced from Jesus, let us own, which does them good; but of this something they have not yet succeeded in getting the right history.

Now, if one feels impatience with people who, like Professor Clifford, lightly run a-muck at an august thing, so a man who is in earnest must feel impatience with those who lightly allege this or that as the true foundation of it. People who gravely offer us about Christianity their stories of the contract in the Council of the Trinity, or of the miraculous resuscitation of the Virgin, are just like Mr. Ruskin telling us in his assured way: "There is not a moment of any day of our lives, when nature is not producing picture after picture and working still upon such exquisite and constant principles of such perfect beauty, *that it is quite certain it is all done for us, and intended for our perpetual pleasure.*" It is *not* quite certain, we have not a particle of certainty about it, and to say that it is certain is utterly fantastic. However, Mr. Ruskin is talking only about the beauties of nature; and here, perhaps, it is an excuse for inventing certainties that what one invents is so

beautiful. But religion is to govern our life. Whoever produces certainties to us on the subject of
religion is bound to take care that they are serious
ones; and yet on no subject is this so little regarded.

And there is no doubt that we touch here on a
real fault both in Christians and in Christian theology;
and that at Christianity's very first start in the world
the heathen philosopher Celsus hit this fault, when
he remarked on the κουφότης τῶν Χριστιανῶν. We
must not translate κουφότης simply *levity*, for the
seriousness of Christianity in morals has been its
charm and its power. Ὅσα σεμνά! as St. Paul says,[1]
—*whatever things are nobly serious!*—may here well
stand for its motto. But the κουφότης Celsus meant
was *a want of intellectual seriousness;* and the reproach
of this was not altogether undeserved by the first
Christians, while it has been abundantly deserved by
Christian theology since. The first Christians misunderstood Jesus and had the multitude's appetite
for miracles, the multitude's inexact observation and
boundless credulity. They it was who supplied the
data which Christian theology took from them without question, and has ever since confidently built
upon. But trained, critical, indifferent minds, which
knew what evidence was and what popular beliefs
were, could not but be struck with the looseness in
the joints of the Christian belief, with the slightness
of evidence for its miraculous data. They *were* struck
with them; and if the old civilisation had not been
on the wane, if a supply of instructed, critical, cool,

[1] Philippians iv. 8.

indifferent minds had continued, Christianity could not have established itself in the precise form it did. For its establishment in that form the extinction of the old civilisation was necessary;—to flood and drown all which this civilisation was, and thought, and knew, with the barbarian nations of the north, men of infantine and untrained mental habit. The infancy of the world was renewed, with all its sweet illusions; and on this new world the popular Christian belief could lay hold freely. Professor Clifford execrates Christianity as an "awful plague," because its success thus involved the ruin of Roman civilisation. It was worth while to have that civilisation ruined fifty times over, for the sake of planting Christianity through Europe in the only form in which it could then be planted there. Civilisation could build itself up again; but what Christianity had to give, and from the first did give in no small measure, was indispensable, and the Roman civilisation could not give it. And Christianity's admixture of popular legend and illusion was sure to be cleared away with time, according to that profound saying of Jesus himself: "There is nothing covered which shall not be uncovered, and hidden which shall not be known."[1]

But the miraculous data supplied by the first Christians became in this manner speedily consecrated, the looseness of the evidence for them soon escaped scrutiny. Theology, the exhibition of Christianity in a scientific and systematic way, took these data as an assured basis. Many theologians have been very

[1] Matthew x. 26.

able men, and their reasonings and deductions have
been very close and subtle. Still they have always
had the defect of going seriously upon data produced
and admitted with a *want of intellectual seriousness*.
But science makes her progress, not merely by close
reasoning and deduction, but also, and much more,
by the close scrutiny and correction of the present
commonly received data. And this scrutiny is just
what theological science has never seriously given ;
and to listen to it, therefore, is, as we said in *Literature and Dogma*, like listening to Cosmas Indico-
pleustes the Christian cosmographer, or any other
early Christian writer in a department of science,
who goes upon data furnished by a time of imperfect observation and boundless credulity. Whatever
acuteness the writer may manifest, yet upon these
data he goes. And Christian writers in other depart-
ments of science have now corrected their old data in
them from top to bottom ; half of these data they
have clean abandoned and the other half they have
transformed. But Christian theologians have not yet
done so in their science of theology, and hence their
unprofitableness.

Mr. Gladstone complains that objectors to the
Athanasian Creed seem to forget, most of them,
" that theology is a science, and that it therefore has
a technical language which is liable to be grossly
misunderstood by those who have never made it the
subject of study." And this is a very usual com-
plaint from our theologians. But the fact is, that
their science is a science going gravely and confidently

upon the uncorrected data of a time of imperfect observation and boundless credulity, and that, there-fore, the more formal and technical it gets, the more hollow it is. And the hollowness of the results ex-hibited by theologians is more apparent than the reason thereof, and a clear-headed man can often perceive that what the theologians say is futile, although he may never have been led to see that the untrustworthiness of their miraculous data is the real cause. Dr. Littledale adjures people to "study theology, instead of practically maintaining, as Dr. Arnold in all sincerity did, that the best preparation for laying down authoritative decisions in theology is to know nothing whatever about it." But Dr. Arnold, who had a sound historical instinct, could tell at once, from the warnings of this instinct, that theology, which is a series of conclusions upon the history in the Bible, had apprehended that history all wrong ; that it was faulty, therefore, in its very base, and so could not be a true theology, a science of the Christian religion, at all. And most certainly it is not the best preparation for forming right judg-ments in a true theology, to have one's head stuffed full of a false.

Moreover, this original vice of Christian theology seems to have affected, where things religious are concerned, the whole mental habit of those who receive it, and to have afflicted them with a malady which cannot be better described than as the κουφότης τῶν Χριστιανῶν, *want of intellectual seriousness* on the part of lovers and defenders of Christianity. Men's experience widens, they get a clearer sense of what fact is and what proof is, they are more aware when they talk nonsense and more shy of talking it; only where religion is concerned does this check of sober reason seem quite to desert them, and levity to reign. We have noticed Cardinal Manning's ground for believing the miraculous resuscitation of the Virgin Mary : that the story is so beautiful. But the same levity is shown by more cautious Catholics discussing the Pope's infallibility, seeking to limit its extent, to lay down in what sense he is really infallible and in what sense he is not ; for in no sense whatever is or can he be infallible, and to debate the thing at all shows a want of intellectual seriousness. The same when Lord Herries thinks to mend matters by saying, that " the Pope is the organ of the Church, and an Almighty Power of infinite wisdom and of infinite truth established his Church to teach all truth unto the end of the world, and as such that Church must be infallible ;" for there is plainly no such thing existing as the said infallible Church, and it is a want of intellectual seriousness to make believe that there is when there is not. The same when Dr. Ward thinks to clear the doctrine of the Real Presence, by talking of "the divine substance in the Host separable from all that group of visible and tangible phenomena which suggest the presence of bread." All that this acute mind effects, by thus gravely cheating itself with words, is to illustrate the κουφότης τῶν Χριστιανῶν, the want of intellectual seriousness found in Christians.   The same, finally, when Mr. Moody, the question being what Christian salvation positively is, tells us his story about Justice and her contract. However honest and earnest Mr. Moody may be, all we can say of a man who at the present juncture bases Christian salvation on a story like that, is that he shows a fatal want of intellectual seriousness.

For Protestantism has the same want of intellectual seriousness as Catholicism, its advantage being, however, that it more possesses in itself the means of deliverance. On this, the advantage of Protestantism, we do not at the present moment insist; we rather point out the weakness, common to it and to Catholicism, of building confidently upon miraculous data lightly admitted. True, Catholicism has more levity in admitting new miraculous data; but Protestantism admits unreservedly one set of miraculous data and builds everything on them, because they are written in a book which, it says, cannot err; and this is levity. At the stage of experience where men are now arrived, it is evident to whoever looks at things fairly that the miraculous data of the Bible have not this unique character of trustworthiness; that they, like other such data, proceed from a medium of imperfect observation and boundless credulity. The story of the magical birth and resuscitation of Jesus was bred in such a medium; and not to see this, to build confidently on the story, is hardly more serious than to admit the story of the magical birth and resuscitation of the Virgin because it is so beautiful.

It is of the utmost importance to be perfectly

honest here.   M. de Laveleye[1] is struck, as any judicious Catholic may well be struck, with the superior freedom, order, stability, and even religious earnestness, of the Protestant nations as compared with the Catholic.   But at the present moment the Protestant nations are living partly upon their past, partly upon their powers of self-transformation ; great care is required to consult and use aright the experience which they offer.   True, their religion has made them what they are, and their religion involved severance from Rome and involved the received Protestant theology.   But it would be a grave mistake to suppose that the secret of the Protestant nations lies in severance from Rome and in the received Protestant theology ; or that, in now merely adopting those from them, a modern nation could find freedom, order, stability, and religious earnestness.   The true force of Protestantism was its signal return to the individual conscience,—to the method of Jesus.   This strengthened the man, this founded him on rock, this invigorated his action on all lines. It induced separation from Rome (so far as this was not due to causes political), and it induced the received Protestant theology.   But a man's conscience does not necessarily tell him right on all points all at once ; and now the conscience of the Protestant nations is beginning to tell them that in their theology of the sixteenth century it did not tell them right.   Conscience told them right in asserting its own general

[1] See his excellent pamphlet : *Le Protestantisme et le Catholicisme*, Brussels, Muquardt.

supremacy as ultimate court of appeal; it did not tell them right in its particular decision that the sixteenth century theology was the true one. Protestantism's secret is undoubtedly its religion; but it has not at this moment a science of religion, or theology, to give to the Catholic nations, for it is working out its own anew. What it has to give them is the sincere, uncompromising return to the method of Jesus, with the deep and firm sense of reality which this return inspires. But if it gives them this, it will have given to the Catholic nations what enables them to do all the rest for themselves.

It is the habit of increased intellectual seriousness, bred of a wider experience and of a larger acquaintance with men's mental history, which is now transforming religion in our country. Intelligent people among the educated classes grow more and more sceptical of the miraculous data which supply the basis for our received theology. The habit is a conquest of the advancing human race; it spreads and spreads; it cannot but be, and will be, on the whole and in the end a boon to us. But many and many an individual it may find unprepared for it, and may act upon him injuriously. Goethe's saying is well known: " All which merely frees our spirit, without giving us the command over ourselves, is deleterious."[1] It is of small use by itself alone, however it may be indispensable this one single current of intellectual seriousness; of small use to those who are untouched

[1] " Alles was unsern Geist befreit, ohne uns die Herrschaft über uns selbst zu geben, ist verderblich."

by the great current of seriousness about conduct.
To a frivolous and sensual upper class, to a raw and
sensual lower class, to feel the greater current may be
more than a compensation for not feeling the lesser.
They do now feel the lesser current, however; and it
removes them farther than ever from the influence of
the greater.

For fear of losing their religious convictions, the
pious part of our people would fain shut off from
themselves the intellectual current, which they fear
might carry them away to shores of desolation.
They may succeed for a longer or a shorter time.
Their love of the old, and their fear of the new, alike
give them energy; and we have repeatedly said that
the nature of the debate as to the miraculous ground
in Christianity is such, that the conviction of its unsoundness must form itself in a man's own mind, it
cannot be forced upon him from without.   It is true,
what apologists are always urging, that there is no
other example of such a success as that of the Christian religion, where the successful religion had an
erroneous belief in miracles for its foundation.   It is
true, what was well pointed out in the *Guardian*,
that the rich crop of non-Christian miracles contemporary with the rise of Christianity, and which is often
brought as proof of the hollowness of the Christian
miracles, may naturally have been called up by the
miracles of Christianity.   The answer, no doubt, is,
that no other religion with an unsound foundation
of miracles has succeeded like Christianity, because
no other religion had, in close conjunction with its

unsound belief in miracles, such an element of soundness as the personality and word of Jesus. And the
suggestion of non-Christian miracles by the Christian
ones only proves a superior force somewhere in the
Christian religion; and this it undoubtedly had, but
not from its miracles. However, a religious man
may still shut his eyes to all this, and may keep
fast his old faith in the Christian miracles. But
before very long the habit of intellectual seriousness
will reach him also, and change him. Not a few
religious people are even now gained by it against
their will, and to their deep distress and bewilder-
ment. So that, whether we look about us at the
religious world or at the irreligious, the conclusion is
the same; people cannot any longer do with Christianity just as it is.

The reader whom the present work has in view is
not the man still striving to be content with the
received theology. With him we do not seek to
meddle. Neither is it intended for a frivolous upper
class in their religious insensibility, nor for a raw
lower class in their religious insensibility, nor for
Liberal secularists at home or abroad, nor for Catholics who are strangers, or very nearly so, to the Bible.
Some or all of these may perhaps come to find the
work useful to them one day, and after they have
undergone a change; but it is not directly aimed at
them. It is meant for those who, won by the modern
spirit to habits of intellectual seriousness, cannot
receive what sets these habits at nought, and will not
try to force themselves to do so; but who have stood

near enough to the Christian religion to feel the
attraction which a thing so very great, when one
stands really near to it, cannot but exercise, and who
have some acquaintance with the Bible and some
practice in using it.

Of such persons there are in this country, and
probably in America also, not a few. The familiarity
with the Bible extends in Protestant countries throughout those large classes which have been religiously
brought up, and is invaluable to them. It is the
excellent fruit which Protestantism gained by its
return at the Reformation to the individual conscience,—to the method of Jesus. The Bible itself
was made the standard, and what the Bible really
said. It matters not that the Protestant's actual in-
terpretation of the Bible has hitherto been little
better than the Catholic's; he has still been conversant with the Bible, has felt its grandeur, has conceived
the just idea that in its right use is salvation. M.
Sainte-Beuve, the finest critical spirit of our times,
conceived of the Bible so falsely, simply from not
knowing it, that he could cheerfully and confidently
repeat the Liberal formula : " Unless we mean to
prefer Byzantinism to progress we must say good-bye
aux vieilles Bibles,—to the old Bibles." Liberals, who
think that religion in general is an obstacle to progress, may naturally, however, be ignorant of the
virtue there is in knowing one's Bible. But Catholics,
although they may love religion, are for the most
part in like case with its Liberal foes in not being
aware what virtue there lies in knowing the Bible.

And therefore a Catholic, who has once come to perceive the want of intellectual seriousness in what his
Church lays down, and in what he has been told of
her infallibility, thinks that there the thing ends, and
that the Christian religion itself has as little intellectual seriousness as the dogmas of his Church. So we
see how many Catholics break violently with religion
altogether, and become its sworn enemies. And even
with Catholics who have been so near to it that they
cannot help feeling its attraction, what they feel is
merely, when the dogmas of their church have lost
credibility for them, a vague sentiment at variance
with their reason ; capable, perhaps, of making them
view with dislike all who raise questions about religion, but not capable of affording them any sure stay.
Therefore Niebuhr might well say that 1517 ought
to precede 1789 ; and even the fanaticism of Exeter
Hall can hardly assert too roundly that the Catholic
nations will never really improve until they know the
Bible better. For easily and always does a religious
Protestant remain aware that religion is not at an end
because the dogmas of a church cannot stand. He
knows that the Bible is behind ; and although he
may be startled on first hearing that what creeds and
confessions have for centuries been giving as the sum
and substance of the Bible is not its sum and substance, yet he knows the vastness and depth of the
Bible well enough to understand that, after all, this
may very likely be quite true.

For such a reader is the present work meant ;—
for a reader who is conversant with the Bible, who

can feel the attraction of the Christian religion, but
who has acquired habits of intellectual seriousness,
has been revolted by having things presented solemnly
to him for his use which will not hold water, and
who will start with none of such things even to reach
what he values. If there are but ten people in the
world who deal with religion fairly, he is resolved to
be one of those ten.

It is the aim of the present volume, as it was the
aim of *Literature and Dogma*, to show to such a man
that his honesty will be rewarded. Plenty of people
there are who labour solely for the diffusion of habits
of intellectual seriousness, at whatever cost. Perhaps
they do well, perhaps ill; at all events I do not, in
the present volume and in its predecessor, write as
one of them. I write to convince the lover of religion
that by following habits of intellectual seriousness he
need not, so far as religion is concerned, lose anything. Taking the Old Testament as Israel's magni-
ficent establishment of the theme: *Righteousness is
salvation!* taking the New as the perfect elucidation
by Jesus of what righteousness is and how salvation
is won, I do not fear comparing even the power over
the soul and imagination of the Bible, taken in this
sense,—a sense which is at the same time solid,—
with the like power in the old materialistic and
miraculous sense for the Bible, which is not.

The solidity itself is indeed an immense element
of grandeur. *To him that ordereth his conversation
right shall be shown the salvation of God!* Or conversely,
and in modern phrase: *Nations and men, whoever is*

shipwrecked, is shipwrecked on conduct! In vain do
philosophical Radicals devise fine new programmes
which leave it out; in vain does France trumpet the
ideas of '89 which are to do instead. Whoever leaves
it out of his programme, whoever fancies that anything else will do instead, is baffled and confounded
by the sure event; experience keeps again and again
sending him back to learn better, like a schoolboy
with an ill-got lesson. France, which was in such
terror of Byzantinism and so resolved to have done
with "the old Bibles," France, with all her eminent
social instincts and gifts, is she not, in her forty and
fifty editions of M. Adolphe Belot's novels, faring
towards the real Byzantinism, a Byzantinism from
which "the old Bibles," perhaps, can alone save her?
For, as it is true that men are shipwrecked on conduct, so it is true that the Bible is the great means
for making men feel this, and for saving them. It
makes them feel it by the irresistible power with
which Israel, the Seer of the Vision of Peace, testifies
it; it saves them by the method and secret of Jesus.

The indispensableness of the Bible and of Christianity, therefore, cannot be exaggerated. In morals,
which are at least three-fourths of life, to do without
them is, as was said in *Literature and Dogma*, exactly
like doing in æsthetics without the art of Greece. To
do with "the common places of morality couched in
modern and congenial language," which is what some
of our Liberal friends propose, answers precisely to
doing with English, French, and German art in
æsthetics. To do with the very best and finest, in

the way of morals, that has outside the Bible been produced, answers to doing, in æsthetics, with Flemish and Italian art. Every lover of art knows that perfection in art, salvation in art, will never be thus reached, will never be reached without knowing Greece. So it is with perfection and salvation in conduct, men's universal concern, *the way of peace;* they are not to be reached without the Bible and Christianity. By the Bible and Christianity, though not by what our missionaries now offer as such, the non-Christian nations will finally be won, and will come to regard their old religions much as a Christian, wide-minded, reverent, and profound, would regard them now. So will be fulfilled the word of Israel's Eternal: *My house shall be called the house of prayer for all nations; there shall be one Eternal, and his name one.*[1] And although we may willingly allow to Professor Rauwenhoff that the mind and life of our Aryan race has deeply modified the religion of Semitic Israel already, and will yet modify it much more, still that cannot prevent the root of the matter for us, in this immense concern of religion, being in the Israel of the Bible, and he is our spiritual progenitor:—*A Syrian ready to perish was thy father.*[2]

Thus neither in respect of the grandeur of the Bible and Christianity, nor in respect of their world-wide importance, will the lover of religion, who brings habits of intellectual seriousness to bear upon them, find that he has to change his notions. Nor will he

[1] Isaiah lvi. 7 ; Zechariah xiv. 9.
[2] Deuteronomy xxvi. 5.

even have to revolutionise his phraseology. He will be aware, indeed, that of the constitution of God we know nothing, and that those who, like Christian philosophers in general, begin by admitting this, and who add, even, that "we are utterly powerless to conceive or comprehend the idea of an infinite Being, Almighty, All-knowing, Omnipotent, and Eternal, of whose inscrutable purpose the material universe is the unexplained manifestation," [1] but then proceed calmly to affirm such a Being as positively as if he were a man they were acquainted with in the next street, talk idly. Nevertheless, admitting that all this cannot be affirmed about the God of our religion, but only that our God is the Eternal not ourselves that makes for righteousness, we yet know also that men inevitably use anthropomorphic language about whatever makes them feel deeply, and the Biblical language about God we may therefore freely use, but as approximative and poetical merely. To seek to discard, like some philosophers, the name of God and to substitute for it such a name as the Unknowable, will seem to a plain man, surely, ridiculous. For *God*,— the name which has so engaged all men's feelings,— is at the same time by its very derivation a positive name, expressing that which is the most blessed of boons to man, Light ; whereas *Unknowable* is a name merely negative. And no man could ever have cared anything about God in so far as he is simply unknowable. "The Unknowable is our refuge and strength, a very present help in trouble," is what would occur

---

[1] Mr. R. A. Proctor, in the *Contemporary Review*.

to no man to think or say. Men cared about God
for the sake of what they knew about him, not of
what they did not. And they knew about him that
he was the Eternal not ourselves that makes for
righteousness, and as such they gave him that name
for what gives light and warmth, *God*. It adds, indeed, to our awe of God that although we are able to
know of him what so greatly concerns us, we know
of him nothing more; but simply to be able to
know nothing of him could beget in us no awe whatever.

Finally, he who most seizes the real significance of
the Bible and of Jesus, will be least disposed to cut
himself off in religion from his fellow-men, to renounce
all participation in their religious language and worship. True, this language is approximative merely
while men imagine it to be adequate; it is *thrown out*
at certain realities which they very imperfectly comprehend. It is materialised poetry, which they give
as science; and there can be no worse science than
materialised poetry. But poetry is essentially concrete; and the moment one perceives that the religious language of the human race is in truth poetry,
which it mistakes for science, one cannot make it an
objection to this language that it is concrete. That
it has long moved and deeply engaged the affections
of men, that the Christian generations before us have
all passed that way, adds immensely to its worth as
poetry. As the Catholic architecture, so the Catholic
worship is likely to survive and prevail, long after
the intellectual childishness of Catholic dogma, and

the political and social mischiefs of the Roman
system, have tired out men's patience with them.
Catholic worship is likely, however modified, to
survive as the general worship of Christians, because
it is the worship which, in a sphere where poetry is
permissible and natural, unites the most of the elements of poetry.

Everything turns on its being at realities that this
worship and its language are aimed. Its anthropomorphic language about God is aimed at a vast,
though ill-apprehended, reality. So is its materialistic language about the death, the rising again, and
the reign of Christ. Baur says that the important
thing is not whether Jesus really rose from the dead
or no; the important thing is, Baur says, that his
disciples believed him to have risen. Mr. Appleton,
in a just and instructive review of the labours of
Strauss, invites our approval for Strauss' early position that what is best in Christianity was not due
to the individual Jesus, but was developed by the
religious consciousness of humanity. But the religious consciousness of humanity has produced in
Christianity not ideas, but imaginations; and it is
ideas, not imaginations, which endure. The religious
consciousness of humanity produced the doctrines of
the Incarnation and of the Real Presence,—beautiful
imaginations, but if Christianity depended upon them
it would dissolve. It will live, because it depends
upon a true and inexhaustibly fruitful idea, the idea
of death and resurrection as conceived and worked
out by Jesus. *Baptized into Christ's death, if by any*

means we might attain to the resurrection from the dead,[1]
is the true, the just, the only adequate account of a
Christian and his religion.   The importance of the
disciples' belief in their Master's resurrection lay in
their believing what was true, although they materialised it.   Jesus *had* died and risen again, but in his
own sense not theirs.   The strength of the Christian
religion lies in its being founded on a truth ; on a
truth which hitherto Christendom has been able to
apprehend only by materialising it, but which it will
one day apprehend better, and which men could
come to apprehend better only by passing through
a materialistic stage.   We can use their language
because it is thrown out at an admirable truth ; only
it is not, as they suppose, their sense for their own
language which is real while our sense is figurative,
but it is our sense which is real, and theirs is merely
figurative.

The freethinking of one age is the common-sense
of the next, and the Christian world will certainly
learn to transform beliefs which it now thinks to be
untransformable.   The way will be found.   And the
new Christianity will call forth more effort in the
individual who uses it than the old, will require more
open and instructed minds for its reception ; and this
is progress.   But we live at the beginning of a great
transition which cannot well be accomplished without
confusion and distress.   I do not pretend to operate
a general change of religious opinion, such as can
only come to pass through the operation of many

[1] Romans vi. 3 ; Philippians iii. 11.

labourers working, all of them, towards a like end, and by the instrumentality, in a very considerable degree, of the clergy. *One man's life, what is it?* says Goethe; but even one man in his short term may do something to ease a severe transition, to diminish violent shocks in it and bitter pain. With this end in view, I have addressed myself to men such as are happily not rare in this country, men of free and active minds, who, though they may be profoundly dissatisfied with the received theology, are yet interested in religion and more or less acquainted with the Bible. These I have endeavoured to help; and they, if they are helped, will in their turn help others. To one country and nation, and to one sort of persons in it, and to one moment in its religious history, have I addressed myself; and if the attempt thus confessedly partial has even a partial success, I am enough rewarded. May even that partial success be looked for? A calmer and a more gradual judgment than that of the immediate present will decide. But however that judgment may go, whether it pronounce the attempt here made to be of solid worth or not, I have little fear but that it will recognise it to have been an attempt conservative, and an attempt religious.

CONTENTS.

CHAP.   PAGE

INTRODUCTION 1

I. THE GOD OF MIRACLES 23

II. THE GOD OF METAPHYSICS . . . 50

III. THE GOD OF EXPERIENCE 96

IV. THE BIBLE-CANON 145

V. THE FOURTH GOSPEL FROM WITHOUT . . 196

VI. THE FOURTH GOSPEL FROM WITHIN . . 244

CONCLUSION 332

GOD AND THE BIBLE.

INTRODUCTION.

MODERN SCEPTICISM will not allow us to rely either on the Epistle of Polycarp, or on the narrative of his martyrdom, as certainly authentic. Nevertheless, a saying from the latter we will venture to use. As Polycarp stood in the amphitheatre at Smyrna just before his martyrdom, with the heathen multitude around crying out against him as an atheistical innovator, the Roman proconsul, pitying his great age, begged him to pronounce the formulas which expressed adherence to the popular religion and abhorrence of Christianity. "Swear," said he, "by the fortune of Cæsar; cry: *Away with the atheists!*" Whereupon Polycarp, says the letter of the Church of Smyrna which relates his martyrdom, looking round with a severe countenance upon the heathen clamourers who filled the amphitheatre, pointed to these with his hand, and with a groan, and casting up his eyes to heaven, cried: "Away with the

Atheists!" This did not give satisfaction, and Polycarp was burnt.

Yet so completely has the so-called atheism of Polycarp prevailed, that we are almost puzzled at finding it called atheism by the popular religion of its own day, by the worshippers of Jupiter and Cybele, of Rome and the fortune of Cæsar. On the other hand, Polycarp's retort upon these worshippers, his flinging back upon their religion the name of atheism, seems to us the most natural thing in the world. And so most certainly will it be with the popular religion of our own day. Confident in its traditions and imaginations, this religion now cries out against those who pronounce them vain: *Away with the atheists!* just as the heathen populace of Asia cried out against Polycarp. With a groan, and casting up his eyes to Heaven, the critic thus execrated might well, like Polycarp, point to his execrators and retort: *Away with the Atheists!* So deeply unsound is the mass of traditions and imaginations of which popular religion consists, so gross a distortion and caricature of the true religion does it present, that future times will hardly comprehend its audacity in calling those who abjure it atheists; while its being stigmatised itself with this hard name will astonish no one.

Let us who criticise the popular theology, however, show a moderation of which our adversaries do not always set us the example. We may not indeed, like the *Times* newspaper, call this established theology "an English, a Protestant, and a reasonable religion." But let us never forget that it professes, as we ourselves have again and again repeated, along with all its pseudo-science and all its popular legend, the main doctrine of the Bible : the pre-eminence of righteousness and the method and secret of Jesus ;— professes it and in some degree uses it. Let us never forget that our quarrel with its pseudo-science and its popular legend is because they endanger this main doctrine, this saving truth, on which our popular religion has in some degree hold. Let us gladly admit that the advance of time and of knowledge has even begun to shake the overweening confidence of our established theology in its own pseudo-science and popular legend, and that its replies to the impugner of them, if still too apt to be intemperate, are yet fast freeing themselves from the insolence and invective of thirty years ago. The strictures on *Literature and Dogma* have certainly not been mild ; yet, on the whole, their moderation has surprised me. An exception ought to be made, perhaps, for the *Dublin Review.* But an Englishman should always ask himself with shame: If Irish Catholicism is provincial in its violence and virulence, whose fault is it ?

To retort, therefore, upon those who have attacked *Literature and Dogma* as anti-christian and anti-religious, to recapitulate their hard words and to give them hard words in return, is not our intention. It is necessary, indeed, to mark firmly and clearly that from our criticism of their theology,—that grotesque mixture, as we have called it, of learned pseudo-science with popular legend,—their outcry does not make us go back one inch; that it is they who in our judgment owe an apology to Christianity and to religion, not we. But when this has once been clearly marked, our business with our assailants is over. Our business is henceforth not with them, but with those for whose sake *Literature and Dogma* was written.

These alone we have in view in noticing criticisms of that book, whatever may be their nature. And there have appeared criticisms of it very different from those blind and angry denunciations of which we have spoken, those denunciations from the point of view of popular and official theology. There have been criticisms deserving, some of them, our high respect; others, not our high respect only, but our warm gratitude also; all of them, our careful attention. Eminently of this sort were the criticisms by Mr. Llewellyn Davies in the *Contemporary Review*, by Professor Rauwenhoff in the Theological Review of Leyden, by M. Albert Réville in the *Academy*, by M. Charles Secrétan in the Swiss Review. But nothing is more tiresome to the public than an author's set vindication of his work and reply to his critics, however worthy they may be of attention; and certainly nothing of this kind should we think of proposing to ourselves. To weigh what his critics say, to profit by it to the best of his judgment, and either to amend or to maintain his work according to his final conviction, is the right course for a criticised author to follow. It is all that the public want him to do, and all that we should in general wish to do ourselves.

But let us recall the object for which *Literature and Dogma* was written. It was written in order to win access for the Bible and its religion to many of those who now neglect them. It was written to restore the use of the Bible to those (and they are an increasing number) whom the popular theology with its proof from miracles, and the learned theology with its proof from metaphysics, so dissatisfy and repel that they are tempted to throw aside the Bible altogether. It was written to convince such persons that they cannot do without the Bible, that the popular theology and the learned theology are alike formed upon a profound misapprehension of the Bible; but that, when the Bible is read aright, it will be found to deal, in a way incomparable for effectiveness, with facts of experience most pressing, momentous, and real.

This conviction of the indispensableness of the Bible, which in *Literature and Dogma* we sought to impart to others, we ourselves had and have. In England the conviction has long prevailed and been nearly universal, but there are now signs of its being shaken. To maintain it, to make it continue to prevail, to hinder its giving way and dying out, is our object. It seemed to us that the great danger to the Bible at present arises from the assumption that whoever receives the Bible must set out with admitting certain propositions, such as the existence of a personal God, the consubstantiality of Jesus Christ with this personal God who is his Father, the miraculous birth, resurrection, and ascension of Jesus.

Now, the nature of these propositions is such that
we cannot possibly verify them.   It seemed to us
that with the uninstructed or ill-instructed masses of
our people this obstacle to the Bible's reception,
which for a long time was an obstacle not ex-
istent for them at all, is, as things now stand, an
obstacle almost insuperable.   Therefore we sought
and seek to show that the Bible is really based upon
propositions which all can verify.

It is true, some deny that there exists the danger
which we apprehend for the Bible.   The masses, say
they, the working men, are not hard-headed, reasoning
people at all; they are eminently people led by their
feelings and passions.   Yes, led by their feelings and
passions towards what flatters their feelings and passions; but religion and the Bible do not flatter their
feelings and passions.   Towards religion and the Bible,
which fill them with superstitious awe no longer, but
which claim to check and control their feelings and
passions, they have plenty of suspiciousness, incredulity, hard-headed common-sense to oppose.   At most,
they will make religion into something which flatters
their feelings and passions.   Thus one hears from
those who know them, and one can see from their
newspapers, that many of them have embraced a kind
of revolutionary Deism, hostile to all which is old,
traditional, established and secure; favourable to a
clean sweep and a new stage, with the classes now in
the background for chief actors.   There is much to
make the political Dissenters, on their part, fall in
with this sort of religion, inasmuch as many of its ends

are theirs too. And we see that they do incline to fall in with it, and to try to use it.

A revolutionary Deism of this kind may grow, not improbably, into a considerable power amongst us; so habituated are the people of this country to religion, and so strongly does their being vibrate to its language and excitements. The God of this religion of the future will be still a magnified and non-natural man indeed, but by no means the magnified and non-natural man of our religion as now current. He may be best conceived, perhaps, as a kind of tribal God of the Birmingham League. Not by any means a *Dieu des Bonnes Gens*, like the God of Béranger, a God who favours garrets, grisettes, gaiety, and champagne; but a *Dieu des Quatre Libertés*, the God of Free Trade, Free Church, Free Labour, and Free Land;—with a new programme, therefore, and with Birmingham for his earthly headquarters instead of Shiloh or Jerusalem, but with the old turn still preserved for commanding to hew Agag in pieces, and with much even of the Biblical worship and language still retained; Mr. Jesse Collings and Mr. Chamberlain dancing before his ark, and Mr. Dale and Mr. George Dawson, in the Birmingham Town Hall, offering up prayer and sacrifice. All this is possible, and perhaps not improbable.

But a revolutionary Deism, based on the supposed rights of man and ardently destructive, is not the real religion of the Bible. It will fail; and its failure, the failure of that attempted application of the Bible which made the Bible flatter their feelings and passions, will discredit the Bible with the masses more than ever, will make them more than ever confront it with a suspiciousness, a hard incredulity, which take nothing upon trust. And fail the application must, for it is just one of those attempts at religion, at setting up something as righteousness which is not, that inevitably as often as we try them break down, and that by breaking down prove the grandeur and necessity of true religion, and testify to what it is. Nothing but righteousness will succeed, and nothing is righteousness but the method and secret and sweet reasonableness of Jesus Christ. But these have nothing to do with the gospel of the rights of man, of the natural claim of every man to a certain share of enjoyment. Political science may create rights for a man and maintain them, may seek to apportion the means of enjoyment. Such is not the function of the Christian religion. Man sincere, man before conscience, man as Jesus put him, finds laid down for himself no rights; nothing but an infinite dying, and in that dying is life.

We persevere therefore in thinking, both that danger, whether from active hostility or from passive indifference, to the continued authority and almost universal use of the Bible in this country there is; and also that the only safe way of meeting this danger is to find, as grounds for men's continued veneration and use of the Bible, propositions which can be verified and which are unassailable. This, then, has been our object: to find sure and safe grounds for the continued use and authority of the Bible.

II.

It will at once be evident how different a design is this, and how much humbler and more limited, from that of those Liberal philosophers whose design is in general to discover and to lay down *truth*, as (after Pilate)[1] they call it. For we start with admitting that truth, so far at least as religion is concerned, is to be found in the Bible, and what we seek is, that the Bible may be used and enjoyed. All disquisitions about the Bible seem to us to be faulty and even ridiculous which have for their result that the Bible is less felt, followed, and enjoyed after them than it was before them. The Bible is in men's hands to be felt, followed, and enjoyed; this conviction we set out with. Men's instinct for self-preservation and happiness guided them to the Bible; now, it is of the essence of what gives safety and happiness to produce enjoyment and to exercise influence. And the Bible has long been enjoyed and enjoyed deeply; its summons to *lay hold of eternal life*, to *seek the kingdom of God*, has been a trumpet-call bringing life and joy to thousands. They have regarded the Bible as a source

---

[1] See John xviii. 37. Pilate asks Jesus: "Art thou a king?" Jesus answers: "Yes, I am a king; a king of whom all who love the truth are the subjects." Jesus says, "*the* truth." He means the doctrine of righteousness as set forth in the Old Testament first, and then interpreted and developed by himself. Pilate catches at the word *truth ;* takes it (as if he had been a member of the British Association) in the sense of *universal knowledge;* drops the article, and asks his disconsolate question : "What is truth ?"

of life and joy, and they were right in so regarding
it; we wish them to be able so to regard it still. All
that we may say about the Bible we confess to be a
failure, if it does not lead people to find the Bible a
source of life and joy still.

Liberal philosophers reproach us with treating the
Bible like an advocate; with assuming that Israel had
a revelation of extraordinary grandeur, that Jesus
Christ said wonderfully profound things, and that
the records of all this are something incomparably
delightful and precious. Now, we say that no inquiries about the Bible can be fruitful that are not
filled with a sense of all this, which Christendom has
always felt and rightly felt, only it has justified its
feelings on wrong grounds. But Liberal investigators
of truth think, some of them, that the Bible often
offends against morality, and at its best only utters
in an old-fashioned and ineffective way the common-
places of morality which belong to all ethical systems;
therefore, say they, the Bible had better be dropped,
and we should try to enounce in modern congenial
language the new doctrines which will satisfy at once
our reason and our imagination. Other investigators of
truth destroy to the best of their ability all the grounds
on which people have accustomed themselves to receive
the Bible as something divine and precious: and then
they think to save everything by a few words of
general respect and esteem for the Bible, or for religion in the abstract. Their negative criticism has
great fulness, ardour, and effect; their positive com-
mendation of the Bible or religion is such as to have

no effect at all. It was this which we blamed in the
Bishop of Natal's treatment of the Bible, now several
years ago. We have no wish to revive a past controversy; but we thought then, and we think still,
that it was a signal fault in Dr. Colenso's book that
it cut away men's usual ground for their religion and
supplied really no other in its place;—for his prayer
of Ram, and his passage from Cicero's *Offices*, and his
own sermon, we must be permitted to regard as being,
under the circumstances, quite comically insufficient.
Mr. Greg, who took up arms for Dr. Colenso, did not
understand this; he does not understand it now.
And no wonder; for his own original book on the
Creed of Christendom, acute and eloquent as his
writing often is, had on the whole the same fault as
Dr. Colenso's work. The upshot of the matter, after
reading him, seemed to be that the Bible was a document hopelessly damaged, and that the new doctrines
which are to satisfy our reason and our imagination
must be sought elsewhere.

The same is to be said of a very learned and exact
book which has appeared lately, having for its title
Supernatural Religion. Hereafter we shall have occasion to criticise several things in this work, but we
now will remark of it only that it has the fault of
leaving the reader, when he closes it, with the feeling that the Bible stands before him like a fair tree
all stripped, torn, and defaced, not at all like a tree
whose leaves are for the healing of the nations. No
doubt this is not the author's design, and no doubt
the current notions assailed by him, the popular view

of the Bible-books and of their composition, are full
of error.   But attacking these throughout two thick
volumes with untiring vigour and industry, and doing
nothing more, he simply leaves the ordinary reader,
to whom the Bible has been the great, often the only,
inspirer of his conduct, his imagination, his feelings,
—he leaves him with the sense that he sees his Bible
with a thousand holes picked in it and fatally discredited as an authority.

These investigators go upon the supposition that
a man's first concern is to know *truth*, and that to
know *truth* about the Bible is to know that much of
it is legendary and much of it of uncertain authorship.   We say, on the other hand, that no one knows
the truth about the Bible who does not know how to
enjoy the Bible ; and he who takes legend for history
and who imagines Moses or Isaiah or David or Paul or
Peter or John to have written Bible-books which they
did not write, but who knows how to enjoy the Bible
deeply, is nearer the truth about the Bible than the man
who can pick it all to pieces but who cannot enjoy it.

Perhaps, however, we ought to say that the author
of *Supernatural Religion*, like Dr. Colenso, tries to provide a substitute for what he destroys.   After declaring that " there is little indeed in the history and
actual achievements of Christianity to support the
claim made on its behalf to the character of a scheme
divinely revealed for the salvation of the human
race," he tells us that after getting rid of Jewish
mythology " we rise to higher conceptions of an infinitely wise and beneficent Being," that " all that we

do know of the regulation of the universe being so perfect and wise, all that we do not know must be equally so," and that "here enters the true and noble faith which is the child of reason." Alas, for our part we should say rather: "Here enter the poor old dead horses of so-called natural theology, with their galvanic movements!" But this is our author's prayer of Ram, his passage from Cicero's *Offices*, his sermon; and he promises us, so far as we understand him, more at a future time in the same style. We say that it is ludicrously insufficient, all of it, to fill the place of that old belief in Christianity's claim to the character of a scheme divinely revealed for the salvation of the human race, which he seeks to expel. We say it is a string of platitudes, without the power of awakening religious emotion and joy, and not a whit more provable, moreover, as scientific fact, than the miracle of the resurrection, or the Johannine authorship of the Fourth Gospel.

We, on the other hand, think that there is everything in the history and actual achievements of Christianity to support its claim to the character of a religion divinely revealed for the salvation of the human race. We look with apprehension on all that diminishes men's attachment to the Bible. But that the Bible is not what men have fancied it, and that to be divinely revealed is not what men have supposed, time and experience are beginning to bear in upon the human mind. Many resist vehemently these intimations from time and experience. This resistance we believe to be utterly vain. We counsel men

to accept them, but we seek to show that the Bible
and the Christian religion subsist, all the while, as
salutary, as necessary, as they ever were supposed to
be ; and that they now come out far more real, and
therefore far more truly grand, than before.

Our adversaries will say, perhaps, that this attempted demonstration is *our* prayer of Ram. And
the test of our work does really lie here. If the
positive side in *Literature and Dogma*, if its attempt
to recommend the Bible, to awaken enthusiasm for
the Bible, on new grounds, proves ludicrously insufficient, weak and vain ; if its negative side, its
attempt to apply to popular religion the confuta-
tions and denials which time and experience suggest,
proves the more prominent, the only operative one,
—if this is so, then our work is, by our own confession and with our own consent, judged ; it is value-
less, perhaps mischievous. We can scarcely, however,
be expected ourselves to admit that this is already
proved. The time for the book's wide working, as
we said on first publishing it, has hardly yet fully
come. At its first appearance it was sure to be laid
hold of by those for whom it was not written, by the
religious world as it is called, the unhesitating re-
cipients of the Christianity popularly current, and to
occasion scandal. But it was not written for those
who at present receive the Bible on the grounds
supplied either by popular or by metaphysical theology. It was written for those who from dissatisfac-
tion with such grounds for the Bible are inclined to
throw the Bible aside.

Into the hands of not a few readers of this sort the book has fallen, both here and abroad, and they have found it of service to them. They have been enabled by it to use and enjoy the Bible, when the common theology, popular or learned, had almost estranged them from it. But many and grave objections have been alleged against the book which has done them this service. Its conclusions about the meaning of the term *God*, and about man's knowledge of God, have been severely condemned ; strong objections have been taken to our view of the Bible-documents in general, to our account of the Canon of the Gospels, to our estimate of the Fourth Gospel. What are the readers who believed they had derived benefit from our book to think of these objections to it, or at least of the more important among them? what weight are they to attach to them? Are they to go back from the way of reading and interpreting the Bible which we had counselled them to follow, and which they had begun to find profit in, or are they to pursue it steadfastly? Puzzled and shaken by some of the objections we may suppose them to be; and yet, if they give ear to the objections, if they do not get the better of them and put them aside, they will lose, we believe, all sure hold on the Bible, they will be more and more baffled, distressed, and bewildered in their dealings with religion. To the extent, there-fore, necessary for enabling such readers to surmount their difficulties, we propose to deal with the re-proaches and objections brought against *Literature and Dogma*.

III.

But first there is one reproach to be noticed, not so much for the reader's sake as for our own : the reproach of irreverent language, of improper and offensive personalities. The parable of the three Lord Shaftesburys, the frequent use of the names of the Bishops of Winchester and Gloucester to point a moral,—every one will remember to have heard of these as serious blemishes in *Literature and Dogma.* To have wounded the feelings of the religious community by turning into ridicule an august doctrine, the object of their solemn faith ; to have wounded the feelings of individuals either by the wanton introduction of their names in a connection sure to be unpleasing to them, or else by offensive ridicule and persistent personal attack, is a crime of which the majority of English reviewers have found us plainly guilty, and for which they have indignantly censured us. The *Guardian* has even been led by our mention of the Archbishop of York, and by our remarks on the Bishops of Winchester and Gloucester, to conclude that the order of bishops has upon us the effect of a red rag upon a bull, and that we cannot contemplate it without becoming infuriated. A word of notice these censures seem to demand.

As regards the three Lord Shaftesburys, we say boldly that our use of that parable shows our indulgence to popular Christianity. Polycarp sternly called the disfigured religion he saw prevalent around him, *atheism.* We have said, and it is important to maintain it, that popular Christianity at present is so wide of the truth, is such a disfigurement of the truth, that it fairly deserves, if it presumes to charge others with atheism, to have that charge retorted upon itself; and future ages will perhaps not scruple to condemn it almost as mercilessly as Polycarp condemned the religion of heathen antiquity. For us, the God of popular religion is a legend, a fairy-tale; learned theology has simply taken this fairy-tale and dressed it metaphysically. Clearly it is impossible for us to treat this fairy-tale with solemnity, as a real and august object, in the manner which might be most acceptable to its believers. But for the sake of the happiness it has given, of its beauty and pathos, and of the portions of truth mixed up with it, it deserves, we have said, and from us it has received and always will receive, a nearly inexhaustible indulgence. Not only have we not called it atheism; we have entirely refused to join our Liberal friends in calling it a degrading superstition. Describing it under the parable of the three Lord Shaftesburys, we have pointed out that it has in it, as thus represented, nothing which can be called a degrading superstition; that it contains, on the contrary, like other genuine products of the popular imagination, elements of admirable pathos and power. More we could not say of it without admitting that it was not a legend or fairy-tale at all, and that its personages were not magnified and non-natural men. But this we cannot admit, although of course its adherents will be satis-

fied with nothing less. It was our object to carry
well home to the reader's mind what a fairy-tale
popular Christianity really is, what a trio of magnified
and non-natural men is its Trinity. The indulgence,
however, due from us to popular Christianity has
been shown, if we have admitted that its fairy-tale,
far from being a degraded superstition, is full of
beauty and power, and that its divinities are magni-
fications of nothing unworthy, but of a sort of character
of which we have an eminent example amongst ourselves, in a man widely beloved and respected, and
whom no one respects more than we do.

As to the bishops, whose sacred order is supposed
to fill us with rage and hatred, it must be modern
bishops that have this effect, for several bishops of
past times are mentioned in *Literature and Dogma* with
veneration. Of three modern bishops, however, the
deliverances are criticised : of the Archbishop of York,
the late Bishop of Winchester, and the Bishop of
Gloucester and Bristol. But the deliverances of all
the three are by no means criticised in the same
manner. Logical and metaphysical reasonings about
essence, existence, identity, cause, design, have from
all time been freely used to establish truths in theology.
The Archbishop of York early acquired distinction
in the study of logic ; that he should follow in theological discussion a line of which St. Anselm, Descartes,
Leibnitz, and Locke have set him the example, is a
matter neither for surprise nor for ridicule. Certainly we hold that this line can lead in theology to
nothing but perplexity and disappointment. We

believe that religion could never have been originated by it, can never be confirmed by it. We say this freely when we see the Archbishop of York adopting it. But we say it without a thought of ridicule or disrespect towards the Archbishop of York, either for his adoption of such a line of argument, or for his management of the line of argument which he has thus chosen to employ.

The case is different with regard to that brilliant and well-known personage, who since the publication of *Literature and Dogma* has passed away from amongst us. We feel more restraint in speaking of the late Bishop of Winchester now that he is dead than we should have felt in speaking of him in his lifetime. He was a man with the temperament of genius ; and to his energy, his presence, his speech, this temperament could often lend charm and power. But those words of his which we quoted, and his public deliverances far too frequently, had a fault which in men of station and authority who address a society like ours, deserve at all times as severe a check as either blame or ridicule can inflict upon them. To a society like ours, a society self-regulating, which reads little that is serious and reflects hardly at all, but which desires to pursue its way comfortably and to think that it has in its customary notions and beliefs about religion, whenever it may be driven to fall back upon them, an impregnable stronghold to which it can always resort ; to such a society men of eminence cannot do a worse service than to confirm and encourage it, with airs of superior knowledge, profound certainty, and oracular assurance, in its illusion. A man of Bishop Wilberforce's power of mind must know, if he is sincere with himself, that when he talks of " doing something for the honour of Our Lord's Godhead," or of " that infinite separation for time and for eternity which is involved in rejecting the Godhead of the Eternal Son,"—he must know that by this singular sort of mixture of unction and metaphysics he is solemnly giving a semblance of conceivability, fixity, and certainty to notions which do not possibly admit of them. He must know this, and yet he gives it, because it suits his purpose, or because the public, or a large body of the public, desire it ; and this is clap-trap.

The *Times*, it is true, speaks of the current Christianity of this country as " an English, a Protestant, and a reasonable religion." The *Times*, however, is a popular newspaper ; and the public, when it reads there things which suit its wishes, is always half-conscious at least that to suit its wishes they are written. But the late Bishop of Winchester was a man in high office and dignity, a man at the same time of great gifts ; he spoke to the English public with authority, and with responsibility proportionate to that authority ; yet he freely permitted himself the use of clap-trap. The use of clap-trap to such a public by such a man ought at least to be always severely treated before the tribunal of letters and science, for it will be treated severely nowhere else. Bishop Wilberforce was a man of a sympathetic temper, a dash of genius, a gift of speech, and ardent energy, who professed to be a guide in a time, a society, a sphere of thought, where the first requisite for a guide is perfect sincerity ;—and he was signally addicted to clap-trap. If by ridicule or by blame we have done anything to discredit a line such as that which he adopted, we cannot regret it. Those who use clap-trap as the late Bishop of Winchester used it, those who can enthusiastically extol him as an ideal bishop, only prove their valuelessness for the religious crisis upon which we are now entering. No talents and acquirements can serve in this crisis without an absolute renunciation of clap-trap. Those who cannot attain to this have no part in the future which is before us. Real insight and real progress are impossible for them ; Jesus would have said of them : *They cannot enter into the kingdom of God.*

With regard to the Bishop of Gloucester and Bristol, we feel an esteem for him as one of the very few public men who in any degree carry on serious studies after having left the University. But he certainly joined himself with the Bishop of Winchester in holding the language on which we have animadverted above, and he laid himself open, therefore, to the same criticism.

Perhaps we ought, finally, to say one word of a remark concerning the late Mr. Maurice, which has given great umbrage to some of his friends. We cannot say that anything Mr. Maurice touched seems to us to have been grasped and presented by him with enough distinctness to give it a permanent value. But his was a pure and fine spirit, perpetually in a

state of ferment and agitation.   On many young men
of ability, agitated by the unsettled mental atmosphere
in which we live, he exercised a great attraction.
Some of them have cleared themselves; and as they
cleared themselves they have come to regard Mr.
Maurice as the author of all the convictions in which
after their ferment and struggle they have found rest.
This is generous in them, and we say with pleasure
that to Mr. Maurice it does honour to have made such
disciples.

And now we have done with these personal
matters, and can address ourselves to our main purpose.

CHAPTER I.

To people disposed to throw the Bible aside *Literature and Dogma* sought to restore the use of it by two considerations; one, that the Bible requires for its basis nothing but what they can verify; the other, that the language of the Bible is not scientific, but *literary.* That is, it is the language of poetry and emotion, approximate language thrown out, as it were, at certain great objects which the human mind augurs and feels after, and thrown out by men very liable, many of them, to delusion and error. This has been violently impugned. What we have now to do, therefore, is to ask whoever thought he found profit from what we said, to examine with us whether it has been impugned successfully; whether he and we ought to give it up, or whether we ought to hold by it firmly and hopefully still.

First and foremost has been impugned the definition which, proceeding on the rule to take nothing as a basis for the Bible but what can be verified, we gave of God. And of this we certainly cannot complain. For we have ourselves said, that without a

clear understanding in what sense this important but
ambiguous term *God* is used, all fruitful discussion in
theology is impossible.   And yet, in theological discussion, this clear understanding is hardly ever cared
for, but people assume that the sense of the term is
something perfectly well known.   "A personal First
Cause, that thinks and loves, the moral and intelligent
governor of the universe," is the sense which theologians in general assume to be the meaning, properly
drawn out and strictly worded, of the term God.
We say that by this assumption a great deal which
cannot possibly be verified is put into the word God;
and we propose, for the God of the Bible and of
Christianity, a much less pretentious definition, but
which has the advantage of containing nothing that
cannot be verified.   The God of the Bible and of
Christianity is, we say: *The Eternal, not ourselves, that
makes for righteousness.*

Almost with one voice our critics have expostulated
with us for refusing to admit what they call a personal
God.   Nothing would be easier for us than, by avail-
ing ourselves of the ambiguity natural to the use of
the term God, to give such a turn to our expressions
as might satisfy some of our critics, or might enable
our language to pass muster with the common religious
world as permissible.   But this would be clean contrary to our design.   For we want to recommend the
Bible and its religion by showing that they rest on
something which can be verified.   Now, in the Bible
God is everything.   Unless therefore we ascertain
what it is which we mean by God, and that what we

mean we can verify, we cannot recommend the Bible
as we desire.   So against all ambiguity in the use of
this term we wage war.   Mr. Llewellyn Davies says
that we ourselves admit that the most proper language
to use about God is the approximative language of
poetry and eloquence, language thrown out at an
object which it does not profess to define scientifically,
language which cannot, therefore, be adequate and
accurate.   If Israel, then, might with propriety call
God "the high and holy one that inhabiteth eternity,"
why, he asks, may not the Bishop of Gloucester with
propriety talk of "the blessed truth that the God of
the universe is a person?"   Neither the one expression nor the other is adequate ; both are approximate.
We answer : Let it be understood, then, that when
the Bishop of Gloucester, or others, talk of the
blessed truth that the God of the universe is a person, they mean to talk, not science, but rhetoric and
poetry.   In that case our only criticism on their
language will be that it is bad rhetoric and poetry,
whereas the rhetoric and poetry of Israel is good.
But the truth is they mean it for science ; they mean
it for a more close and precise account of what Israel
called poetically "the high and holy one that inhabiteth eternity;" and it is false science because
it assumes what it cannot verify.   However, if it
is not meant for science, but for poetry, let us treat
it as poetry; and then it is language not professing to be exact at all, and we are free to use it
or not to use it as our sense of poetic propriety
may dictate.   But at all events let us be clear about

one thing : Is it meant for poetry, or is it meant for science ?

If we were asked what in our own opinion we had by *Literature and Dogma* effected for the benefit of readers of the Bible, we should answer that we had effected two things above all. First, that we had led the reader to face that primary question, so habitually slurred over, what " God " means in the Bible, and to see that it means the Eternal not ourselves that makes for righteousness. Secondly, that we had made him ask himself what is meant by " winning Christ," " knowing Christ," " the excellency of the knowledge of Christ," and find that it means laying hold of the method and secret of Jesus. And of these two things achieved by us, as we think, for the Bible-reader's benefit, the first seems to us the more important. Sooner or later he will find the Bible fail him, unless he is provided with a sure meaning for the word " God." Until this is done, and to keep steadily before his mind how loosely he and others at present employ the word, we even recommend him to allow to the word no more contents than by its etymology it has, and to render it " The Shining." Archbishop Whately blames those who define words by their etymology, and ridicules them as people who should insist upon it that sycophant shall mean " fig-shewer " and nothing else. But etymological defini-tion, trifling and absurd when a word's imported meaning is sure, becomes valuable when the imported meaning is unfixed. There was at Athens a practice, says Festus, of robbing the fig-orchards ; a law was passed to check it; under this law vexatious informations were laid, and those who laid them were called *sycophants*, fig-informers, or, if Archbishop Whately pleases, fig-shewers. Then the name was transferred to vexatious informers or to calumniators generally, and at last to a cheating impostor of any sort. The wider new meaning thus imported into the word was something quite clear, something on which all were agreed; and thenceforward to insist on limiting *sycophant* to its old etymological sense of fig-informer would have been ridiculous.

But the case is different when the fuller meaning imported into a word is something vague and loose, something on which people are by no means agreed. It is then often an excellent discipline to revert to the etymology; and to insist on confining ourselves to the sense given by this, until we get for our word a larger sense clear and certain. "The Shining is our hope and strength." "O Shining, thou art my Shining, early will I seek thee!" "My soul, wait thou only upon The Shining, for my expectation is from him!" "The fool hath said in his heart: There is no Shining!"[1] This will not give us satisfaction. But it will thereby stimulate us all the more to find a meaning to the word "God" that does give us satisfaction; and it will keep vivid in our minds the thought how little we ourselves or others have such a meaning for the word at present.

Lord Lyttelton lately published in the *Contemporary Review* a disquisition on "Undogmatic and Un-

[1] Ps. xlvi. 1; lxiii. 1; lxii. 5; xiv. 1.

sectarian Teaching," which signally illustrates the utility of this etymological discipline. Lord Lyttelton is very severe upon those whom he calls "the shallow sciolists and apostles of modern Unsectarianism;" and very favourable to dogma, or the determined, decreed and received doctrine of so-called orthodox theology. He draws out a formal list of propositions beginning with: "God is, God made the world, God cares for men, God is the Father of men," and ending with: "The Deity of God is in one sense One in another Threefold, God is One in Three Persons." He defies any one to show where in this list that which is universal ends and that which is dogmatic begins. And his inference apparently is, that therefore the last propositions in the series may be freely taught. But if he examines his thoughts with attention he will find that he cannot tell where the character of his propositions changes because he has been using the word "God" in the same sense all through the series. Now, the sense given to this word governs the sense of each and all of his propositions, but this sense he omits to furnish us with. Until we have it, we may agree that his latter propositions are dogmatic, but we cannot possibly concede to him that his earlier propositions have universal validity. Yet the whole force of his series of propositions, and of the argument which he founds upon it, depends on this: whether his definition of God, which he does not produce, is unchallengeable or no. Till he produces it, his readers will really best enable themselves to feel the true force of Lord Lyttelton's propositions by sub-

stituting for the word God its strict etymological
equivalent Shining,—the only definition to which,
until the fuller definition is produced and made good,
the word has any right. The propositions will then
run : "The Shining is, The Shining made the world,
The Shining cares for men, The Shining is the Father
of men ;" and so on to the final proposition : "The
Shining is One in Three Persons." That entire incon-
clusiveness, of which we are by these means made
fully aware, exists just as much in Lord Lyttelton's
original propositions, but without being noticed by
himself or by most of his readers.

Resolutely clear with himself, then, in using this
word "God," we urge our reader to be, whatever
offence he may give by it. When he is asked in a
tone of horrified remonstrance whether he refuses to
believe in a personal God, let him steadily examine
what it is that people say about a personal God, and
what grounds he has for receiving it. People say
that there is a personal God, and that a personal
God is a God who thinks and loves. That there is
an Eternal not ourselves which makes for righteousness and is called God, is admitted ; and indeed so
much as this human experience proves. For the
constitution and history of things show us that happiness, at which we all aim, is dependent on righteousness. Yet certainly we did not make this to be so,
and it did not begin when we began, nor does it end
when we end, but is, so far as we can see, an eternal
tendency outside us, prevailing whether we will or
no, whether we are here or not. There is no diffi-

culty, therefore, about an Eternal not ourselves that makes for righteousness, and to which men have transferred that ancient high name, *God*, the Brilliant or Shining, by which they once adored a mighty object outside themselves, the sun, which from the first took their notice as powerful for their weal or woe. So that God is, is admitted; but people maintain, besides, that he is personal and thinks and loves. "The Divine Being cannot," they say, "be without the perfection which manifests itself in the human personality as the highest of which we have any knowledge." Now, "the deeper elements of personality are," they add, "existence, consciousness of this existence and control over it." These, therefore, they say, God must have. And that the Eternal that makes for righteousness has these, they account (though their language is not always quite consistent on this point) a fact of the same order and of as much certainty as that there is an Eternal that makes for righteousness at all. "It is this power itself," says M. Albert Réville, "this not ourselves which makes for righteousness, that constantly reveals to us the fact that it is a Spirit, that is to say, not merely an influence, but life, consciousness, and love." Religion, it is affirmed, religion, which is morality touched with emotion, is impossible unless we know of God that he is a person who thinks and loves. "If the not ourselves which makes for righteousness," says M. Réville, "is an unconscious force, I cannot feel for it that sacred emotion which raises morality to the rank of religion. Man no longer worships powers of which he has discovered the action to be impersonal." All this sort of argumentation, which M. Réville manages with great delicacy and literary skill, is summed up in popular language plainly and well by a writer in the *Edinburgh Review.* "Is the Power around us not a person; is what you would have us worship a thing? All existing beings must be either persons or things; and no sophistries can deter us from the invincible persuasion which all human creatures possess, that *persons* are superior to *things.*"

Now, before going farther, we have one important remark to make upon all this. M. Réville talks of those who *have discovered* the action of God to be impersonal. In another place he talks of *denying* conscious intelligence to God. The Edinburgh Reviewer talks of those who would have us worship a *thing.* We assure M. Réville that we do not profess to have discovered the nature of God to be impersonal, nor do we deny to God conscious intelligence. We assure the Edinburgh Reviewer that we do not assert God to be a *thing.* All we say is that men do not know enough about the Eternal not ourselves that makes for righteousness, to warrant their pronouncing this either a person or a thing. We say that no one has discovered the nature of God to be personal, or is entitled to assert that God has conscious intelligence. Theologians assert this and make it the basis of religion. It is they who assert and profess to know, not we. We object to their professing to know more than can be known, to their insisting we shall receive

it, to their resting religion upon it. We want to rest
religion on what can be verified, not on what cannot.
And M. Réville himself seems, when he lets us see
the bottom of his thoughts, to allow that a personal
God who thinks and loves cannot really be verified,
for he says : "It is in vain to ask how we can verify
the fact that God possesses consciousness and intelligence." But we are for resting religion upon some
fact of which it shall not be in vain to ask whether
we can verify it. However, the theologians' conception of God is represented as a far more satisfying
one in itself than ours, and as having, besides, much
to make its truth highly probable, at any rate, if not
demonstrable. And the reader of *Literature and
Dogma* may think, perhaps, that we have been over-
cautious, over-negative; that we are really, as M.
Réville says, "decidedly too much afraid of the idea
of the personality of God." He may think, that
though we have given him as his foundation something verifiable and sure, yet that what we have
given him is a great deal less than what the theologians offer, and offer with such strong and good
reasons for its truth, that it becomes almost certain
if not quite, and a man is captious who will not
accept it.

Descartes, as is well known, had a famous philosophical method for discovering truths of all kinds ;
and people heard of his method and used to press
him to give them the results which this wonderful
organ had enabled him to ascertain. Quite in a contrary fashion, we sometimes flatter ourselves with

the hope that we may be of use by the very absence
of all scientific pretension, by our very want of "a
philosophy based on principles interdependent, sub-
ordinate and coherent ; " because we are thus obliged
to treat great questions in such a simple way that
any one can follow us, while the way, at the same
time, may possibly be quite right after all, only over-
looked by more ingenious people because it is so very
simple.

Now, proceeding in this manner, we venture to
ask the plain reader whether it does not strike him
as an objection to our making God a person who
thinks and loves, that we have really no experience
whatever, not the very slightest, of persons who think
and love, except in man and the inferior animals. We
for our part are by no means disposed to deny that
the inferior animals, as they are called, may have
consciousness, that they may be said to think and
love, in however low a degree. At any rate we can
see them before us doing certain things which are
like what we do ourselves when we think and love,
so that thinking and loving may be attributed to
them also without one's failing to understand what
is meant, and they may conceivably be called persons who think and love. But really this is all the
experience of any sort that we have of persons who
think and love,—the experience afforded by ourselves
and the lower animals. True, we easily and naturally
attribute all operations that engage our notice to
authors who live and think like ourselves. We
make persons out of sun, wind, love, envy, war,

fortune; in some languages every noun is male or
female. But this, we know, is figure and personifi-
cation. Being ourselves alive and thinking, we
naturally invest things with these our attributes,
and imagine all action and operation to proceed as
our own proceeds. This is a tendency which in
common speech and in poetry, where we do not
profess to speak exactly, we cannot well help following, and which we follow lawfully. In the language
of common speech and of poetry, we speak of the
Eternal not ourselves that makes for righteousness,
as if he were a person who thinks and loves. Naturally we speak of him so, and there is no objection
at all to our so doing.

But it is different when we profess to speak
exactly, and yet make God a person who thinks and
loves. We then find what difficulty our being
actually acquainted with no persons superior to ourselves who think and love brings us into. Some,
we know, have made their God in the image of the
inferior animals. We have had the God Apis and
the God Anubis; but these are extravagances. In
general, as God is said to have made man in his own
image, the image of God, man has returned the
compliment and has made God as being, outwardly
or inwardly, in the image of man. What we in
general do is to take the best thinking and loving of
the best man, to better this best, to call it *perfect*,
and to say that this is God. So we construct a
magnified and non-natural man, by dropping out all
that in man seems a source of weakness and inserting

its contrary, and by heightening to the very utmost all that in man seems a source of strength, such as his thought and his love. Take the account of God which begins the Thirty-nine Articles, or the account of God in any Confession of Faith we may choose. The same endeavour shows itself in all of them : to construct a man who thinks and loves, but so immensely bettered that he is a man no longer. Then between this magnified man and ourselves we put, if we please, angels, who are men etherealised. The objection to the magnified man and to the men etherealised is one and the same : that we have absolutely no experience whatever of either the one or the other.

Support, however, is obtained for them from two grounds ;—from metaphysical grounds, and from the ground of miracles. Let us take first the ground said to be given by miracles. Interferences and communications of such a kind as to be explainable on no other supposition than that of a magnified and non-natural man, with etherealised men ministering to him, are alleged to have actually happened and to be warranted by sure testimony. And there is something in this. If the alleged interferences and communications have happened, then by this supposition they may fairly be explained. If the progress of the natural day was really stopped to enable the chosen people to win a great victory over its enemies, if a voice out of the sky really said when Jesus was baptized : *This is my beloved Son*,—then the magnified and non-natural man of popular religion,

either by himself or with angels, etherealised men,
for his ministers, is a supposition made credible,
probable, and even almost necessary, by those
incidents.

II.

Thus we are thrown back on miracles; and the
question is, are we to affirm that God is a person who
thinks and loves because miracles compel us? Now,
the reader of *Literature and Dogma* will recollect that
half-a-dozen pages of that book, and not more, were
taken up with discussing miracles. The *Guardian*
thinks this insufficient. It says that solid replies are
demanded to solid treatises, and that we ought to
have taken Dr. Mozley's Bampton Lectures on
Miracles, and given, if we could, a refutation to them.
It tartly adds, however, that to expect this of us
"would be to expect something entirely at variance
with Mr. Arnold's antecedents and with his whole
nature." Well, the author of *Supernatural Religion*
has occupied half a thick volume in refuting Dr.
Mozley's Bampton Lectures. He has written a solid
reply to that solid treatise. Sure we are that he has
not convinced the *Guardian*, but it ought at least to
be pleased with him for having so far done his duty.
For our part, although we do justice to Dr. Mozley's
ability, yet to write a refutation of his Bampton
Lectures is precisely, in our opinion, to do what
Strauss has well called "going out of one's way to
assail the paper fortifications which theologians
choose to set up." To engage in an *à priori* argu-

ment to prove that miracles are impossible, against an adversary who argues *à priori* that they are possible, is the vainest labour in the world. So long as the discussion was of this character, miracles were in no danger. The time for it is now past, because the human mind, whatever may be said for or against miracles *à priori*, is now in fact losing its reliance upon them. And it is losing it for this reason : as its experience widens, it gets acquainted with the natural history of miracles, it sees how they arise, and it slowly but inevitably puts them aside.

Far from excusing ourselves for the brevity and moderation with which the subject of miracles is in *Literature and Dogma* treated, we are disposed to claim praise for it. It is possible to spend a great deal too much time and mental energy over the thesis that miracles cannot be relied on. The thesis, though true, is merely negative, and therefore of secondary importance. The important question is, what becomes of religion,—so precious, as we believe, to the human race,—if miracles cannot be relied on? We ought never so to immerse ourselves in the argument against miracles as to forget that the main question lies beyond, and that we must press forward to it. As soon as we satisfy ourselves that on miracles we cannot build, let us have done with questions about them and begin to build on something surer. Now, it is in a much more simple and unpretending way than controversialists commonly follow that we satisfy ourselves that we cannot build upon miracles.

For it is possible, again, to exaggerate untruly the

demonstrative force of the case against miracles. The logical completeness of the case for miracles has been vaunted, and vaunted falsely; some people are now disposed to vaunt falsely the logical completeness of the case against miracles. Poor human nature loves the pretentious forms of exact knowledge, though with the real condition of our thoughts they often ill correspond. The author of *Supernatural Religion* asserts again and again that miracles are contradictory to a complete induction. He quotes Mr. Mill's rule: "Whatever is contradictory to a complete induction is incredible," and quotes Mr. Mill's account of a complete induction : "When observations or experiments have been repeated so often and by so many persons as to exclude all supposition of error in the observer, a law of nature is established ;" and he asserts that a law of nature of this kind has been established against miracles. He brings forward that famous test by which Paley seeks to establish the Christian miracles, his "twelve men of known probity and good sense relating a miracle wrought before their eyes, and consenting to be racked and burned sooner than acknowledge that there existed any falsehood or imposture in the case," and he asserts that no affirmation of any twelve men would be sufficient to overthrow a law of nature, or to save, therefore, the Christian miracles.

Now, these assertions are exaggerated and will not serve. No such law of nature as Mr. Mill describes has been or can be established against the Christian miracles ; a complete induction against them, there-

fore, there is not.   Nor does the evidence of their
reporters fail because the evidence of no men can
make miracles credible.   The case against the Christian miracles is that we have an induction, not
complete, indeed, but enough more and more to
satisfy the mind, and to satisfy it in an ever increasing number of men, that miracles are untrustworthy.
The case against their reporters is, that more and
more of us see, and see ever more clearly, that these
reporters were not and could not be the sort of
picked jury that Paley's argument requires, but that,
with all the good faith in the world, they were men
likely to fall into error about miracles, to make a
miracle where there was none, and that they did fall
into error and legend accordingly.

This being so, we have no inclination, even now,
either to dwell at excessive length on the subject of
miracles, or to make a grand show of victoriously de-
monstrating their impossibility.   But we have to ask
ourselves, if necessary, again and again, whenever
anything is made to depend upon them, how their
case really and truly stands, whether there can be
any prospect, either for ourselves or for those in
whose interest *Literature and Dogma* was written, of
returning to a reliance upon them.   And the more
we consider it the more we are convinced there is
none ; and that the cause assigned in *Literature and
Dogma* as fatal to miracles ;—that the more our experience widens, the more we see and understand the
process by which they arose, and their want of
solidity,—is fatal to them indeed.   The time has

come when the minds of men no longer put as a
matter of course the Bible-miracles in a class by themselves.   Now, from the moment this time commences,
from the moment that the comparative history of all
miracles is a conception entertained and a study
admitted, the conclusion is certain, the reign of the
Bible-miracles is doomed.

III.

Let us see how this is so.   Herodotus relates,
that, when the Persian invaders came to Delphi, two
local heroes buried near the place, Phylacus and
Autonous, arose, and were seen, of more than mortal
stature, fighting against the Persians.[1]   He relates,
that before the onset at Salamis the vision of a
woman appeared over an Æginetan ship, and cried
in a voice which all the Grecian fleet heard : "Good
souls, how long will ye keep backing ?"[2]   He relates,
that at Pedasus, in the neighbourhood of his own
city Halicarnassus, the priestess of Athene had a
miraculous sprouting of beard whenever any grievous
calamity was about to befall the people around ; he
says in one place that twice this miraculous growth
had happened, in another that it had happened
thrice.[3]   Herodotus writes here of times when he
was himself alive, not of a fabulous antiquity.   He
and his countrymen were not less acute, arguing,
critical people than the Jews of Palestine, but much
more.   Herodotus himself, finally, is a man of a
beautiful character and of pure good-faith.

[1] Herod. viii. 38, 39.   [2] Herod. viii. 84.   [3] Herod. viii. 104.

But we do not believe that Phylacus and Autonous arose out of their graves and were seen fighting with the Persians; we know by experience, we all say, how this sort of story grows up. And that after the Crucifixion, then, many dead saints arose and came out of the graves and went into the holy city and appeared unto many, is not this too a story of which we must say, the moment we fairly put it side by side with the other, that it is of the same kind with it, and that we know how the sort of story grows up? That the Phantom-woman called to the Æginetan crew at Salamis, *How long will ye keep backing?* we do not believe any the more because we are told that all the Grecian fleet heard it. We know, we all say, by experience, that this is just the sort of corroboration naturally added to such a story. But we are asked to believe that Jesus after his death actually cried to Paul on his way to Damascus: *It is hard for thee to kick against the pricks,* because the bystanders are said to have heard it, although to be sure in another place, with the looseness natural to such a story, the bystanders are said *not* to have heard this voice. That the Salamis story and the Damascus story are of one kind, and of what kind, strikes us the moment that we put the two stories together.

The miraculous beard of the priestess of Pedasus is really just like the miraculous dumbness of Zacharias, the father of John the Baptist. The priestess of Pedasus, however, is said by Herodotus in one place to have twice had her marvellous beard, in another to have had it thrice; and the discrepancy

proves, we all say, how loose and unhistorical this
kind of story is. But yet when Jesus is in the Second
Gospel said to have healed as he departed from
Jericho one blind man who sate by the wayside, and
in the First Gospel to have healed as he departed
from Jericho two blind men who sate by the wayside,
there is here, we are asked to believe, no discrepancy
really at all. Two different healings are meant,
which were performed at two different visits to
Jericho. Or perhaps they were performed at one
and the same visit, but one was performed as Jesus
entered the city, and the other as he left it. And
the words of St Mark : "And he came to Jericho ;
and as he went out of Jericho blind Bartimæus sate
by the wayside," really mean that Bartimæus sate
there as Jesus went *in* to Jericho, and two other
blind men sate by the wayside as he went *out*. How
arbitrary, unnatural, and vain such an explanation is,
what a mere device of our own to make a solid
history out of a legend, we never feel so irresistibly
as when we put the Jericho story by the side of
others like it.

Yet still, in new and popular books, this precious
device for reconciling inconsistent accounts of the
same thing, — the hypothesis that the incident did
really happen more than once, — is furbished up and
brought out afresh. So strong, so persistent, so
desperate is the endeavour to make that wonderful
mixture of truth and fiction, which the Four Gospels
give us, into one uniform strain of solid history. The
attempt must fail. It will impair the understanding

of all who make it, it will mar the reputation of every critic who makes it, and yet will disappoint them after all. The kindest thing one can do to an intelligent reader of the Bible is to convince him of the utter hopelessness of any such attempt, to bring him speedily and once for all to a state of settled clearness on the subject. And this will be done, not so well directly, by arguing how improbable such an hypothesis as that incidents should exactly repeat themselves in itself is, as indirectly, by showing from examples how very prone is the human imagination to reproduce striking incidents a second time, although the incidents have in truth occurred only once.

To save the exactness of the Gospel narratives, the stories of the healing of the blind men at Jericho are made to pass, we have seen, for the stories of two separate miracles. But a more remarkable instance still of the actual production of an incident twice, is alleged in regard to the clearing the Temple of buyers and sellers. The Fourth Gospel, as is well known, puts the clearance at the beginning of Christ's career. The Synoptics put it at the end, shortly before his arrest. Probably the Synoptics are right; for the act was one which, coming from an unknown man, would have merely seemed extravagant and exasperating, whereas, coming from Jesus after his line of teaching and reforming had become familiar, it would have had significance and use. But be this as it may ; at any rate, if the act was done at the outset of the career of Jesus, then the Synoptics, one would say, must have made a mistake; if at the close, then the author of the Fourth Gospel. Not at all ! The same striking incident with all its circumstances really happened, we are told, twice : first at the outset of Christ's career, and then again at its close. Neither the Synoptics, therefore, nor the author of the Fourth Gospel are in error.

Now, this seems surprising. But some who are lovers of the Bible may be inclined to try and believe it, may seek to cling to such an explanation, may argue for its possibility à *priori*. Crumble to bits, sooner or later, such explanations will. That which may convince a man, once and for ever, of their hollowness, and save him much loss of time and distress of mind, is the application of such a piece of experience as the following :—

Some years ago a newly-married couple were during their honeymoon travelling in the Alps. They made an excursion on Mont Blanc ; the bride met with an accident there, and perished before her husband's eyes. The other day we had, strange to relate, just this touching story over again. Again a newly-married couple were in the Alps during their honeymoon, again Mont Blanc was the scene of an excursion, again the bride met with an accident, again she perished in her husband's sight. Surprising, but there was the fact ! People talked of it, the telegraph spread it abroad. But ours is a time of broad daylight and searching inquiry. The matter drew attention, and in a few days the telegraph announced that the second accident had never really happened at all, that it was a mere doubling and reflection of the first. Men's imagination reiterates in this way things which strike it, and loose relation narrates the doubled fact seriously. As our experience widens, it brings us more and more proof that this is so; and one day a signal example is decisive with us. The Mont Blanc story, or some story of the kind, comes with a sort of magic to make the scales fall from our eyes. It is still possible *à priori* that the Temple may have been cleared twice, and that there is no mistake in the Gospel reports. The induction against it is not a complete induction. But it is henceforth complete enough to serve; it convinces us. In spite of the *à priori* possibility, we cannot any longer believe in the double clearance of the Temple, and in the exactitude of both the accounts in the Gospels, even though we would.

IV

It is this impossibility of resting religion any more on grounds once supposed to be safe, such as that the Gospel narratives are free from mistake and that the Gospel miracles are trustworthy, which compels us to look for new grounds upon which we may build firmly. Those men do us an ill turn, and we owe them no thanks for it, who compel us to keep going back to examine the old grounds, and declaring their want of solidity. What we need is to have done with all this negative, unfruitful business, and to get to religion again;—to the use of the Bible upon new grounds which shall be secure. The old grounds cannot be used safely any more, and if one opens one's eyes one must see it. Those who inveigh against us could see it, if they chose, as plainly as we do ; and they ought to open their eyes and see it, but they will not. And they want us to go on trusting foolishly to the old grounds as they do, until all tumbles in, and there is a great ruin and confusion. Let us not do so. Let those who have read *Literature and Dogma* with satisfaction be sure that what is in that book said against miracles, kept though it be within the narrowest limits possible, is indispensable, and requires so little space just because it is so very certain. Let him accustom himself to treat with steadiness, with rigorous simplicity, all the devices to save those unsaveable things, the Bible miracles.

To reduce the miraculous in them to what are thought reasonable dimensions is now a favourite attempt. But if anything miraculous is left, the whole miracle might as well have been left ; if nothing, how has the incident any longer the proving force of a miracle ? Let us treat so absurd an attempt as it deserves. Neander supposes that the water at the marriage-feast at Cana was not changed by Jesus into wine, but was only endued by him with wine's brisk taste and exhilarating effects. This has all the difficulties of the miracle, and only gets rid of the poetry. It is as if we were startled by the extravagance of supposing Cinderella's fairy godmother to have actually changed the pumpkin into a coach and six, but suggested that she did really change it into a one-horse brougham. Many persons, again, feel

now an insurmountable suspicion (and no wonder) of
Peter's fish with the tribute-money in its mouth, and
they suggest that what really happened was that
Peter caught a fish, sold it, and paid the tribute with
the money he thus got. This is like saying that all
Cinderella's godmother really did was to pay a cab
for her godchild by selling her vegetables. But then
what becomes of the wonder, the miracle? Were
there ever such apologists as these? They impair the
credit of the Evangelists as much as we do, for they
make them transform facts to an extent wholly incompatible with trustworthy reporting. They impair
it more; for they make them transform facts with a
method incompatible with honest simplicity.

Simple, flexible common-sense is what we most
want, in order to be able to follow truly the dealings
of that spontaneous, irregular, wonderful power which
gives birth to tales of miracle,—the imagination. It
is easy to be too systematic. Strauss had the idea,
acute and ingenious, of explaining the miracles of the
New Testament as a reiteration of the miracles of the
Old. Of some miracles this supplies a good explanation. It plausibly explains the story of the Trans-
figuration, for instance. The story of the illumined
face of Jesus,—Jesus, the prophet like unto Moses,
whom Moses foretold,—might naturally owe its origin
to the illumined face of Moses himself. But of other
miracles, such as the walking on the Lake of Genne-
saret or the cursing of the barren fig-tree, Strauss'
idea affords no admissible explanation whatever. To
employ it for these cases can only show the imper-

turbable resolution of a German professor in making
all the facts suit a theory which he has once adopted.
But every miracle has its own mode of growth and
its own history, and the key to one is not the key
to others. Such a rationalising explanation as that
above quoted of the money in the mouth of Peter's
fish is ridiculous. Yet a clue, a suggestion, however
slight, of fact, there probably was to every miracle;
and sometimes, not by any means always, this clue
may be traced with likelihood.

The story of the feeding of the thousands may well
have had its rise in the suspension, the comparative
extinction, of hunger and thirst during hours of rapt
interest and intense mental excitement. In such
hours a trifling sustenance, which would commonly
serve for but a few, will suffice for many. Rumour
and imagination make and add details, and swell the
thing into a miracle. This sort of incident, again, it
is as natural to conceive repeating itself, as it is unnatural to conceive an incident like the clearance of
the Temple repeating itself. Or to take the walking
on the Sea of Galilee. Here, too, the sort of hint of
fact which may have started the miracle will readily
occur to every one. Sometimes the hint of fact, lost
in our Bibles, is preserved elsewhere. The Gospel of
the Hebrews,—an old Gospel outside the Canon of
Scripture, but which Jerome quotes and of which we
have fragments,—this Gospel, and other records of
like character, mention what our Four Gospels do
not: a wonderful light at the moment when Jesus
was baptized. No one, so far as we know, has yet re-

marked that in this small and dropped circumstance, —a weird light on Jordan seen while Jesus was baptized,—we not improbably have the little original nucleus of solid fact round which the whole miraculous story of his baptism gathered.

He does well, who, steadily using his own eyes in this manner, and escaping from the barren routine whether of the assailants of the Bible or of its apologists, acquires the serene and imperturbable conviction, indispensable for all fruitful use of the Bible in future, that in travelling through its reports of miracles he moves in a world, not of solid history, but of illusion, rumour, and fairy-tale. Only, when he has acquired this, let him say to himself that he has by so doing achieved nothing, except to get rid of an insecure reliance which inevitably some day or other would have cost him dear, of a staff in religion which must sooner or later have pierced his hand.

One other thing, however, he has done besides this. He has discovered the hollowness of the main ground for making God a person who thinks and loves, a magnified and non-natural man. Only a kind of man magnified could so make man the centre of all things, and interrupt the settled order of nature in his behalf, as miracles imply. But in miracles we are dealing, we find, with the unreal world of fairy-tale. Having no reality of their own, they cannot lend it as foundation for the reality of anything else.

CHAPTER II.

THE GOD OF METAPHYSICS.

THERE remain the grounds for asserting God to be a person who thinks and loves which are supplied by metaphysics.

"Continuo auditæ voces, vagitus et ingens."

At the mention of that name *metaphysics*, lo, essence, existence, substance, finite and infinite, cause and succession, something and nothing, begin to weave their eternal dance before us! with the confused murmur of their combinations filling all the region governed by *her*, who, far more indisputably than her late-born rival, political economy, has earned the title of the Dismal Science. Yet even here we will ask the reader of *Literature and Dogma*, if he does not disdain so unsophisticated a companion, to enter with us. And here, possibly, we may after all find reason to retract, and to own that the theologians are right. For metaphysics we know from the very name to be the science of things which come after natural things. Now, the things which come after natural things are things not natural. Clearly, therefore, if any science is likely to be able to demonstrate to us the magnified

and non-natural man, it must be the science of non-
naturals.

II.

Professor Huxley's interesting discourse the other
day at Belfast drew attention to a personage who
once was in the thoughts of everybody who tried to
think,—René Descartes.   But in this great man there
were, in truth, two men.   One was the anatomist,
the physicist, the mechanical philosopher who exclaimed : " Give me matter and motion, and I will
make the world ! " and of whom Pascal said that the
only God he admitted was a God who was useless.
This is the Descartes on whom Professor Huxley has
asked us to turn once more our eyes : and no man
could ask it better or more persuasively.

But there is another Descartes who had of late
years been much more known, both in his own country
and out of it, than Descartes the mechanical philosopher, and that is the Descartes who is said to have
founded the independence of modern philosophy and to
have founded its spiritualism. He began with universal
doubt, with the rejection of all authority, with the resolve to admit nothing to be true which he could not
clearly see to be true.   He ended with declaring that
the demonstration of God and the soul was more completely made out than that of any other truth whatever, nay, that the certitude and truth of every science
depended solely on our knowledge of the true God.[1]

[1] " Je reconnais très clairement que la certitude et la vérité de
toute science dépend de la seule connaissance du vrai Dieu."

Here we have the Descartes who is commonly said to have founded modern philosophy. And who, in this our day of unsettlement and of impatience with authority, convention, and routine, who, in this our day of new departures, can fail to be attracted by the author of the *Méthode*, and by his promises? "*Je n'admets rien qui ne soit nécessairement vrai;* I admit nothing which is not necessarily true." "*Je m'éloigne de tout ce en quoi je pourrais imaginer le moindre doute;* I put aside everything about which I can imagine there being the smallest doubt." What could we, who demand that the propositions we accept shall be propositions we can verify, ask more? "*Il n'y a que les choses que je conçois clairement et distinctement qui aient la force de me persuader entièrement; Je ne puis me tromper dans les jugements dont je connais clairement les raisons;* Only those things which I conceive clearly and distinctly have the power thoroughly to persuade me; I cannot be mistaken in those judgments of which I clearly know the reasons." What can be better? We have really no other ground for the certainty of our convictions than this clearness.

Will it be said, however, that there is here an opening, at any rate, for unsoundness, and that in the following sentence, for example, we can plainly see how? "*Toutes les choses que nous concevons clairement et distinctement sont vraies de la façon dont nous les concevons;* All things that we conceive clearly and distinctly are true as we conceive them." There is an ambiguity, is there not, about "clearly and distinctly;" a man may say or fancy he sees a thing clearly and distinctly, when he does nothing of the kind? True, this is so; a man may deceive himself as to what constitutes clearness and distinctness. Still, the test is good. We can only be sure of our judgments from their clearness and distinctness, though we may sometimes fancy that this clearness and distinctness is present when it is not.

At any rate, that first and greatest rule of Descartes, never to receive anything as true without having clearly known it for such, is for us unchallengeable. How vain and dangerous did we find Butler's proposal that we should take as the foundation of our religion something for which we had a low degree of probability! In this direction, assuredly, Descartes does not err. "Inasmuch as my reason convinces me," says he, "that I ought to be as careful to withhold my belief from things not quite certain and indubitable as from those which I plainly see to be false, it will be a sufficient ground to me for rejecting all my old opinions if I find in them all some opening for doubt." Certainly this is caution enough; to many it will even seem excess of caution.

It is true, the doubts which troubled Descartes and which have troubled so many philosophers,—doubts, whether this world in which we live, the objects which strike our senses, the things which we see and handle, have any real existence,—are not exactly the doubts by which we ourselves have been most plagued. Indeed, to speak quite frankly, they are doubts by which we have never been tormented at all. Our trouble has rather been with doubts whether things

which people assured us really existed or had really
happened, but of which we had no experience ourselves and could not satisfy ourselves that any one
else had had experience either, were really as people
told us. But probably this limited character of our
doubting arose from our want of philosophy and
philosophical principles, which is so notorious, and
which is so often and so uncharitably cast in our
teeth. Descartes could look out of his window at
Amsterdam, and see a public place filled with men
and women, and say to himself that he had yet no
right to be certain they were men and women, because
they might, after all, be mere lay figures dressed up
in hats and cloaks. This would never have occurred,
perhaps, to the generality of mankind ; to us, at any
rate, it never would have occurred. But if this sort
of scrupulosity led Descartes to establish his admirable rules : " I admit nothing which is not necessarily true ; " " Only those things which I conceive
clearly and distinctly have the power to convince
me ; " we cannot regret that he was thus scrupulous.
Men, all of them, as many as have doubts of any
kind and want certainty, find their need served when
a great man sets out with these stringent rules to
discover what is really certain and verifiable. And
we ourselves accordingly, plain unphilosophical people
as we are, did betake ourselves once to Descartes with
great zeal, and we were thus led to an experience
which we have never forgotten. And perhaps it may
be of use to other plain people, for the purpose of the
enquiry which at present occupies us,—the enquiry

whether the solid and necessary ground of religion is the assurance that God is a person who thinks and loves,—to follow over again in our company the experience which then befell us.

Every one knows that Descartes, looking about him, like Archimedes, for a firm ground whereon he might take his stand and begin to operate, for one single thing which was clearly certain and indubitable, found it in the famous "*Cogito, ergo sum;* I think, therefore I am." If I think, said he, I am, I exist; my very doubting proves that I, who doubt, am. "After thinking it well over and examining it on all sides, to this conclusion I cannot but come; I cannot but consider it settled that this proposition, *I am, I exist,* is necessarily true every time that I pronounce it or that I conceive it in my mind." The discovery of this axiom appears to have filled Descartes with a profound sense of certitude and of satisfaction. And the axiom has been hailed with general approval and adopted with general consent. Locke repeats it as self-evident, without taking the trouble to assign to Descartes the authorship of it: "If I doubt of all other things, that very doubt makes me perceive my own existence and will not suffer me to doubt of that." Thinker after thinker has paid his tribute of admiration to the axiom; it is called the foundation of modern philosophy.

Now we shall confess without shame,—for to the prick of shame in these matters, after all the tauntings and mockings we have had to undergo, we are by this time quite dead,—we shall confess that from this

fundamental axiom of Descartes we were never able
to derive that light and satisfaction which others
derived from it. And for the following reason. The
philosopher omits to tell us what he exactly means
by to *be*, to *exist*. These terms stand for the most
plain, positive, fundamental of certainties, which is
established for us by the fact that we think. Now
what to *think* means we all know ; but even if we did
not, Descartes tells us. " A thing which thinks," says
he, " is a thing which doubts, which understands,
which conceives, which affirms, which denies, which
wishes, which declines, which imagines also, and
which feels." So far so good. But Descartes does
not tell us what those other terms *be* and *exist* mean,
which express that fundamental certainty established
for us by the fact of our thinking ; and this we do
not so clearly know of ourselves without being told.
Philosophers know, of course, for they are always
using the terms. And perhaps this is why Descartes
does not trouble himself to explain his terms, I *am*,
I *exist*, because to him they carry an even more clear
and well-defined sense than the term, I *think*. But to
us they do not ; and we suspect that the majority of
plain people, if they consented to examine their minds,
would find themselves to be in like case with us.

To get a clear and well-defined sense for the terms,
I *am*, I *exist*, in the connection where Descartes uses
them, we are obliged to translate them at a venture
into something of this kind : " I feel that I am alive."
And then we get the proposition : " I think, therefore
I feel that I am alive." This asserts our conscious-

ness to depend upon our thinking rather than upon
anything else which we do.   The assertion is clear, it
is intelligible, it seems true ; and perhaps it is what
Descartes meant to convey.   Still, it is disappointing
to a plain man, who has been attracted to Descartes
by his promises of perfect clearness and distinctness,
to find that his fundamental proposition, his first
great certainty, is something which we cannot grasp
as it stands, but that we have to translate it into
other words in order to be able to grasp it.

Perhaps, too, this translation of ours does not,
after all, represent what Descartes himself meant by
" I am, I exist."   Perhaps he really did mean something more by the words, something that we fail to
grasp.   We say so, because we find him, like philosophers in general, often speaking of essence, existence, and substance, and in speaking of them he lays
down as certain and evident many propositions which
we cannot follow.   For instance, he says : " We have
the idea of an infinite substance, eternal, all-knowing,
all-powerful, the creator of all things, and with every
possible perfection."   Again, he says : " The ideas
which represent substances to us are undoubtedly
something more, and contain in themselves, so to speak,
more objective reality, that is to say, they partake by
representation in more degrees of being or perfection,
than those which represent to us modes or accidents
only."   " Undoubtedly," says he, this is so ; he intro-
duces it too with saying : " It is evident."   So our
guide, who admits nothing which is not necessarily
true, and puts aside everything about which he can

imagine there being the smallest doubt, lays down
that we have the idea of an *infinite substance ;* and
that of *substances* we have ideas distinguished from
ideas of modes or accidents by their possessing more
being, and this is equivalent to possessing more perfection. For when we assert that one thing is more
perfect than another, this means, Descartes informs us,
that it has more reality, more *being*.

All this, I say, our guide finds certain and not
admitting of the least doubt. It is part of the things
which we conceive with clearness and distinctness,
and of which, therefore, we can be persuaded
thoroughly. Man is a finite substance, that is, he
has but a limited degree of being, or perfection.
God is an infinite substance, that is, he has an un-
limited degree of being, or perfection. Existence
is a perfection, therefore God exists; thinking and
loving are perfections, therefore God thinks and
loves. In short, we have God, a perfect and infinite
Being, eternal, all-knowing, all-powerful, the creator
of all things, and having every perfection we can
think of for him. And all this turns upon the words
is, being. Infinite being, necessary being, being in
itself, as opposed to our own finite, contingent,
dependent being, is something, says Descartes, that
we clearly conceive. Now something cannot come
from nothing, and from us this infinite being could
never have come ; therefore it exists in itself, and is
what is meant by God.

Not Descartes only, but every philosopher who
attempts a metaphysical demonstration of God, will

be found to proceed in this fashion, and to appeal at
last to our conception of *being, existing.* Clarke starts
with the proposition that something must have existed
from eternity, and so arrives at a self-existent cause,
which must be an intelligent *Being;* in other words,
at God as a person who thinks and loves. Locke
lays it down that " we know there is some real being,
and that nonentity cannot produce any real being,"
and so brings us to an eternal, powerful, knowing
Being; in other words, God as a person who thinks
and loves. Of the God thus arrived at, Locke, like
Descartes, says that, "the evidence is, if I mistake
not, equal to mathematical certainty." St. Anselm
begins with an essential substantial good and great,
whereby, he says, it is absolutely certain, and whoever likes can perceive it, that all the multifarious
great and good things in the world get their goodness
and greatness; and thus again we come to a one *Being*
essentially great and good, or Divine Person who
thinks and loves.

Now here it is, we suppose, that one's want of
talent for abstract reasoning makes itself so lament-
ably felt. For to us these propositions, which we are
told are so perfectly certain, and he who will may
perceive their truth,—the propositions that we have
the idea of an infinite substance, that there is an
essential substantial good and great, that there is
some real being, that a self-existent cause must have
been from eternity, that substances are distinguished
in themselves and in our ideas of them from modes
or accidents by their possessing more being,—have

absolutely no force at all, we simply cannot follow their meaning. And so far as Descartes is concerned, this, when we first became aware of it, was a bitter disappointment to us. For he had seemed to promise us something which even *we* could understand, when he said that he put aside everything about which he could imagine there being the smallest doubt, and that the proof of things to us was in the perfect clearness and distinctness with which we conceived them.

However, men of philosophical talents will remind us of the truths of mathematics, and tell us that the three angles of a triangle are undoubtedly equal to two right angles, yet very likely from want of skill or practice in abstract reasoning we cannot see the force of *that* proposition, and it may simply have no meaning for us. And perhaps this may be so. But then the proposition in question is a deduction from certain elementary truths, and the deduction is too long or too hard for us to follow, or, at any rate, we may have not followed it or we may have forgotten it, and therefore we do not feel the force of the proposition. But the elementary assertions in geometry even we can apprehend; such as the assertion that two straight lines cannot enclose a space, or that things which are equal to the same are equal to each other. And we had hoped that Descartes, after his grand promises of clearness and certainty, would at least have set out with assertions of this kind, or else with facts of the plainest experience; that he would have started with something we might apprehend as we apprehend that three and two make five, or that fire burns. Instead of this, he starts with propositions about *being*, and does not tell us what *being* is. At one time he gives us hopes we may get to know it, for he says that to possess more being is to possess more perfection; and what men commonly mean when they talk of perfection, we think we can discover. But then we find that with Descartes to possess more perfection means to possess, not what men commonly call by that name, but to possess more being. And this seems to be merely going round in a circle, and we have to confess ourselves fairly puzzled and beaten.

So that when even Fénélon says, that most attractive of theologians: "It is certain that I conceive a Being, infinite, and infinitely perfect,"—that is to say, infinitely *being*, we have to own with sorrow and shame that we cannot conceive this at all, for want of knowing what *being* is. Yet it is, we repeat, on the clearness and certainty of our conceptions of *being*, that the demonstration of God,—the most sure, as philosophers say, of all demonstrations, and on which all others depend,—is founded. The truth of all that people tell us about God, turns upon this question what *being* is. Philosophy is full of the word, and some philosophies are concerned with hardly anything else. The scholastic philosophy, for instance, was one long debate about *being* and its conditions. Great philosophers, again, have established certain heads or "categories" as they call them, which are the final constitutive conditions of things, into

which all things may at last be run up; and at
the very top of these categories stands *essence* or
being.

Other metaphysical terms do not give us the same
difficulty. Substance, for example, which is the
Latin translation of essence or being, merely means
being in so far as *being* is taken to be the subject of
all modes and accidents, that which stands under
them and supplies the basis for them. Perhaps *being*
does really do this, but we want first to know what
being is. Spirit, which they oppose to matter, means
literally, we know, only breath, but we use it for a
being which is impalpable to touch as breath is.
Perhaps this may be right, but we want first to know
what *being* is. Existence, again, means a stepping
forth, and we are told that God's essence involves
existence, that is, that God's *being* necessarily steps
forth, comes forth. Perhaps it does, but we require
first to know what *being* is.

Till we know this, we know neither what to affirm
nor what to refuse to affirm. We refused to affirm
that God is a person who thinks and loves, because
we had no experience at all of thinking and loving
except as attached to a certain bodily organisation.
But perhaps they are not attached to this, but to
being, and we ourselves have them, not because we
have a bodily organisation, but because we partake of
being. Supreme *being*, therefore *being* in itself, which
is God, must think and love more than any of us.
Angels, too, there may be, whole hierarchies of them,
thinking and loving, and having their basis in *being*.

In the same way, again, our difficulties about the
Real Presence may vanish. In bread there is, perhaps, an essence or substance separable from what
the theologians call "that group of visible and
tangible phenomena which suggest the presence of
bread," in other words, from that assemblage of
certain atoms in a certain combination which we
think is the bread; and in the Sacred Host this
essence or substance is not substance of bread but
divine substance. All this may be so; only we cannot possibly verify any of it until we know what
being is; and we want to rest religion upon something which we can verify. And we thought that
Descartes, with his splendid promises, was going to
help us here; but just at the very pinch of the
matter he fails us.

After all, plain, simple people are the great
majority of the human race. And we are sure, as
we have said, that hundreds and thousands of people,
if their attention were drawn to the matter, would
acknowledge that they shared our slowness to see at
once what *being* is, and, when they found how much
depended on seeing it, would gladly accompany us in
the search for some one who could give us help. For
on this we ourselves, at any rate, were bent:—to discover some one who could tell us what *being* is. Such
a kind soul we did at last find; and in these days we
need hardly add that he was a German professor.

III.

But not a professor of logic and metaphysics. No, not Hegel, not one of those great men, those masters of abstruse reasoning, who discourse of being and non-being, essence and existence, subject and object, in a style to which that of Descartes is merely child's play. These sages only bewildered us more than we were bewildered already. For they were so far advanced in their speculations about being, that they were altogether above entertaining such a tyro's question as what *being* really was.

No, our professor was a mere professor of words, not of ontology. We bethought ourselves of our old resource, following the history of the human spirit, tracking its course, trying to make out how men have used words and what they meant by them. Perhaps in the word *being* itself, said we to ourselves, there may be something to tell us what it at first meant and how men came to use it as they do. *Abstracta ex concretis*, say the etymologists; the abstract has been formed out of the concrete. Perhaps this abstract *being*, also, has been formed out of some concrete, and if we knew out of what, we might possibly trace how it has come to be used as it has. Or has indeed the mystic vocable no natural history of this sort, but has dropped out of heaven, and all one can say of it is that it means *being*, something which the philosophers understand but we never shall, and which explains and demonstrates all sorts of hard problems, but to philosophers only, and not to the common herd of mankind ? Let us enquire, at any rate.

So, then, the natural history of the word was what we wanted. With a proper respect for our Aryan forefathers, first we looked in Sanscrit dictionaries for information. But here, probably from our own ignorance and inexperience in the Sanscrit language, we failed to find what we sought. By a happy chance, however, it one day occurred to us to turn for aid to a book about the Greek language,—a language where we were not quite so helpless as in Sanscrit,—to the "Principles of Greek Etymology,' by Dr. George Curtius, of Leipsic.[1] He it was who succoured a poor soul whom the philosophers had driven well-nigh to despair, and he deserves, and shall have, our everlasting gratitude.

In the book of Dr. Curtius we looked out the Greek verb *eimi, eis, esti*, the verb which has the same source as the English verb *is*. Shall we ever forget the emotion with which we read what follows :— "That the meaning, addressed to the senses, of this very old verb substantive was *breathe*, is made all but certain by the Sanscrit *as-u-s*, life-breath, *asu-ra-s*, living, and the Sanscrit *ás*, mouth, parallel with the Latin *os*. The Hebrew verb substantive *haja* or *hawa* has, according to Renan (*De l'Origine du Langage*, 4th ed., p. 129), the same original signification. The three main meanings succeed one another in the following order : *breathe, live, be ?* Here was some

---

[1] *Grundzüge der Griechishen Etymologie*, von Georg Curtius, 3d edit., Leipzig 1869.

F

light at last ! We get, then, for the English *is*,—the French and Latin *est*, the Greek *estin* or *esti*,—we get an Indo-European root *as*, breathe.

To get even thus much was pleasant, but what was our joy to find ourselves put by Dr. Curtius, in some words following those we have quoted, on the trace of a meaning for the mysterious term *being* itself? Dr. Curtius spoke of a root synonymous with *as*, the root *bhu*, in Greek φυ, and referred his readers to No. 417. To No. 417 we impatiently turned. We found there the account of the Greek verb φύω, φύομαι, I beget, I grow. This word is familiar to us all in our own words *future* and *physics*, in the French *fus*, in the Latin *fui*. All these are from an Indo-European root *bhu*, "be," which had primarily that sense of "grow" which its Greek derivative has kept. "The notion *be* attaches to this root," says Dr. Curtius, "evidently on the foundation only of the more primitive *grow*." If the root *as*, breathe, gives us, then, our *is*, *essence*, the root *bhu*, grow, gives us our *be*, *being*. Is, essence and entity, am, be and being, here we have the source of them all ! as in another Indo-European root, *sta*, stand, we have, as everybody knows, the source of our words *existence*, *substance*. Our composite verb substantive in English, like the verb substantive in Latin, employs both the root *as* and the root *bhu* ; we have *is* and *be*, as the Latin has *est* and *fui*. The French verb substantive manages to employ,—so M. Littré in his admirable new dictionary points out,—the roots *as*, *bhu*, and *sta*, all three.

Now, then, it remained for us to ask, how these harmless concretes, *breathe*, *grow*, and *stand*, could ever have risen into those terrible abstracts, *is*, *be*, and *exist*, which had given us so much torment. And really, by attending to the natural course followed by the human mind, to men's ways of using words and arriving at thoughts, this was not so very hard to make out. Only, when once it was made out, it proved fatal to the wonderful performances of the metaphysicians upon their theme of *being*. However, we must not anticipate.

Men took these three simple names of the foremost and most elementary activities in that which they knew best and were chiefly concerned with,—in themselves,—they took *breathing*, *growing*, *standing forth*, to describe *all* activities which were remarked by their senses or by their minds. So arose the verb substantive. Children, we can observe, do not connect their notions at all by the verb, the word expressing activity. They say, "horse, black," and there they leave it. When man's mind advanced beyond this simple stage, and he wanted to connect his notions by representing one notion as affecting him through its appearing or operating in conjunction with another notion, then he took a figure from the activity that lay nearest to him and said : " The horse breathes (is) black." When he got to the use of abstract nouns his verb still remained the same. He said : " Virtue breathes (is) fair ; Valour growing (being) praiseworthy." Soon the sense of the old concrete meaning faded away in the new employ-

ment of the word. That slight parcel of significance
which was required had been taken, and now this
minimum alone remained, and the rest was left unregarded and died out of men's thoughts.

We may make this clearer to ourselves by observ-
ing what has happened in the French and Dutch
words for our common word *but*. *But* is in French
mais, the Latin *magis*, our word *more*; in Dutch it is
maar, our word *more* itself. *Mais* and *maar* were
originally used, no doubt with the sense of their
being a check, or stop, given to something that had
been said before, by the *addition* to it of something
fresh. The primitive sense of addition faded away,
the sense of check remained alone. And so it was
with *as* and *bhu*, the primitive *breathe* and *grow*.
Whatever affected us by appearing to us, or by acting on us, was at first said by a figure to breathe and
grow. The figure was forgotten; and now *as* and
bhu no longer raised the idea of breathing and growing, but merely of that appearance or operation,—a
kind of shadow of breathing and growing,—which
these words *as* and *bhu* had at first been employed to
convey. And for breathing and growing other words
than *as* and *bhu* were now found, just as, in French,
mais now no longer means *more*, but for *more*, another
word has been found : *plus*. Sometimes, however, as
in the case of the Greek verb γίγνομαι, ἐγενόμην, we
see the same word continuing to be used both in its
old full sense and in its new shrunk sense ; γενέσθαι
may mean both *to be born* and *to be*. But the user
employed it, probably in the two different accep-

tations, as if he had been employing two different words ; nor did its use as hardly more than a copula necessarily raise in his mind the thought of its originally fuller significance.

Nor were these primitive verbs, *as* and *bhu*, used only as a copula, to connect, in the manner we have described, the attribute with its subject. They were also used as themselves expressing an attribute of the subject. For when men wanted strongly to affirm that action or operation of things, that image of their own life and activity, which impressed itself upon their mind and affected them, they took these same primitive verbs and used them emphatically. Virtue *is*, they said ; Truth does not cease to *be*. Literally : Virtue *breathes* ; Truth does not cease to *grow*. A yet more emphatic affirmation of this kind was supplied by the word *exist*. For to exist is literally to step forth, and he who steps forth gives a notable proof of his life and activity. Men said, therefore : Duty *exists*. That is, according to the original figure : Duty steps forth, stands forth.

And the *not ourselves*, mighty for our weal or woe, which so soon by some one or other of its sides attracted the notice of man, this also man connected with whatever attributes he might be led to assign to it, by his universal connective, his now established verbs *as* and *bhu*, his *breathe* and *grow* with their blunted and shadowy sense of breathing and growing. He said : God *breathes* angry ; our God *breathes* a jealous God. When he wanted to affirm emphatically that this power acts, makes itself felt, lasts, he said :

God *is*, God *exists*. In other words : God *breathes*,
God *steps forth*.

Israel conceived God with a solemnity and a seriousness unknown to other nations, as "The not ourselves that makes for righteousness." "When I speak
of this unique God of Israel," asked Moses, "how shall
I name him?" And the answer came (we will give it
in the words of the literal Latin version, printed
under the Hebrew in Walton's noble Polyglott Bible):
Dixit Deus ad Mosen : *Ero qui ero.*   Et dixit: Sic
dices filiis Israel : *Ero* misit me ad vos."   "*I will
breathe* hath sent me unto you;" or, as the Arabic version well renders this mystic name : *The Eternal, that
passeth not.*   For that this is the true meaning of the
name there can be no doubt :—The *I will go on living,
operating, enduring.*   "God here signifies of himself,"
says Gesenius, "not simply that he is he who is, for
of this every one must perceive the frigidity, but he
signifies emphatically that he is *he who is always the
same*, that is, the Immutable, the Eternal."   To the
like effect Dr. Kalisch, in his valuable Commentary,
after reciting the series of more fanciful and metaphysical interpretations, rests finally in this, the simple
and the undoubtedly true one : "He that changeth
not, and that faileth not."

"*I will breathe* hath sent me unto you!"   Still the
old sensuous image from the chief and most striking
function of human life, transferred to God, taken to
describe, in the height and permanency of its beneficent operation, this mighty *not ourselves*, which in its
operation we are aware of, but in its nature, no.

And here is, indeed, the grand conclusion to be drawn from this long philological disquisition, from our persistent scrutiny of the primitives *as* and *bhu*, breathe and grow: that by a simple figure they declare a perceived energy and operation, nothing more. Of a *subject*, as we call him, that performs this operation, of the nature of something outside the range of plants and of animals, which do indeed grow and breathe, and from which the figure in *as* and *bhu* is borrowed, they tell us nothing. But they have been falsely supposed to bring us news about the primal nature of things, to declare a subject in which inhered the energy and the operation we had noticed, to indicate a fontal category or supreme constitutive condition, into which the nature of all things whatsoever might be finally run up.

For the original figure, as we have said, was soon forgotten; and *is* and *be*, mysterious petrifactions, remained in language as if they were autochthons there, and as if no one could go beyond or behind them. Without father, without mother, without descent, as it seemed, they yet were omnipresent in our speech, and indispensable. Allied words in which the figure was manifest, such as existence and substance, were thought to be figures from the world of sense pressed into the service of a metaphysical reality enshrined in *is* and *be*. That imposing phrase of the metaphysicians for summing up the whole system of things, *substance and accident*,—phenomena, and that which stands under phenomena and in which they inhere,—must surely, one would think, have provoked question, have aroused misgivings,—people must surely have asked themselves what the *that* which stands under phenomena was,—if the answer had not been ready : *being.* And *being* was supposed to be something absolute, which stood under all things. Yet *being* was itself all the while but a sensuous figure, *growing,* and did not of necessity express anything of a thing's nature, expressed only man's sense of a thing's operation.

But philosophers, ignorant of this, and imagining that they had in *being* a term which expressed the highest and simplest nature of things, stripped off, to use a phrase of Descartes, when they wanted to reach the naked truth of a thing, one of the thing's garments after another, they stripped away this and that figure and size for bodies, this and that thought and desire for mind, and so they arrived at the final sub-stances of bodies and of mind, their *being* or *essence,* which for bodies was a substantial essence capable of infinite diversities of figure and size, for mind a substantial essence capable of infinite diversities of thought and desire. And that for bodies and for mind they thus got a highest reality merely negative, a reality in which there was less of reality than in any single body or mind they knew, this they did not heed, because in *being* or *essence* they supposed they had the supreme reality.

Finally, in considering God they were obliged, if they wanted to escape from difficulties, to drop even the one characteristic they had assigned to their sub-stance, that of admitting modes and accidents, and thus to reduce, in fact, their idea of God to nothing at all. And this they themselves were much too acute, many of them, not to perceive ; as Erigena, for instance, says : " *Deus non immerito nihilum vocatur ;* God may be not improperly called nothing." But this did not make them hesitate, because they thought they had in pure *being*, or *essence*, the supreme reality, and that this *being* in itself, this *essence* not even serving as substance, was God. And therefore Erigena adds that it is *per excellentiam*, by reason of excellency, that God is not improperly called nothing : " *Deus per excellentiam non immerito nihilum vocatur.*"

To such a degree do words make man, who invents them, their sport ! The moment we have an abstract word, a word where we do not apprehend both the concrete sense and the manner of this sense's application, there is danger. The whole value of an abstract term depends on our true and clear conception of that which we have abstracted and now convey by means of this term. *Animal* is a valuable term because we know what breathing, *anima* is, and we use animal to denote all who have this in common. But the *être* of Descartes is an unprofitable term, because we do not clearly conceive what the term means. And it is, moreover, a dangerous term, because without clearly conceiving what it means, we nevertheless use it freely. When we at last come to examine the term, we find that *être* and *animal* really mean just the same thing : *breather*, that which has vital breath.

How astounding are the consequences if we give to *être* and its cognates this their original sense which

we have discovered !　*Cogito, ergo sum*, will then be :
" I think, therefore I breathe." A true deduction
certainly ; but *Comedo, ergo sum*, " I eat, therefore I
breathe," would be nearly as much to the purpose !
Metaphysics, the science treating of *être* and its conditions, will be the science treating of breathing and
its conditions. But surely the right science to treat
of breathing and its conditions is not metaphysics,
but physiology ! " God *is*," will be, God *breathes ;*
exactly that old anthropomorphic account of him
which our dogmatic theology, by declaring him to be
without body, parts, or passions, has sought to banish !
And even to adore,—like those men of new lights,
the French revolutionists, haters of our dogmatic
theology,—even to adore, like Robespierre, the *Être
Suprême*, will be only, after all, to adore the Supreme
Animal ! So perfidiously do these words *is* and *be*,—
on which we embarked our hopes because we fancied
they would bring us to a thinking and a loving,
independent of all material organisation,—so perfidiously do they land us in mere creature-worship of
the grossest kind. Nay, and perhaps the one man
who uses that wonderful abstract word, *essence*, with
propriety, will turn out to be, not the metaphysician
or the theologian, but the perfumer. For while
nothing but perplexity can come from speaking of
the *breathing* of the Divine Nature, there is really
much felicity in speaking of the *breathing* of roses.

IV.

Dismayed, then, at the consequence of a rash use of *being* and *essence*, we determined henceforth always to subject these vocables, when we found them used in a way which caused us any doubt, to a strict examination. Far from remaining, as formerly, in helpless admiration of the philosophers, when upon the foundation of these words they built their wonderful cloud-houses and then laughed at us for not being able to find our way through them, we set ourselves to discover what meaning the words, in men's use of them, really did and could contain. And we found that the great thing to keep steadily in mind is that the words are, as we have shown, figure. Man applied this image of breathing and growing, taken from his own life, to all which he perceived, all from which he felt an effect; and pronounced it all to be living too. The words, therefore, which appear to tell us something about the life and nature of all things, do in fact tell us nothing about any life and nature except that which breathing and growing go in some degree to constitute; the life and nature, let us say, of men, of the lower animals, and of plants. Of life or nature in other things the words tell us nothing, but figuratively invest these things with the characters of animal and vegetable life. But what do they really tell us of these things? Simply that the things have an effect upon us, that they operate.

The names themselves, then, *being* and *essence*, tell

us something of the real constitution of animals and plants, but of nothing else. However, the real constitution of a thing it may happen that we know, although these names convey nothing of it and help us to it not at all. For instance, a chemist knows the constitution, say, of common ether. He knows that common ether is an assemblage of molecules each containing four atoms of carbon, ten of hydrogen, and one of oxygen, arranged in a certain order. This we may call the being or essence, the *growing* or *breath*, of common ether. That is to say, to the real constitution of a thing, when we know it, we often apply a figurative name originally suggested by the principal and prominent phenomena of our own constitution.

This in the case of bodies. When we speak of the being or essence of bodies, it may be that we know their real constitution and give these names to it. But far oftener men say that bodies have *being*, assert that bodies *are*, without any knowledge, either actual or implied, of the real constitution of the bodies, but merely meaning that the bodies are seen, heard, touched, tasted, or smelt by us, affect our senses in some way or other. And to bodies, thus acting upon us and affecting us, we attribute being or *growing*, we say that they are or *breathe*, although we may know nothing of their constitution. But we apply to their action a figurative name originally suggested by the principal and prominent activities of our own constitution.

And we proceed just in the same way with what are not bodies. Men abstract, say, from a number of brave and self-denying actions, which have come within their experience, the quality which in these actions strikes them. Some men abstract inexactly and ill what they thus perceive, others exactly and well. But whether they abstract it exactly or inexactly, alike they talk of the *being* of what they have thus abstracted; alike they say that courage and duty have *growing* or being, alike they assert that courage and duty *breathe* or are. They apply to the working of their abstraction figurative names, drawn originally from the principal and prominent workings of their own life.

Or, again, they become aware of a law of nature, as it is called,—of a certain regular order in which it is proved, or thought to be proved, that certain things happen. To this law, to the law, let us suppose, of gravitation, they attribute *being;* they say that the law of gravitation is, exists, *breathes, steps forth.* That is, they give to the regularly ordered operation which they perceive, figurative names borrowed from the principal and prominent functions of their own life.

Or, finally, they become aware of a law of nature which concerns their own life and conduct in the highest degree,—of an eternal not ourselves that makes for righteousness. For this is really a law of nature, collected from experience, just as much as the law of gravitation is; only it is a law of nature which is conceived, however confusedly, by very many more of mankind as affecting them, and much more nearly. But it has its origin in experience, it appeals to experience, and by experience it is, as we believe, verified. A writer whom we name with esteem because he has so firmly grasped the truth, that what Jesus Christ cared for was to change the inner man of each individual, not to establish organisations of any sort, Mr. Dunn says, that the God of popular religion, the personal God who thinks and loves, is as much verifiable by experience as our eternal power that makes for righteousness. Possibly he imagines us to mean by *power* some material agent, some body, some gas; and such a divine agent making for righteousness is no more verifiable by experience, we confess, than a divine person, who thinks and loves, making for it. We no more pretend to know the origin and composition of the power that makes for righteousness than of the power that makes for gravitation. All we profess to have ascertained about it is, that it has effect on us, that it operates.

Some deny that it operates. *The fool hath said in his heart: There is no God.* But we maintain that experience is against the fool, that righteousness is salvation. As far as man's experience reaches, it comes out, and comes out ever more clearly, both by the operation of the law itself and by man's inward sense of affinity and response to it, that our welfare, which we cannot but pursue, is inextricably and unalterably, and by no procuring of ours but whether we will or no, dependent on conduct. Mr. Dunn does not surely think that we have the same experience of God as a person who thinks and loves, which we have of this? He says that a great many people have believed that God is a person who thinks and loves. Undoubtedly they have ; just as a great many people have believed this or that hypothesis about the system of nature. But the question is, whether they had any such good grounds from experience for accepting these things as true, as there are for accepting as true the law of gravitation and the law of righteousness, the Eternal that makes for righteousness.

It is said, again, that *eternal*,—that which never had a beginning, and can never have an end,—is a metaphysical conception not given by experience. Yes indeed, *eternal*, as that which never had a beginning and can never have an end, is, like the final substance or subject wherein all qualities inhere, a metaphysical conception to which experience has nothing to say. But eternal, *ævi-ternus*, the age or life-long, as men applied it to the Eternal that makes for righteousness, was no metaphysical conception. From all they could themselves make out, and from all that their fathers had told them, they believed that righteousness was salvation, and that it would go on being salvation from one generation of men to another. And this is the only sound sense in which we can call the law of righteousness, or the law of gravitation, or any other law which we may perceive, eternal. From all that we hear or can make out it holds good ; and we believe, therefore, that it will go on holding good.

Well, then, men become aware from experience,— that source of all our knowledge,—they become aware of a law of righteousness. And to this law they

attribute *being*. They say that the law of conduct,
the eternal not ourselves which makes for righteousness, is, exists,—*breathes, steps forth.* That is to say,
they give to the steadfast, unchanging, widely and
deeply working operation which they perceive, figurative names borrowed from the principal and prominent
operations of their own life.

Being and *essence* men in this way attribute to what
they perceive, or think they perceive, to be a law of
nature. But, long before they perceive it as a law of
nature, they dimly and obscurely are conscious of its
working; they feel its power by many a sharp lesson.
And imagination coming in to help, they make it, as
they make everything of which they powerfully feel
the effect, into a human agent, at bottom like themselves, however much mightier,—a human agent that
feels, thinks, loves, hates. So they made the sun into
a human being; and even the operation of chance,
fortune. And what should sooner or more certainly
be thus made into a human being, but far mightier
and more lasting than common man, than the operation which affects men so widely and deeply,—for it
is engaged with conduct, with at least three-fourths
of human life,—the *not ourselves* that makes for righteousness?

Made into a human being this was sure to be, from
its immense importance, its perpetual intervention.
But this does not make the personifying, anthropomorphic process, the less the explanation of the attributed human qualities in this case, than it is the
explanation of them in others. Yet we will have it,

very many of us, that the human qualities are in the
one case really there and inherent, but in all the
other cases they are the mere work of man's plastic
and personifying power. What was the Apollo of
the religion of the Greeks? The law of intellectual
beauty, the eternal not ourselves that makes for intellectual beauty. By a natural and quite explicable
working of the human spirit, a heightened, glorified
human being, thinking and loving, came to stand for
the operation of this power. Who doubts this? But
the thinking and loving Apollo of the Greeks, and
every other example of the like kind except one, this
natural working of the human spirit is supposed to
explain; only the thinking and loving Jehovah of the
Hebrews shall not be explained by this working, but
a person who thinks and loves he really is!

To return, then, to our much abused primitives.
What is the conclusion of the whole matter about
them? It is this:—They were supposed to give us
for conscious intelligence, for thinking and loving, a
basis or subject independent of bodily constitution.
They do in fact give us nothing beyond bodily phenomena; but they transfer by a figure the phenomena
of our own bodily life to all law and operation. On
a fine and subtle scale they still carry on that personifying anthropomorphic process, native in man and
ineradicable, which in all the early religions of the
world we can see going forward on a scale gross and
palpable.

So it appears, that when we talk of the *being* of
things, we use a fluid and literary expression, not a rigid

and scientific one. And in every case where anything is
made to depend upon the use of the words *is* and *be*,
we ought to examine what is said, and see what sense
they can really, in that particular case, bear. For
instance, Descartes says, that what makes him certain
of the truth of his fundamental proposition, " I think,
therefore I am, *Je pense, donc je suis*," is that he sees
quite clearly that in order to think one must be :—
" *Pour penser il faut être.*" And *être* really means to
breathe ; and we do, indeed, see quite clearly that, in
order to think, we must breathe. And this is the
clearest sense the words can have. Nevertheless, it
is not the sense Descartes meant to give them. Well,
then, they can also bear the sense that because we
think, we feel ourselves to be alive. And probably
this is what Descartes alleges that he and all of us
can see quite clearly. So when philosophers tell us,
in their grand language, that " from our actual thought
we affirm our actual existence," let us simple people
interpret, and say, that this means that because we
think, we feel ourselves to be alive; and let us concede,
with due admiration for those who clothe the thing
in such imposing language, that we can clearly see
this also to be true. Only let us remember exactly
what it is that we have seen to be true. And when
the philosophers go on to tell us, further, that " as
we affirm our actual existence from our actual thought,
similarly, the idea we have of the infinite and infinitely perfect Being, that is, of God, clearly involves
his actual existence ;" let us again put the thing into
easier language, and propound it to ourselves that as,

because we think, we feel ourselves to be alive, similarly, because we think of God, God feels himself to
be alive. Probably we shall not be disposed to concede that we can clearly see this to be true; nor,
perhaps, would the philosophers allege it as certain,
if they had accustomed themselves to inquire in all
cases what *being*, *existing*, really mean.

V.

Armed with this key of the real signification of our
two poor little words, *is* and *be*, let us next boldly
carry the war into the enemy's country, and see how
many strong fortresses of the metaphysicians, which
frown upon us from their heights so defiantly, we can
now enter and rifle. For *is* and *be*, we have learnt,
either mean *breathe* and *grow*, or else they mean
operate. But when the metaphysicians start with
their at least certainly knowing that *something is*, they
always have in their minds:—"Something thinks
which neither breathes nor grows, and we know of a
subject for thinking which neither breathes nor grows,
and that subject is being, *être*." But they are unaware
that being, *être*, are two words which simply mean
breathing and growing. And then, with two supposed data of a cogitative substance and an incogita-
tive substance, the metaphysicians argue away about
the necessary mutual relations of these two in the
production of things, and form all manner of fine
conclusions. But all the knowledge they do really
set out with in their *something is* amounts to this:

"We are aware of *operation.*" And this neither
tells them anything about the origin and production of things, nor enables them to conclude anything.

Now, if we keep this in mind, we shall see the
fallacy of many reasonings we meet with. The
Edinburgh Review says : "All existing things must
be persons or things ; persons are superior to things ;
do you mean to call God a thing ?" The ambiguity
is in *things.* He who asserts this or that to be a person or a thing,—endued, that is, with what we call
life or not endued with it,—pronounces something
concerning its constitution. And when we pronounce
that God has *being,* that God *is,* we may mean by this
that God has growth, that God breathes ; and then
we do assert something concerning God's constitution,
and affirm God to be a person not a thing. But we
may also mean, when we pronounce that God has
being, that God *is,* simply that God operates, that the
Eternal which makes for righteousness has operation.
And then we assert nothing about God's constitution
whatever, we neither affirm God to be a person nor
to be a thing. And, indeed, we are not at all in a
position to affirm God to be either the one or the
other. He who pronounces that God must be a
person or a thing, and that God must be a person
because persons are superior to things, talks as idly
as one who should insist upon it that the law of gravitation must be either a person or a thing, and should
lay down which of the two it must be. Because it is
a law, is it to be pronounced a thing and not a person,

and therefore inferior to persons? and are we quite
sure that a bad critic, suppose, is superior to the law
of gravitation? The truth is, we are attempting an
exhaustive division into things and persons, and attempting to affirm that the object of our thought is
one or the other, when we have no means for doing
anything of the kind, when all we can really say of
our object of thought is, that it *operates*.

Or to take that favourite and famous demonstration of Anselm and Descartes, that if we have the
idea of a perfect being, or God,—that is to say, of an
infinite substance, eternal, all-knowing, all-powerful,
the creator of all things, and with every possible
perfection,— then this perfect being must exist.
Existence, they argue, is a perfection, and besides,
our imperfect finite being could never have given to
itself the idea of a perfect infinite being. But we
have this idea quite clearly and distinctly, and therefore there must exist some other being besides ourselves from whom we must have received it. All
this, again, tumbles to pieces like a house of cards
the moment we press it. The ambiguity lies in the
words *perfect being, infinite substance*. Of a *not ourselves* we are clearly aware;—but a clear idea of an
infinite substance, a perfect being, knowing and thinking and yet not breathing and growing? And this
idea we could not have given to ourselves, because it
is a clear idea of an infinite substance, full of perfection; and we are a finite substance, full of imperfection? But after examining *is* and *be*, we are sure
that no man has a clear idea of an infinite substance,

knowing and thinking. And the idea which he thus describes is an idea which, in the only state wherein he really has it, he may perfectly well have given to himself. For it is an idea of a man hugely magnified and improved.

The less and more in ourselves of whatever we account good, gives us a notion of what we call perfection in it. We have degrees of pleasure and we talk of perfect, infinite pleasure ; we have some rest, and we talk of perfect, infinite rest ; we have some knowledge, and we talk of perfect, infinite knowledge; we have some power, and we talk of perfect, infinite power. What we mean is, a great deal of pleasure, rest, knowledge, power ; as much of them as we can imagine, and without the many lets and hindrances to them which we now experience. Our idea of a perfect being, all-knowing, all-powerful, is just like that idea of a myriagon, of which Descartes himself speaks somewhere. Of a pentagon, or five-sided figure, we have a distinct idea. And we talk of our idea of a myriagon, or ten-thousand-sided figure, too ; but it is not a clear idea, it is an idea of something very big, but confused. Such is our idea of an infinite substance, all-knowing, all-powerful. Of a bounded man, with some knowledge and power, we have a distinct idea ; of an unbounded man, with all knowledge and all power, our idea is not clear ; we have an idea of something very wise and great, but confused. And granting that clear ideas prove themselves, this alleged clear and distinct idea of an infinite substance, all-knowing and all-powerful, is one of those cases where an idea is fancied to be clear and distinct when it is not.

But people insist that perfect ideas *must* have being quite independently of us and our experience, and must inhere, therefore, in a source, a subject, an infinite substance, which is God. For we have, say they, the idea of a perfect circle; yet this idea cannot be given us by experience, because in nature there is no such thing as a perfect circle. We have the idea of a perfect good; yet this idea cannot be given us by experience, because in nature there is no such thing as a perfect good. But let us ask ourselves whether even the circle and the triangle were first, probably, pure conceptions in the human mind, and then applied to nature? or whether these forms were not first observed in nature, and then refined into pure conceptions? And was perfect good, in like manner, or perfect beauty, first a pure conception in the human mind, and then applied to things in nature? or were things more or less good and beautiful first observed in experience, and goodness and beauty then refined into pure conceptions? Because, in that case, our ideas of a perfect circle and a perfect good are simply the imagination of a still rounder circle and a still better good than any which we have yet found in experience. But experience gave us the ideas, and we have no need to invent something out of experience as the source of them.

Finally, let us take the grand argument from design. Design, people say, implies a designer. The ambiguity lies in the little termination *er*, by which we mean a *being* who designed. We talk of a being, an *être*, and we imagine that the word gives us conscious intelligence, thinking and loving, without bodily organisation; but it does not. It gives us one of two things only ;—either it gives us breathing and growing, or it gives us effect and operation. Design implies a designer? Human design does ; it implies the presence of a being who breathes and thinks. So does that of the lower animals, who, like man himself, breathe, and may be said to think. A very numerous class of works we know, which man and the lower animals make for their own purposes. When we see a watch or a honeycomb we say : It works harmoniously and well, and a man or a bee made it. But a yet more numerous class of works we know, which neither man nor the lower animals have made for their own purposes. When we see the ear, or see a bud, do we say : It works harmoniously and well, and a man or one of the lower animals made it? No ; but we say : It works harmoniously and well, and an infinite eternal substance, an all-thinking and all-powerful being, the creator of all things, made it. Why? Because it works harmoniously and well. But its working harmoniously and well does not prove all this ; it only proves that it works harmoniously and well. The well and harmonious working of the watch or the honeycomb is not what proves to us that a man or a bee made them ; what proves this to us is, that we know from experience that men make watches and bees make honeycombs. But we do not know from experience that an infinite eternal substance, all-thinking and all-powerful, the creator of all things, makes ears and buds. We know nothing about the matter, it is altogether beyond us. When, therefore, we are speaking exactly, and not poetically and figuratively, of the ear or of a bud, all we have a right to say is: It works harmoniously and well.

VI.

We besought those who could receive neither the miracles of popular theology nor the metaphysics of learned theology, not to fling away the Bible on that account, but to try how the Bible went if they took it without either the one or the other, and studied it without taking anything for granted but what they could verify. But such indignant and strenuous objection was made in the religious world to this proposal, and in particular it was so emphatically asserted that the only possible basis for religion is to believe that God is a person who thinks and loves, that the readers of *Literature and Dogma* who had taken our advice and had begun to find profit from it, might well be supposed to feel alarm and to hesitate, and to ask whether, after all, they were doing well in following our recommendation. So we had to look again at the reasons for laying down as the foundation of religion the belief that God is a person who thinks and loves. And we found reasons of two kinds alleged: reasons drawn from miracles, and reasons drawn from metaphysics. But the reasons from miracles we found, after looking at miracles again, that we could not rely on, that fail us sooner or later they surely must. And now we find the same thing with the reasons drawn from metaphysics.

The reasons drawn from miracles one cannot but dismiss with tenderness, for they belong to a great and splendid whole,—a beautiful and powerful fairy-tale, which was long believed without question, and which has given comfort and joy to thousands. And one abandons them with a kind of unwilling disenchantment, and only because one must.

The reasons drawn from metaphysics one dismisses, on the other hand, with sheer satisfaction. They have convinced no one, they have given rest to no one, they have given joy to no one. People have swallowed them, people have fought over them, people have shown their ingenuity over them; but no one has ever enjoyed them. Nay, no one has ever really understood them. No one has ever fairly grasped the meaning of what he was saying, when he laid down propositions about finite and infinite substance, and about God's essence involving existence. Yet men of splendid ability have dealt in them. But the truth is, the reasons from metaphysics for the Divine Personality got their real nourishment and support out of the reasons from miracles. Through long ages the inexperience, the helplessness, and the agitation of man made the belief in a magnified and non-natural man or men, in etherealised men,—in short, in preternatural beings of some sort or other,—inevitable. And, the preternatural having been supposed to be certainly there, the metaphysics, or science of things coming after natural things and no longer natural, had to come in to account for it. But the miracles proving to be an unsubstantial ground of reliance, the metaphysics will certainly not stand long. Now, an unsubstantial ground of reliance men more and more perceive miracles to be; and the sooner they quite make up their mind about it, the better for them. But if it is vain to tamper with one's understanding, to resist one's widening experience, and to try to think that from miracles one can get ground for asserting God to be a person who thinks and loves, still more vain is it to try to think one can get ground for this from metaphysics.

And perhaps we may have been enabled to make this clear to ourselves and others, because we, having no talent for abstruse reasoning and being known to have none, were not ashamed, when we were confronted by propositions about essence and existence, and about infinite substance having undoubtedly more objective reality than finite substance, we were not ashamed, I say, instead of assenting with a solemn face to what we did not understand, to own that we did not understand it, and to seek humbly for the meaning of the little words at the bottom of it all; and so the futility of all the grand superstructure was revealed to us. If the German philosopher, who writes to us from Texas reproaching us with wasting our time over the Bible and Christianity, "which are certainly," says he, "disappearing from heart and mind of the cultured world," and calling us to the

study of the great Hartmann, will allow us to quote
the Bible yet once more, we should be disposed to
say that here is a good exémplification of that text:
"*Mansueti delectabuntur ;* The meek-spirited shall be
refreshed."

But to our reader and to ourselves we say once
again, as to the metaphysics of current theology,
what we said as to its miracles.   When we have
made out their untrustworthiness, we have as yet
achieved nothing, except to get rid of an unsafe stay
which would inevitably have sooner or later broken
down with us.   But to use the Bible, to enjoy the
Bible, remains.   We cannot use it, we cannot enjoy
it, more and more amongst us, if its use and enjoyment require one first to take for granted something
which cannot possibly be verified.   Whether we will
or not, this is so ; and more and more will mankind,
the religious among them as well as the profane, find
themselves in this case.   "In good truth," said
Pascal to the Jesuits, " the world is getting mistrustful, and no longer believes things unless they
are evident to it."   In the seventeenth century,
when Pascal said this, it had already begun to be
true ; it is getting more widely true every day.
Therefore we urge all whom the current theology,
both popular and learned, repels (for with those
whom it does not repel we do not meddle), we urge
them to take as their foundation in reading the Bible
this account of God, which can be verified : "God is
the eternal power, not ourselves, which makes for
righteousness," instead of this other : "God is a

person who thinks and loves," which cannot. We advise them to eschew as much as possible, in speaking about God, the use of the word *Being*, which even strict thinkers are so apt to use continually without asking themselves what it really means. The word is bad, because it has a false air of conveying some real but abstruse knowledge about God's nature, while it does not, but is merely a figure. *Power* is a better word, because it pretends to assert of God nothing more than effect on us, operation. With much of the current theology our unpretending account of God will indeed make havoc; but it will enable a man, we believe, to use and enjoy the Bible in security. Only he must always remember that the language of the Bible is to be treated as the language of letters, not science, language approximative and full of figure, not language exact.

Many excellent people are crying out every day that all is lost in religion unless we can affirm that God is a person who thinks and loves. We say, that unless we can verify this, it is impossible to build religion successfully upon it; and it cannot be verified. Even if it could be shown that there is a low degree of probability for it, we say that it is a grave and fatal error to imagine that religion can be built on what has a low degree of probability. However, we do not think it can be said that there is even a low degree of probability for the assertion that God is a person who thinks and loves, properly and naturally though we may make him such in the language of feeling; the assertion deals with what is

so utterly beyond us. But we maintain, that, start-
ing from what may be verified about God,—that he
is the Eternal which makes for righteousness,—and
reading the Bible with this idea to govern us, we
have here the elements for a religion more serious,
potent, awe-inspiring, and profound than any which
the world has yet seen. True, it will not be just
the same religion which prevails now; but who
supposes that the religion now current can go on
always, or ought to go on? Nay and even of that
much-decried idea of God as *the stream of tendency by
which all things fulfil the law of their being*, it may be
said with confidence that it has in it the elements of
a religion new, indeed, but in the highest degree
hopeful, solemn, and profound. But our present
business is not with this. Our present business is
with the religion of the Bible; to show a new aspect
of this, wherein it shall appear true, winning, and
commanding.

And if our reader has for a time to lose sight of
this aspect amid negations and conflicts,—necessary
negations, conflicts without which the ground for a
better religion cannot be won,—still by these waters
of Babylon, let him remember Sion! After a course
of Liberal philosophers proposing to replace the
obsolete Bible by the enouncement in modern and
congenial language of new doctrines which will satisfy
at once our reason and imagination, and after reading
these philosophers' grand conclusion that there is
little indeed in the history and achievements of
Christianity to support the claim made on its behalf

to the character of a scheme divinely revealed for the salvation of the human race, a man may of a truth well say : "*My soul hath dwelt among them that are enemies unto peace !* and may with longing remember Sion. But we will not quarrel with him if he says and does the same thing after reading us, too, when we have kept him so long at the joyless task of learning what not to believe. But happily this part of our business is now over. In what follows, we have to defend ourselves, and secure him, against the Liberal philosophers who accuse us of teaching him to believe too much.

CHAPTER III.

THE GOD OF EXPERIENCE.

AMONG German critics of the Bible, a sort of criticism which we may best, perhaps, describe as a *mechanical* criticism, is very rife. For negative purposes this criticism is particularly useful. It takes for granted that things are naturally all of a piece and follow one uniform rule; and that to know that this is so, and to judge things by the light of this knowledge, is the secret for sure criticism. People do not vary; people do not contradict themselves; people do not have under-currents of meaning; people do not divine. If they are represented as having said one thing to-day and its seeming opposite to-morrow, one of the two they are credited with falsely. If they are represented as having said what in its plain literal acceptation could not hold good, they cannot have said it. If they are represented as speaking of an event before it happened, they did not so speak of it,—the words are not theirs. Things too, like persons, must be rigidly consistent, must show no conflicting aspects, must have no flux and reflux, must not follow a slow, hesitating, often obscure line of growth; no, the character which we assign to them they must have always, altogether, and unalterably, or it is not theirs.

This mechanical character strongly marked a criticism in the *Westminster Review* upon *Literature and Dogma.* The reviewer's line ran as follows:— "Israel's first conception of God was that of an unseen but powerful foe, whose enmity might be averted by the death of victims;" therefore the God of Israel cannot have been, as we represent him, the Eternal which makes for righteousness. "The original and current idea of righteousness in Israel was largely made up of ceremonial observances;" we must not say, therefore, that to Israel was revealed the Eternal that loveth righteousness. We, again, say that the world cannot do without the Bible, and we desire to bring the masses to use the Bible. But no! Israel went to ruin, and Christendom is far from perfect; therefore the Bible cannot be of much use. "Take," says the *Westminster* Reviewer, "the commentary afforded by Israel's history on the value of the Bible! The Bible failed to turn the hearts of those to whom it was addressed; how can it have an efficacy for the regeneration of our masses?" In a like strain the author of *Supernatural Religion:* "There is little, indeed, in the history and actual achievements of Christianity to support the claim made on its behalf to the character of a scheme divinely revealed for the salvation of the human race."

On persons and their sayings this sort of criticism
does execution in very short and sharp fashion.
Jesus said of the daughter of Jairus : " She is not
dead, but sleepeth." Well, then, " we have here, by
the express declaration of Jesus, a case of mere suspension of consciousness." Jesus said, *sleepeth ;* and
how, then, *can* the girl have been more than asleep ?
If Jesus is reported to have said : " Before Abraham
was, I am," or to have said : " Therefore doth my
Father love me because I lay down my life that
I may take it again," these speeches *must* have
been invented for him after his death, when the
Resurrection had become a matter of Christian belief,
or when the dogma of the Godhead of the Eternal
Son wanted proving. That they should have arisen
in any other way is " wholly inexplicable." It is
" wholly inexplicable " to this kind of criticism that
Jesus should have both said of the Gentile centurion :
" I have not found so great faith in Israel," and also
said to the Canaanitish woman : " It is not meet to
take the children's bread and cast it to the dogs,"
because the two sayings show a different tendency,
and the same man does not utter two sayings showing
a different tendency. Either the first saying must have
been put into the mouth of Jesus by a Pauline universalist, or the second by a Judaic particularist. If
Jesus speaks of the destruction of Jerusalem, then
the speech must have been invented for him after
Jerusalem was destroyed ; for it is " wholly inexplicable " that a man should speak of a thing before
it happens. To suppose otherwise, to suppose, as

we do, that Jesus foretold to his disciples that they
should see Jerusalem destroyed, that he varied his
line according to the occasion and the hearer, that
he foresaw his own death, and that he dealt with the
terms *living* and *dying* in a profound manner easily
misapprehended, — to suppose all this is to "invest
Jesus with attributes of prescience and quasi-omni-
science which we can only characterise as divine,"
and is therefore inadmissible.

One of the many reproaches brought against
Literature and Dogma is, that its conception of the
development of our religion is wanting in vigour
and rigour. Certainly the sort of criticism we are
now noticing does not err by want of vigour and
rigour. It has abundance of both, and it does its
work with great thoroughness. The only thing to be
said against it is, that the growth of human things,
and above all of immense concerns like religion, does
not exactly proceed with vigour and rigour; rather
it follows an order of development loose and wavering.
And to impose, therefore, on the growth of religion
and Christianity a method of development of great
vigour and rigour, to criticise its productions and
utterances with the notion that we shall reach the
truth about them by applying to them such a method,
is most probably to criticise them all wrong.

And it would not be difficult to show that this
method is, in fact, fallacious in each of the points
where we have been just now seeing it draw its conclusions. But we are here solely concerned with
whatever may be supposed to check and disconcert

the reader of *Literature and Dogma* after that book had
seemed to put him in a way of reading the Bible with
profit.   Now certainly nothing could check and disconcert him so much as to find that the God of Israel,
the God of the Bible, cannot be taken to be the
Eternal that loveth righteousness.   For in place of
the magnified and non-natural man given by miracles
and metaphysics, but who cannot be verified, we had
advised our reader to take as the God of the Bible,
and the foundation of the whole matter of his Christianity, the Eternal that loves righteousness, makes
for righteousness.   This Eternal can be verified indeed, but now we are told that he is not the God of
the Bible.   Or, at any rate, he is not the God of
Israel and of the Old Testament; the God of Israel
and of the Old Testament is something quite different.
This objection, then, we must deal with, and must
establish in spite of it, if we can, our assertion that
the God of Israel and of the Bible is the Eternal that
makes for righteousness.

II.

The *Westminster* Reviewer objects to us that "Israel
must have had a faculty for abstract thought quite
unparalleled if his conception of a God came to pass
as Mr. Arnold describes it.   A people in a very early
stage of civilisation is so deeply absorbed in the study
and practice of morality that they discover that there
is a law, which is not themselves, which makes for it,
which law they proceed to worship!   Can improbability go further!"   This, says the Reviewer, is the

à *priori* argument against "the opinion that Israel's
God was not a person, but the deification of a natural
law." But certainly we do not opine,—and the
reader of *Literature and Dogma* will hardly have supposed us to opine,—that Israel's God was the *conscious*
deification of a natural law. To attack, therefore, the
improbability of this, is merely to tilt against a
phantom of one's own creating. Unquestionably,
that Israel, as we see him in the earliest documents
of the Old Testament, should have been likely to sit
down and say to himself : " I perceive a great natural
law, the law of righteousness, ruling the world ; I
will personify this law as a God,—the one and only
God; I will call it Jehovah, build a sanctuary for it,
and invent a worship for it ; "—that this should have
happened is utterly improbable. One can almost as
well conceive Israel saying that he was aware of the
law of gravitation, and felt disposed to deify it and
to erect a temple to it.

But if one has certain facts before one, one naturally
asks oneself how they can have come about. Israel
is always saying that in the Eternal he puts his trust,
and that this Eternal is righteous, and loves righteousness. He is always saying that among the gods of
other people there is no God like the Eternal, none
that can do what the Eternal does, and that whoever
runs after another God shall have great trouble.
These are his ruling thoughts. Where did he get
them? They were given him, says popular theology,
by a magnified and non-natural man, who was in
constant communication with him, walked in the

garden where he was, talked to him, showed him even, on one occasion, his bodily parts, and worked miracle after miracle for him. And this is Israel's own account of the matter. But how many other religions also, besides Israel's, present us with personages of this kind ! And we hold that the personages are not real, but have their origin in the play of the human imagination itself. How, then, did the God of Israel, with the special characters that we find in him, actually arise ?

Now, it may be contended either that these special characters, which we assign to him, are not really there ; or that they have come there by chance, and nothing can be inferred from them ; or, finally, both that the characters are there, and that it was the pressure upon the mind of Israel which made him give to his religion, and to his Eternal, that unique type which we profess to find in them. Let us examine these alternatives, so important to the reader of *Literature and Dogma*.

We must go to Sir John Lubbock or to Mr. Tylor for researches concerning what is called " prehistoric man," human nature in its inchoate, embryo, and as yet unformed condition. Their researches concerning this are profoundly interesting. But for our present business we have not to go back higher than historic man,—man who has taken his ply, and who is already much like ourselves. With inchoate, prehistoric man, the great objects of nature and the pleasure or pain which he experienced from them may probably enough have been the source of religion. In those

times arose his name for God : *The Shining.* So may
have originally commenced the religion of even the
most famous races,—the religion of Greece, the religion
of Israel. But into the thoughts and feelings of man
in this inchoate stage we cannot, as we now are, any
longer fully enter. We cannot really participate in
them ; the religion of man in this stage does not
practically concern us. Man's religion practically
concerns us from that time only when man's real
history has commenced ; when moral and intellectual
conceptions have invaded the primordial nature-
worship, have, in great measure, superseded it, and
given a new sense to its nomenclature. The very
earliest Bible-religion does not go higher than a time
of this kind, when already moral and intellectual conceptions have entered into religion. And no one will
deny that, from the very first, those conceptions
which are moral rather than intellectual,—the idea of
conduct and of the regulation of conduct,—appear in
Bible-religion prominently.

Let us for a moment leave Bible-religion, and let
us turn to the people who, after the Hebrews, have
had most influence upon us,—to the Greeks. Greek
history and religion begin for us, as do the religion
and history of the Hebrews, at a time when moral
and intellectual ideas have taken possession of the
framework given originally, it may be, by nature-
worship. The great names of Hellenic religion, Zeus
and Phœbus, come, as every one knows, from the sun
and air, and point to a primordial time of nature-
worship. But Greek history and religion begin with

the sanctuaries of Tempe and of Delphi, and with the
Apolline worship and priesthood which in those sanctuaries under Olympus and Parnassus established
themselves.   The northern sanctuary of Tempe soon
yielded to Delphi as the centre of national Hellenic
life and of Apolline religion.   Now, we all are accustomed to think of Apollo as the awakener and
sustainer of genius, as the power illuminating and
elevating the soul through intellectual beauty.   And
so from the very first he was.   But in those earliest
days of Hellas, and at Delphi, where the hardy and
serious tribes of the Dorian Highlands made their
influence felt, Apollo was not only the nourisher of
genius,—he was also the author of every higher moral
effort.   He was the prophet of his father Zeus, in the
highest view of Zeus, as the source of the ideas of
moral order and of right.   For to this higher significance had Zeus and Phœbus,—those names derived
merely from sun and air,—by this time risen.   They
had come to designate a Father, the source of the
ideas of moral order and of right; and a Son, his
prophet, purifying and inspiring the soul with these
ideas, and also with the idea of intellectual beauty.

But it is with the ideas of moral order and of right
that we are at this moment concerned.   These ideas
are in human nature; but they had, says the excellent
historian of Greece, Dr. Curtius, "especially been a
treasure in the possession of the less gay and more
solitary tribes in the mountains of Northern Greece."
These were Delphi's first pupils.   And the graver
view of life, the thoughts which give depth and so-

lemnity to man's consciousness,—the moral ideas, in short, of conduct and righteousness,—were the main elements of early Greek religion. *Soberness* and *righteousness*, to which the words written up on the temple at Delphi called all comers,[1] were thus the primal rule of Hellenic religion. For a long while, in the great poets of Hellas, the power of this influence shows itself. From Pindar, Æschylus, and Sophocles, may be quoted sentences as religious as those which we find in Job or Isaiah. And here, in this bracing air of the old religion of Delphi,—this atmosphere of ideas of moral order and of right,— the Athenians, Ionian as they were, imbibed influences of character and steadiness, which for a long while balanced their native vivacity and mobility, distinguished them profoundly from the Ionians of Asia, and gave them men like Aristides and Pericles.

Every one knows, however, that this archaic severeness of Hellenic religion, this early preoccupation with conduct and righteousness, did not last. There were elements of mobility and variety in men's dispositions which proved fatal to it. The manner in which this came about we have not here to trace ; all we are now concerned with is the fact that it was so. It had come to be so even by the time when, with the Persian War, the brilliant historic period of Greece begins. Even by this time the living influence of Delphi had ceased. Bribes had discredited its sanctity ; seriousness and vital power had left it.

---

[1] See Plato, *Erastæ*, cap. vii. τοῦτ᾽ ἄρα, ὡς ἔοικε, τὸ ἐν Δελφοῖς γράμμα παρακελεύεται, σωφροσύνην ἀσκεῖν καὶ δικαιοσύνην.

Delphi had come to be little more than a name, and what continued to exist there was merely a number of forms. The predominance, for Hellas, of a national religion of righteousness, of grave ideas of conduct, moral order, and right, outweighing all other ideas, disappeared with the decline of Delphi, never to return. Still, indeed, these ideas inspired poetry; and Greek poetry was now more religious than Greek religion, and partly supplied its place. Finally, they ceased even to inspire poetry, and took refuge with philosophic thinkers.

We by no means say that they disappeared from life. They are, we repeat, in human nature; they cannot disappear wholly. But a religion founded on them, a religion of soberness and righteousness, ceased to be set up before the eyes of all men, ceased to stand in the minds of all men for the great primary concern of human life, as it had stood before the minds of the grave forefathers of Hellas in the shadow of their Parnassian sanctuary. And to this extent, of course, the ideas were weakened and effaced in life;—that they were no longer impressively presented as life's first concern by a national religion, itself the great and solemn centre of men's thoughts. We by no means, again, say that for this there were no compensations. Other aspects of life presented themselves than the aspect in which life appears exclusively concerned with soberness and righteousness. Many a line of activity did these new aspects suggest to the Hellenic genius, and with what brilliant success it followed them we all know. Still, the fact remains.

In Greece, as the national history went on, the all-importance of conduct and righteousness pressed no longer upon the Hellenic spirit, and upon Hellenic religion, as their omnipresent and central idea. In the later days of the national life of Hellas it was a religious solemnity, witnessed with transport and celebrated by the first artist of the time, to see the courtesan Phryne enter the sea at Eleusis, and represent there, to an innumerable multitude of spectators, *Venus Anadyomene,*—Venus issuing from the waves.[1] To this had come the religion of Delphi and the art of Olympia. And it was at Eleusis that this happened, the old seat of the mysteries ;—those highest means possessed by Greek religion for deepening and ennobling men's thoughts about life and death. The time had been when the religious solemnities at Eleusis were of a character to draw from Pindar a strain such as we now call Biblical,—a strain like that of Job, or Isaiah, or the Psalms. "Blessed is the man who hath beheld these things before he goeth under the earth ! he knoweth the end of man's life, and he knoweth its God-given beginning."

III.

Not long after Phryne's religious performance at Eleusis came the last days, too, of the national life of the Jews, under the successors of Alexander. The religious conceptions of the Jews of those days are well given by the Book of Daniel. How popular and

[1] See Athenæus, lib. xiii. p. 590.

prevalent these conceptions were, is proved by their vitality and power some two centuries later at the Christian era, and by the large place which they fill in the New Testament. We are all familiar with them; with their turbid and austere visions of the Ancient of Days on his throne, and of the Son of Man coming with the clouds of heaven to give the kingdom to the saints of the Most High, and to bring in everlasting righteousness. Here, then, is the last word of the religion of the Hebrews, when their natural life is coming to an end, when their career has been, for the most part, run; when their religion has had nearly all the development which, within the limits of their national life, belonged to it. This, we say, is its last word: *To bring in everlasting righteousness.*[1]

Let us now go back to the commencement of Hebrew history. The beginnings of Hebrew national life may not inaptly be paralleled with the beginnings of Greek national life,—with that epoch when the infant Hellenic tribes met in federation under the religious shadow of Tempe or Delphi, and set before their eyes the law of "soberness and righteousness." Such an epoch in the career of the Hebrew race is well given by the history of Abraham. The religion of Abraham, this founder and father of the Hebrew people, is a religion, as King Abimelech says, of "integrity of heart and innocency of hands."[2] The God of Abraham has chosen Abraham and his race, because, God says: "I know Abraham, that he will

[1] Dan. ix. 24.   [2] Gen. xx. 5.

command his children and his household after him,
and they shall keep the way of the Eternal to do
righteousness and judgment." [1]   So that the Hebrew
people and Hebrew history, when they begin, begin,
like the Hellenic people and like Hellenic history,
with a religion of soberness and righteousness. And
the after-decline of this religion in Greece we have
seen. But in Judæa, at the close of the national
history, what do we find to be the condition of this
religion? Has it weakened, has it grown obsolete,
has it fallen out of sight and out of mind? So far
from it, that it has grown into an enthusiasm, turbid,
passionate, absorbing, and all-pervasive, to *bring in
everlasting righteousness.*

How was the long intervening period filled between
the call of Abraham at the beginning of Israel's
national history, and the Book of Daniel at its close?
Let us take, as a mid-point, that wonderful collection,
ranging over so many years, reflecting so many ex-
periences, contributed by so many voices, and answering so profoundly to the religious consciousness of
Israel: the Book of Psalms. Two things are equally
manifest, on the very face of the Book of Psalms,—
Israel's attachment to his religion, and that religion's
character. One may dip into the Psalms where one
will, and be sure to find them not far off.

First, as to the attachment and strong reliance
with which Israel's religion inspired him. "In the
Eternal put I my trust," [2] is the constant burden of
his song. "My hope hath been in thee, O Eternal;

[1] Gen. xviii. 19.   [2] Ps. xi. 1.

I have said, Thou art my God!" "Blessed are the people whose God is the Eternal!" They who run after another God shall have great trouble."[1]

And then as to the character, expressed briefly and generally, of this God of Israel, this Eternal. There is really no doubt about it. "The Eternal loveth the thing that is right!"[2] Ten thousand variations are played on the one theme, but the theme is that. "The Eternal alloweth the *righteous*, but the *wicked* his soul hateth,"[3] says David. "Unto the ungodly saith God: Why dost thou take my covenant in thy mouth, whereas thou hatest to be *reformed*?"[4] "My help cometh of God, who preserveth them that are *true of heart*."[5] "I will wash my hands in *innocency*, O Eternal, and so will I go to thine altar."[6] As in the days of Abimelech, so it was still: the religion of the Hebrew people was a religion of integrity of heart and innocency of hands. "Put thou thy trust in the Eternal, and be *doing good*."[7] "If I incline unto *wickedness* with my heart, the Eternal will not hear me."[8] No; for this is the essential character of Israel's Eternal, to love the thing that is *right*, to abhor that which is *evil*.

Do we want a somewhat fuller account of what *right* is, that we may be sure it does not mean a mere performance of ceremonies? Here it is :—"Come ye children, and hearken unto me; I will teach you the fear of the Eternal. Keep thy tongue from evil, and

---

[1] Ps. xxxi. 14; xxxiii. 12; xvi. 4.   [2] Ps. xxxvii. 28.
[3] Ps. xi. 5.   [4] Ps. l. 16, 17.   [5] Ps. vii. 10.
[6] Ps. xxvi. 6.   [7] Ps. xxxvii. 3.   [8] Ps. lxvi. 18.

thy lips that they speak no guile; eschew evil and
do good, seek peace and pursue it."[1]   Or of what
evil is, — what is the course of those who do not
"understand and seek after God;" that we may be
sure evil does not mean a mere omission of ceremonies,
or a sparing to smite God's enemies who happen to
be also one's own?   "Their mouth is full of cursing
and bitterness, their feet are swift to shed blood,
destruction and unhappiness is in their ways, and the
way of peace have they not known."[2]   In a plain
way, all this points well enough, and with perfect
clearness, to just what we universally mean by right
and wrong, good and evil.   It points to morals, conduct; to a man's behaviour, way and walk in life.
And this was what Israel meant by religion: to
attend to one's way and walk in life, and to regulate
them according to the commandments of the Eternal
that loveth righteousness.   "I called mine own ways
to remembrance," he says, "and turned my feet unto
Thy testimonies."[3]   And they who do so, maintains
he, "shall want no manner of thing that is good."[4]
"*That* shall bring a man peace at the last."[5]   "To
him that ordereth his conversation right shall be
shown the salvation of God."[6]

But the *Westminster* Reviewer says that we are
not to rely much on what comes from prophets and
psalmists, "on the most spiritual utterances of the

---

[1] Ps. xxxiv. 11, 13, 14.
[2] Ps. xiv. (Prayer Book Version), 6, 7 ; and Rom. iii. 14-17.
[3] Ps. cxix. 59.   [4] Ps. xxxiv. 10.
[5] Ps. xxxvii. 38.   [6] Ps. l. 23.

most spiritual part of the nation, of men who were
at once reformers and poets." "They were," says
he, "innovators, unorthodox free-thinkers." What
they alleged about righteousness by no means proves
that righteousness was the religion of Israel.

And perhaps this sort of argument can, in some
cases, be used fairly enough. Pindar may have lofty
passages about the end and the God-given beginning
of man's life. Socrates and Plato may have their
minds still bent on those ideas of moral order and of
right which were the treasure of the primitive and
serious tribes of early Hellas. They may harp still
upon the old-fashioned doctrines recommended from
the temple at Delphi. Yet, if the Greek nation and
its religion have taken quite another line, these utterances of philosophers and poets will not justify us
in saying that the religion of Greece was a religion
of righteousness. But we have a right to give Israel
the benefit of the utterances of its prophets and
psalmists. And why? Because the nation adopted
them. So powerfully did the inmost chords of its
being vibrate to them, so entirely were they the very
truth it was born to and sought to find utterance for,
that it adopted them, made them its standards, the
documents of the most profound and authentic expression of the national consciousness, its religion. Instead of remaining literature and philosophy, isolated
voices of sublime poets and reforming free-thinkers,
these glorifications of righteousness became Jewish
religion, matters to be read in the synagogue every
Sabbath-day. So that while in Greece it was a

religious solemnity to behold a courtesan enter the
sea, in Judæa it was a religious solemnity to hear
that "the righteous Eternal loveth righteousness."

What we claim, then, for Israel, when we say that
he had the intuition of the Eternal Power, not ourselves, that makes for righteousness, when we say
that to him were entrusted the oracles of God, that
to him our religion was first revealed, is this :—that
the ideas of moral order and of right, which are in
human nature, which appear in a recognisable shape,
whatever may be their origin, as soon as man is
sufficiently formed for him to have a history at all, to
be intelligible to us at all, to stand related to us as
showing a like nature with ourselves, — that these
ideas so laid hold upon Israel as to be the master-
element in his thoughts, the sheet-anchor of his life.
And these ideas have such a range that they take in
at least three-fourths of human life. It matters
nothing that Israel could give no satisfying and
scientific account of the way in which he came by these
ideas ; that he could only give legendary and fanciful
accounts of it. It matters nothing that the practical
application he gave to these ideas was extremely
crude and limited, that they were accompanied in him
by gross imperfection. It matters nothing that there
may be shown to have hung about them any number
of waifs and strays from an earlier and unripe stage,
survivals from a time of nature-worship, or of any
other passage which preceded, with Israel, the entrance upon his real history. If from the time he
was formed, and distinguishable, and himself, if from

one end of the Bible to the other, we find him impressed, awe-struck, absorbed by the idea of righteousness, whatever alloys he may mix with it, and however blindly he may deal with it; if we find him, —and it is indisputable that we do find him,—thus fascinated, it is enough, and he has the intuition.

His very shortcomings prove the force of the intuition within him, since all the wear and tear of them could not rase it out. "*Cogitavi vias meas, et converti pedes meos in testimonia Tua;* I called mine own ways to remembrance, and turned my feet unto Thy testimonies." [1] Israel is the great, standing, unsilenceable, unshaken witness to the necessity of minding one's ways, of conduct. And whatever else he may have done, or not done, he can assuredly plead: *Cogitavi vias meas.* "Sacrifices work a conception in which morality has no part," says the *Westminster* Reviewer; "sacrifices existed in Israel *ab origine.*" Even in his historic time there hung about Israel traces of an inchoate and dark stage, remains of an early "conception of God as an unseen but powerful foe, whose enmity might be averted by the death of victims." It may have been so; but, "Still," Israel can answer, "still, all hampered with these survivals of a lower world: *Cogitavi vias meas!*" "Though righteousness," pursues the *Westminster* Reviewer, "entered largely into Israel's conception of the Eternal, yet that conception contained much that conflicts with righteousness. The God of Israel often appears as more patriotic than righteous; blesses

[1] Ps. cxix. 59.

Jael, for instance, for the treacherous murder of
Sisera." True ; but true, also, that with all this
mixture : *Cogitavi vias meas !* "Israel's God," the
objector goes on, "is a magnified and non-natural
man, not impassive and uniform like a law of nature,
but angry and then repenting him, jealous and then
soothed." Nevertheless, with this crude anthropomorphic conception of God : *Cogitavi vias meas !*
"Israel's religion deals in ecstasy, enthusiasm, evoca-
tions of the dead." *Cogitavi vias meas !* "The current
idea of righteousness in Israel was largely made
up of ceremonial observances." *Cogitavi vias meas !*
Finally, in spite of all this thinking upon his ways,
Israel misdirected them. "The Bible," cries the
Westminster Reviewer, "failed to turn the hearts of
those to whom it was addressed ; the commentary
afforded by Israel's history on the value of the Bible !"
True, as Israel managed his profession of faith, it did not
save him ; but did he on that account drop it ? *Cogitavi,
cogitavi vias meas !*

IV.

The *Westminster* Reviewer will now, perhaps,
understand what we mean by saying that the Hebrew
people had the revelation and intuition of the Eternal
that makes for righteousness. We do not mean that
this people had a clear and adequate idea of rightness
in conduct as a law of nature, that they then proceeded to personify this law and deify it, and that
they deified it in their Jehovah. If this were what
we meant, all the criticisms of the *Westminster*

Reviewer upon the shortcomings of Jehovah and Jahvism in the Old Testament would take effect. But perhaps our saying that Israel had the *revelation* of the Eternal that makes for righteousness is the stumbling-block. Let us try, then, so to draw out what we mean by this, that to the Reviewer and to others it may appear as simple and certain as it does to ourselves.

For let us now conceive man, so far as this is possible for us, just as the investigation of his beginnings and the actual observation of the state of certain savages shows him to us, in his inchoate, prehistoric, almost pre-human condition. In this time of ignorance his gods have their origin. We are accused of introducing in the *not ourselves* which presses, we say, upon man's spirit, a refined metaphysical conception. It is so far from this, that it is one of the first pieces of man's experience, and dates from the most primitive time. It is whatever appears to man as outside himself, not in his own power, and affecting him whether he will or no. Now, the more helpless and inexperienced man is, the greater is the number to him of things not in his own power. Who can trace or divine all the possibilities of hope and fear in this wide field? But we know and can easily understand how on certain great and prominent objects of nature, exercising a powerful influence on human life,—such as the sun, for instance,—hope and fear fastened, and produced worship. And we know, too, and can well understand, how by a natural impulse men were moved to represent in a human form like their own, the powers which attracted their hope, fear, and worship; as Xenophanes says that if horses, oxen, and lions could paint or model, they would certainly make gods in their own image,—horses in that of horses, oxen in that of oxen. And even when men did not represent their gods in human form, they still supposed in them human thoughts and passions.

In those times arose names like Eloah, Elohim, *The Mighty;* or Deus, God, *The Shining.* And then, too, in those days of bounded view and of apprehensive terror, grew up and prevailed "the conception of God," to use the *Westminster* Reviewer's words, "as a foe whose enmity might be averted by the death of victims." Such, he asserts, was Israel's first conception of God; and although here he speaks positively of things beyond the ken of any certain knowledge, yet we are not concerned to dispute the probability of his conjecture, that with the inchoate and primordial Israel it may have been so. For "the gods," as Xenophanes again says, "did not from the first show to men all things; but in time, by searching, men came to a discovery of the better."

Such a "better" was reached at a point where human history and human religion, in the only sense which our race can now attach to the word *religion,* first began. It was reached when the ideas of conduct, of moral order and of right, had gathered strength enough to declare and establish themselves. Long before, indeed, during man's chaotic and rudimentary time, these ideas must have been at work; and as they were no conscious creation of man's will, but solicited him and ripened in him whether he

would or no, we may truly and fitly call them the
Spirit of God brooding over chaos, moving silently
upon the human deep.   Then these ideas found and
took possession of the framework of the older, and,
—for so we may call them,—the as yet irreligious
religions.   In many an imagining and legend men
gave voice to their half-recollection of stages and
moments in man's dim ante-natal time, mixing it and
colouring it with their later experience.

From the older religions were handed on ceremonial and rite, which have, in truth, their proper
origin, not in the moral stirrings of man's nature at
all, but in the stirrings which we call æsthetic.
Many practices, even, were not at once dropped,
which had their proper origin in darkness and disease
of the moral feelings, in blind and pusillanimous
terror.   Of this kind were human sacrifices, such as
Abraham's sacrifice of Isaac.   Nevertheless God by the
very cradle of Hebrew history, the God of Abraham,
the God of "integrity of heart and innocency of hands,"
is no longer "a foe whose enmity might be averted
by the death of victims."   The God of Abraham is a
friend ; and the intended sacrifice is no longer an act
of selfish terror to avert a powerful foe's enmity, it is
an act of faithful devotion to the supposed will of an
all-wise and all-good friend.   To this extent in its very
cradle did the one true religion, Israel's religion, the
religion of righteousness, succeed in transforming the
baneful and false usage which clung to it from the
times of darkness out of which it emerged, until the
day came for the disappearance of the usage altogether.

In a like "better" did the history and religion of
Hellas also, as we have seen, take their rise; a
"better" brought about by the ideas of moral order
gathering strength and making themselves felt.
Then the nature-deities of ruder times, Zeus and
Phœbus, became the Father of judgment and of
right, and his Prophet-Son. At that moment, therefore, the Eternal who makes for righteousness, the
God of Israel, who is, as St. Paul said to the Athenians,
not far from every one of us, seemed offering to reveal
himself to Greece also. But it was for a moment
only. Other aspects of life than the moral aspect
came into view and into favour with the Greeks;
other tendencies than the tendency which disposes
men to preoccupy themselves with conduct, and with
its divine sanctions, prevailed. "They did not like,"
says the Hebrew Paul austerely, "to retain God in
their knowledge, and so God gave them over to a
reprobate mind."[1] This is, no doubt, a stern sentence. What the Greeks were and what they accomplished, and how brilliant a course they ran after
their religion had passed out of its brief moment of
accord with that of Israel, we know; and with that
knowledge we shall not be forward to utter against
them hard censures. But thus much, at least, we
may say, notwithstanding all the glory and genius of
Greece, notwithstanding all the failure and fanaticism
of Israel; thus much we may well say, whenever we
contrast the heart and mind of the Græco-Roman
world in its maturity with the interior joys of

[1] Rom. i. 28.

Israel : *They that run after another God shall have great trouble.*

Israel, on the contrary, advanced from the God of Abraham, the Mighty who requires integrity of heart and innocency of hands, to the God of Moses, the Eternal who makes for righteousness unalterably. Then the law in its primitive shape, an organism having for its heart the Ten Commandments, arose. It formulated, with authentic voice and for ever, the religion of Israel, as a religion in which ideas of moral order and of right were paramount. And so things went on from Moses to Samuel, and from Samuel to David, and from David to the great pro- phets of the eighth century and to the Captivity, and from that to the Restoration, and from the Restora- tion to Antiochus and the invasion of Greek culture, to the Maccabees and the Book of Daniel, and from thence to the Roman conquest, and from that to John the Baptist ; until all the wonderful history received its solution and consummation in Jesus Christ. Through progress and backsliding, amid infectious contact with idolatry, amid survival of old growths of superstition, of the crude practices of the past ; amid multiplication of new precepts and observances, of formalism and ceremonial ; amid the solicitation of new aspects of life ; in material prosperity, and in material ruin ; more and more the great governing characteristics of the religion of Israel accentuated and asserted themselves, and forced themselves on the world's attention : the God of this religion, with his eternal summons to keep judgment and do jus-

tice ; the mission of this religion, to bring in everlasting righteousness.

And this native, continuous, and increasing pressure
upon Israel's spirit of the ideas of conduct and of its
sanctions, we call his intuition of the Eternal that
makes for righteousness, the revelation to him of the
religion of this Eternal. Really, we do not know
how else to account for the evident fact of the pressure, than by supposing that Israel had an intuitive
faculty, a natural bent for these ideas; that their truth
was borne in upon him, revealed to him. How else are
we to explain their pressure on him ? We put aside all
the preternatural;—a magnified and non-natural man,
walking in gardens, speaking from clouds, sending
dreams, commissioning angels. We give an explanation which is natural. But we say that this natural
explanation is yet grander than the preternatural one.

Some people, however, when they have got rid of
the preternatural in religion, seem to think that they
are bound to get rid, as much as they can, of the
notion of there being anything grand and wonderful
in religion at all ; at any rate, to reduce this element
of what is grand and wonderful to the very smallest
dimensions. They err. They impede the acceptance
of even the real truths which they have to tell the
world, because the world feels that on the main
matter they are wrong. They act imprudently,
therefore ; but they really fail, besides, to appreciate
and explain their facts. We have already, in *Literature and Dogma*, mentioned Professor Kuenen's explanation of the morality in Bible-religion from the

simple and severe life of the primitive Beni-Israel as
nomads of the desert. But whoever will read in M.
Caussin de Perceval's Arabian History the Moàllacas
of the poets among the Arabs before Mahomet, will
find this poetry extremely licentious, in spite of the
nomad life led in the desert by the Arab tribes. And
the reformation of Mahomet is undoubtedly a reformation largely inspired by the Bible of the Beni-
Israel. On the other hand, we find Semitic people
without the nomad life,—the Semitic people of great
cities,—developing a worship such as Herodotus has
described to us in that of Mylitta.[1]

Professor Kuenen's excellent History is now published in English. We may all read there of a
religious revival in Hebrew religion under Samson
and Samuel, and how by degrees Jahvism grew in
spirituality, and the age of ecstasy and of the Witch
of Endor gave place to the prophets of the eighth
century, conscious of a real inner call. Well, but
what is the reason of all this advance, this "development of monotheism," as people call it? Professor
Kuenen thinks that it is largely due to "the influence
of the war between Baal and Jahveh upon the minds
of those who had remained loyal to Jahveh." So, we
are told, arose the deep gulf of separation between
Jahveh and the heathen "nonentities," as the Hebrew
prophets call them.

So?—but how? Not out of mere blind obstinacy,
not from having fought for a God called Jahveh,
against a God called Baal, so long and so hard that

[1] *Herodotus,* i. 199.

his champions grew bent on sticking to Jahveh, and found out all manner of perfections for him. Israel adhered to Jahveh for the same reason which had at first made him take to the worship of Jahveh :— that Jahveh was the Eternal Power that makes for righteousness, was the centre and source of those ideas of moral order and of conduct which are, we repeat, in human nature, but which pressed on Israel's spirit with extraordinary power. This alone gives us a natural, intelligible clue to the development of the religion of the Bible.

But even suppose that we reject all notion of a special bent or intuition in Israel determining the course of his religion. Suppose that we allow him to have had not one whit more bent than other people for the ideas of moral order and of right, but that his religion came to be what it was by the mere force of external circumstances and from accident. Still we shall have a religion insisting on the idea of righteousness with an energy and impressiveness absolutely unparalleled. We shall have a fact which cannot be accounted for through any intelligible process of cause and effect, and which is due to mere chance ;—but we shall have the fact all the same. In Israel's religion, far and away more than in the religion of any other ancient people, the Eternal Power that makes for righteousness is impressive and para-mount. And of Israel, therefore, the distinction assigned by the word of this Eternal will hold true :— *You only have I known of all the families of the earth.*[1]

---

[1] Amos iii. 2.

V.

But now, as if it were not enough to have a *Westminster* Reviewer on one's hands, there comes a *Quarterly* Reviewer besides, and strikes his blow at *Literature and Dogma.* After some animadversions on our reasoning faculty, which are probably just, and some compliments to the clearness of our diction, which we hesitate to accept, because it is the very simplicity of our understanding that incapacitates us for the difficult style of the philosophers, and drives us to the use of the most ordinary phraseology,— after these preliminaries, the *Quarterly* Reviewer says that we have no right to call our "enduring power, not ourselves, which makes for righteousness," a verifiable fact at all, or to talk of Israel's intuition of it. And why? "Because," says the *Quarterly* Reviewer, "the origin of the moral perceptions in man is assigned by some to intuition, by others to education, and by Mr. Darwin to a social instinct, arising out of evolution and inheritance."

Let us assure the *Quarterly* Reviewer that, for our purpose, whether a man assigns the origin of the moral perceptions to intuition, or to education, or to evolution and inheritance, does not matter two straws. And really we are almost astonished at having to explain this, so clear does it seem to us. For surely, because we may choose to say that the English people have an intuitive sense for politics, we are not therefore to be understood as settling the question about the origin of political perceptions, whether they proceed from intuition, or from education, or from evolution and inheritance. Nay, and we thought that on this very point we had said in *Literature and Dogma* all that was necessary ; but we find it is not so. We find a great many people imagining that if Mr. Darwin is right in assigning the origin of the moral perceptions to evolution and inheritance, in that case everything we have said about an enduring power which makes for righteousness, and about Israel's recognition of this power, must necessarily fall to the ground. Come, then, let us make it clear to the reader of *Literature and Dogma*, that these imaginations are quite vain, and that he would do very ill to be moved by them.

So let us take Mr. Darwin's doctrine and see how innocent it is, and how entirely unaffected religion is by it. But we will not take it from the mouth of that illustrious philosopher himself, because to so many religious people he is a bugbear. Neither will we take it from M. Littré, as we did in *Literature and Dogma*, for the sake of softening a little the stern hearts of the Comtists ; for M. Littré's name is not more acceptable to the religious world than Mr. Darwin's. No, we will take it from one of the clearest of thinkers, and one of the most religious of men,— Pascal. "What is nature?" says Pascal. "Perhaps a first habit, as habit is a second nature." *Qu'est ce que la nature ? Peut-être une première coutume, comme la coutume est une seconde nature.* Here, briefly and admirably expressed, is the famous doctrine of Mr. Darwin.

And now suppose that our moral perceptions and rules are all to be traced up, as evolutionists say, to habits due to one or other of two main instincts,— the reproductive instinct and the instinct of self-preservation. Let us take an example of a moral rule due to each instinct. For a moral rule traceable, on our present supposition, to the instinct of self-preservation, we cannot do better than to take "the first commandment with promise :" *Honour thy father and thy mother.* We say that it makes not the smallest difference to religion whether we suppose this commandment to be thus traceable or not.

For let it be thus traceable, and suppose the original natural affection of the young to their parents to be due to a sense of dependence upon them, and of benefit from them. And then, when the dependence and benefit end, when the young can shift for themselves, the natural affection seems in the lower animals, as they are called, to pass away. But in man it is not thus evanescent. For at first, perhaps, there were some who from weakness or from accident felt the dependence and received the benefit longer than others, and in such was formed a more deep and strong tie of attachment. And while their neighbours, so soon as they were of adult vigour, heedlessly left the side of their parents and troubled themselves about them no more, and let them perish if so it might happen, these few remained with their parents, and grew used to them more and more, and finally even fed and tended them when they grew helpless. Presently they began to be shocked at

their neighbours' callous neglect of those who had
begotten them and borne them; and they expostulated with their neighbours, and entreated and pleaded
that their own way was best. Some suffered, perhaps,
for their interference; some had to fight for their
parents to hinder their neighbours maltreating them;
and all the more fixed in their new feelings did
these primitive gropers after the Fifth Commandment become.

Meanwhile this extending of the family-bond, this
conquering of a little district from the mere animal
life, this limiting of the reign of blind, selfish impulse,
brought, we may well believe, more order into the
homes of those who practised it, and with more order
more well-doing, and with both more happiness. And
when they solicited their more inhuman neighbours
to change their ways, they must always have had to
back them the remembrance, more or less alive in
every man, of an early link of affection with his
parents; but now they had their improved manner
of life and heightened well-being to back them too.
So the usage of the minority gradually became the
usage of the majority. And we may end this long
chapter of suppositions by supposing that thus there
grew at last to be communities which honoured their
fathers and mothers, instead of,—as, perhaps, if one
went back far enough, one would find to have been
the original practice,—eating them.

But all this took place during that which was, in
truth, a twilight ante-natal life of humanity, almost as
much as the life which each man passes in the womb

before he is born. The history of man as man proper,
and as distinguished from the other animals,—the real
history of our race, and of its institutions,—does not
begin until stages such as that which we have been
describing are passed, and feelings such as that of which
we have been tracing the growth are formed. Man and
his history begin, we say, when he becomes distinctly
conscious of feelings which, in a long preparatory
period of obscure growth, he may have been forming.
Then he calls his habit, acquired by a process which
he does not recollect, *nature ;* and he gives effect to it
in fixed customs, rules, laws, and institutions. His
religion consists in acknowledging and reverencing
the awful sanctions with which this right way for
man has, he believes, been invested by the mighty
not ourselves which surrounds us. And the more emphatically he places a feeling under the guardianship
of these sanctions, the more impressive is his testimony to the hold it has upon him. When Israel
fixed the feeling of a child's natural attachment to its
parents by the commandment : *Honour thy father and
thy mother, that thy days may be long in the land which
the Eternal thy God giveth thee,* he showed that he had
risen to regard this feeling,—slowly and precariously
acquired though by our supposition it may have been,
—as a sure, solid, and sacred part of the constitution
of human nature.

But as well as the supposition of a moral habit and
rule evolved out of the instinct of self-preservation,
we are to take the supposition of a moral habit and
rule evolved out of the reproductive instinct. And

here, indeed, in the relations between the sexes, we are on ground where to walk right is of vital concern to men, and where disasters are plentiful. Who first, in the early and tentative up-struggling of our race, who first discerned them, this peril of disaster, this necessity for taking heed to one's steps? Who was he, that, amid the promiscuous concubinage of man's commencements, — if we are to suppose that out of the sheer animal life human life had to evolve itself and rise,—who was he that first, through attachment to his chance companion or through attachment to his supposed offspring, gathered himself together, put a bridle on his vague appetites, marked off himself and his, drew the imperfect outline of the circle of home, and fixed for the time to come the rudiments of the family? Who first, amid the loose solicitations of sense, obeyed (for create it he did not) the mighty *not ourselves* which makes for moral order, the stream of tendency which was here carrying him, and our embryo race along with him, towards the fulfilment of the true law of their being? — became aware of it, and obeyed it? Whoever he was, he would soon have had imitators; for never was a more decisive step taken towards bringing into human life greater order, and, with greater order, greater well-doing and happiness. So the example was followed, and a habit grew up, and marriage was instituted.

And thus, again, we are brought to the point where history and religion begin. And at this point we first find the Hebrew people, with polygamy still clinging

to it as a survival from the times of ignorance, but
with the marriage-tie solidly established, strict and
sacred, as we see it between Abraham and Sara.
Presently this same Hebrew people, with that aptitude
which, we say, characterised it for being profoundly
impressed by ideas of moral order, placed in the
Decalogue the marriage-tie under the express and
solemn sanction of the Eternal, by the Seventh Commandment : *Thou shalt not commit adultery.*

Now, we might jump at once from here to the end
of Jewish history, and show Jesus Christ renewing
by his method the Seventh Commandment as he did
also the Fifth, renewing them and extending them,
clearing casuistry and formalism away from them, and
making them look as fresh and impressive in this new
light as in their old light they had in Israel's best
days looked to him.   But let us first, after hearing
Israel in the Decalogue on the relation of the sexes,
take Israel in the middle of his career, as the Book
of Proverbs discovers him to us.   There he touches
on that great and often-arising theme in what our
philosophers call " sociology :" *the strange woman.*
And this is his sentence on the man who is be-
witched by her : *He knows not that the dead are there,
and that her guests are in the depths of hell.*[1]

Now, we ask the *Quarterly* Reviewer to consider
this saying of Israel, led up to by the Seventh Commandment in the earlier days of his history, and con-
summated by such things as the review of the Seventh
Commandment by the well-known sentence of Jesus

[1] Proverbs ix. 18.

in the later.[1] Religion, we know, arises when moral ideas are touched with emotion. Now, this may be the case with moral ideas from whatever source they were at first derived. And that people, amongst whom it is the case eminently, are the chosen people of religion. We have granted the supposition that moral perceptions and habits in what concerns the relation of the sexes were originally formed for Israel, as for everybody else, by evolution and inheritance. We will grant, besides, that religious worship and many of its names and ceremonies arose out of ignorant hope and fear in man's rudimentary time. But, for us now, religion is, we say, morality touched with emotion, lit up and enkindled and made much more powerful by emotion. And when morality is thus touched with emotion, it is equally religion, whether it have proceeded from a magnified and nonnatural man in the clouds, or arisen in the way we have supposed. And those in whom it appears thus touched with emotion most, are those whom we call endued with most bent for religion, most feeling, most apprehension ; as one man and one race seem to turn out to have more gift, without any conscious intending and willing of it, for one thing, and another man and another race for another. Now such a bent, such a feeling, when it declares itself, we call an intuition. And we say that Israel had such an intuition of

[1] Matt. v. 27, 28. Compare : "Not in the lust of concupiscence, *as the Gentiles who know not God ;*" "The time past may suffice us *to have wrought the will of the Gentiles* when we walked in lasciviousness," etc.—1 Thess. iv. 5 ; 1 Pet. iv. 3.

religion, that he shows it in the special matter with which we are now dealing, and in others of like kind, and that this people is, therefore, the chosen people of religion.

For how does a bent or feeling of this kind for moral perceptions declare itself, when it has grown strong enough to declare itself? It declares itself by the accent and power with which its utterances are made;—the accent of conviction in the speaker himself, the power of impressiveness on those who hear him. Moral perceptions, and rules securing and establishing them, take, on the supposition we are here following, a long while to build up. There is a backwards and forwards with them; often it looks as if they would never have strength to get established at all. However, at last there comes some one like Israel, and lays down a sentence like the Seventh Commandment, and reinforces it by such deliverances as that of the Book of Proverbs, and that of the Sermon on the Mount. He thus, we say, takes a lead in what vitally concerns conduct and religion, which for ever remains to him and for ever is proving its reality.

For, again, a moral perception does not always, and for all persons, retain the vividness it had at the moment when it established itself in a rule like the Seventh Commandment. Human nature has many sides, many impulses; our rule may seem to lose ground again, and the perception out of which it grew may seem to waver. Practice may offer to it a thousand contradictions, in what M. Taine calls the *triste défilé*, the dismal procession of the Haymarket, and in what a sage or a saint might, perhaps, in like manner call the dismal procession of the Bois de Boulogne. Not practice alone is against the old strictness of rule, but theory; we have argumentative systems of free love and of re-habilitation of the flesh. Even philosophers like Mr. Mill, having to tell us that for special reasons they had in fact observed the Seventh Commandment, think it right to add that this they did, "although we did not consider the ordinances of society binding, on a subject so entirely personal." So arises what these same philosophers would call a disintegration of that moral perception on which the Seventh Commandment is founded. What we have to ask, then, is: Was this perception, and the rule founded on it, really a conquest for ever, placing human nature on a higher stage; so that, however much the perception and rule may have been dubious and unfounded once, they must be taken to be certain and formed now? And whatever now makes the perception or the rule fluctuating, does it tend, so far, not to emancipate man, but to replace him in the bondage of that old, chaotic, dark, almost ante-human time, from which slowly and painfully he had emerged when the real history and religion of our race began? And whatever, on the other hand, reinvigorates the perception, does it tend to man's freedom, safety, and progress? Because, if this is so, the accent of clear and decisive conviction in Israel's comment on the theory of Free Love is invaluable. *He knows not that the dead are there, and that her guests are in the depths of hell.*

Here, then, let us summon the most naturalistic, the freest, the calmest of observers on these matters, —Goethe.   He is speaking to the Chancellor von Müller against over-facility in granting divorce.   He says : "What culture has won of nature we ought on no account to let go again, at no price to give up.   In the notion of the sacredness of marriage, Christianity has got a culture-conquest of this kind, and of price-less value, although marriage is, properly speaking, unnatural."   Unnatural, he means, to man in his rudimentary state, before the fixing of moral habits has formed the right human nature.   Emancipation from the right human nature is merely, therefore, return to chaos.   Man's progress depends on keeping such "culture-conquests" as the Christian notion of the sacredness of marriage.   And undoubtedly this notion came to Christianity from Israel.   Such was Israel's genius for the ideas of moral order and of right, such his intuition of the Eternal that makes for righteousness, that he felt without a shadow of doubt, and said with the most impressive solemnity, that Free Love was,—to speak, again, like our modern philosophers,—fatal to progress. *He knows not that the dead are there, and that her guests are in the depths of hell*.

And now, perhaps, the *Quarterly* Reviewer will suffer us to speak of Israel's intuition of the Eternal that makes for righteousness, even though moral per-ceptions and habits may have originally been evolved as Mr. Darwin supposes.   And the *Westminster* Re-viewer will let us repeat that the word of this Eternal concerning Israel, as distinguished from every other

nation of antiquity, is true, in spite of Israel's sacrifices and polygamy : *You only have I known of all the
families of the earth.*

VI.

Finally, a very different writer from the *Westminster* Reviewer,—M. Charles Secrétan, in the *Revue
Suisse,*—is at one with the *Westminster* Reviewer in
denying the possibility of basing on experimental
grounds the claim of the Bible and of its religion to
our acceptance. "The Power making for righteousness," says M. Charles Secrétan, "the Secret of Jesus,
are not really experimental notions which any man
can verify. The contrary is true. The Secret and
the Power are objects of *faith* only. Experience
offers every day abundant contradictions to the reality
of this Power."

Now on this point it is certainly indispensable that
the reader of *Literature and Dogma* should be in no
doubt. For the fundamental thesis of that book is,
that righteousness is salvation verifiably, and that
the secret of Jesus is righteousness verifiably ; and
that the true faith which the Bible inculcates is the
faith that this is so. But unquestionably the common
notion among religious people is M. Charles Secrétan's :
that experience is altogether against the saving power
of righteousness or of the secret of Jesus, but that
their saving power will be proved to a man after he
is dead by a great judgment, and by a system of re-
wards and punishments in accordance with them ;
and that faith is the belief that this will really

happen. And unquestionably all this is taken from
Israel himself, who in his latter days consoled himself, as we can see in the Book of Daniel, by the idea
of a resurrection, judgment, and recompense of this
sort, and for whom faith came to be the belief that it
all would certainly happen.

Jesus Christ, we say, made it the great object of
his teaching to clear and transform this *extra-belief*
of his countrymen. Upon that, however, we will not
insist now; neither will we now ourselves set about
proving that experimentally righteousness is salvation,
and experimentally the secret of Jesus is righteousness, independently of the soundness or unsoundness
of the *extra-belief* of Jews or Christians. On the experimental character of these truths, which are the
undoubted object of religion, we have elsewhere said
what is necessary. But they are the matter of an
immense experience which is still going forward. It
is easy to dispute them, to find things which seem to
go against them; yet, on the whole, they prove themselves, and prevail more and more. And the idea of
their truth is in human nature, and every one has
some affinity for them, although one man has more and
another less. But if any man is so entirely without
affinity for them, so subjugated by the conviction that
facts are clean against them, as to be unable to entertain
the idea of their being in human nature and in experience, for him *Literature and Dogma* was not written.

We suppose, therefore, the reader of *Literature and
Dogma* to admit the idea of these truths being in
human nature and in experience. Now, we say that

the great use of the Bible is to animate and fortify faith in them, against whoever says that "experience offers every day abundant contradictions to their reality." The truth that righteousness is salvation has double power upon mankind by the inspiration of the sublime witness borne to it by Israel in his best days. This is why these Scriptures are truly said to be "written for our learning, that we through patience and comfort of the Scriptures might have hope."[1] True, in his later days Israel had taken refuge in an ideal world to ensure the triumph of righteousness, had imagined his apocalyptic Ancient of Days to be necessary and his Son of Man coming in the clouds, his *crisis*, his *anastasis*, and his Messianic reign of the saints. All this was, in a certain way, a testimony to the ideas of moral order and of right. But Israel's best, his immortal testimony to them, is the testimony borne in his earlier days and in his prime, when his faith is in the triumph of the ideas themselves, not in a phantasmagoric restitution of all things to serve them. *As the whirlwind passeth, so is the wicked no more, but the righteous is an everlasting foundation. As righteousness tendeth to life, so he that pursueth evil pursueth it to his own death.*[2]

This imperishable faith of the true Israel, clouded in his later days, resumed and perfected by Jesus Christ, but from the first only half understood and mixed with natural errors by his disciples, makes the glory and the grandeur of the Old Testament. It has an answer,—a far better answer than any we

[1] Rom. xv. 4.   [2] Prov. x. 25 ; xi. 19.

could give, — to every objection of M. Charles
Secrétan. "The power making for righteousness is
not really," says M. Secrétan, "an experimental
notion, which any man can verify; the contrary is
true." Let Israel answer. *The Eternal upholdeth the*
righteous; though he fall he shall not be cast away, for
the Eternal upholdeth him with his hand. I have been
young and now am old, and yet saw I never the righteous
forsaken. I myself have seen the ungodly in great power,
and flourishing like a green bay-tree; I went by, and lo,
he was gone![1] "Experience," pursues M. Secrétan,
"offers every day abundant contradictions to the
reality of this power." What says Israel? *I should*
utterly have fainted, but that I believe verily to see the
goodness of the Eternal in the land of the living.[2] Israel
would not allow time enough for the demonstration
of his truth that righteousness is salvation; hence his
later disappointments and illusions. But for any one
who believes that this truth is a profound law of
human nature, Israel's faith in it during his best days
opens a boundless source of joy, courage, and enthusiasm; and it is a source such as no other people of
antiquity offers. So that here, again, is confirmation
of that unique rank emphatically assigned to Israel
by the Eternal that makes for righteousness: *You*
only have I known of all the families of the earth.

[1] Ps. xxxvii. 24, 25, 35, 36.   [2] Ps. xxvii. 13.

VII.

The *Spectator* asks : How are we to know that Israel meant what he said when he pronounced righteousness to be salvation, if we contend that he did not speak literally when he brings in God talking, thinking, and loving? Surely because in the one case he is on ground of experience where we can follow him, but on the other he is not. Therefore, when he says : *There ariseth light for the righteous,*[1] his words present no difficulty, and we can take them as they stand ; but when he speaks of God walking in a garden, we are driven to find for the words some other origin than his actual experience. And whoever attends to the history of the human spirit, will soon see that such an origin is not hard to find.

The *Spectator* asks, again, where in Wordsworth, whose personifying language about nature we produced to illustrate Israel's personifying language about God, we can point to language which speaks of nature in the "mood of real expectation and confidence common in the Psalms." Why, where Wordsworth says : *Nature never did forsake the heart that loved her.* Or where, asks the *Spectator*, can we find language which "treats distrust in the promises of nature as a sin?" Why, in plain prose, without going to the poets for it at all ; in one of the profoundest and most impressive passages to be found in Butler, in his sermon on *The Ignorance of Man.* "If things afford to man,"

[1] Ps. xcvii. 11.

says Butler, "the least hint or intimation that virtue
is the law he is born under, scepticism itself should
lead him to the most strict and inviolable performance
of it ; *that he may not make the dreadful experiment of
leaving the course of life marked out for him by nature,
whatever that nature be, and entering paths of his own, of
which he can know neither the danger nor the end.*"
What can be more solemn and grand? it is grand
with the grandeur of Greek tragedy. But Israel had
more than a hint or intimation that virtue is the law
man is born under. He had an irresistible intuition
of it. Therefore he breaks into joy, which Butler
and Greek tragedy do not. Nevertheless, the greatness of Butler, as we hope one day to show, is in his
clear perception and powerful use of a "course of life
marked out for man by nature, whatever that nature
be." His embarrassment and failure is in his attempt
to establish a perception as clear, and a use as powerful, of the popular theology. But from Butler, and
from his treatment of *nature* in connection with
religion, the idea of following out that treatment
frankly and fully, which is the design of *Literature
and Dogma*, first, as we are proud to acknowledge,
came to us ; and, indeed, our obligations of all kinds
to this deep and strenuous spirit are very great.

From our use of the proof from happiness, accusa-
tions have been brought against us of eudæmonism,
utilitarianism. We are reproached, by a foreign
critic, with utilitarianism, with making, "conformably
to the tradition of the English school" (the *Westminster* Reviewers will hear with astonishment what

company they have been keeping!) "self-interest the
spring of human action." Utilitarianism! Surely a
pedant invented the word; and oh, what pedants
have been at work in employing it! But that joy
and happiness are the magnets to which human life
inevitably moves, let not the reader of *Literature and
Dogma* for a moment confuse his mind by doubting.
The real objection is to low and false views of what
constitutes happiness. *Pleasure* and *utility* are bad
words to employ, because they have been so used as
to suggest such views. But *joy* and *happiness*, on the
whole, have not. We may safely say, then, that joy
and happiness are the magnets to which human life
irresistibly moves. The men of positive experience
are for us here, but so are the chief men of religion
too. St. Augustine :—"Act we *must* in pursuance of
that which gives most delight." Pascal :—"However
different the means they employ, all men without
exception tend towards one object, — happiness."
Barrow :—"The sovereign good, the last scope of our
actions, the top and sum of our desires,—happiness."
Butler :—"It is manifest that nothing can be of consequence to mankind, or any creature, but happiness."
This truth cannot be gainsaid ; and to reject the truth
itself, because of frequent perversions of it, is a fatal
error. From theologians of the Unitarian school the
cry against eudæmonism comes loudest. To champion
anti-eudæmonism, and to champion the metaphysical
personality of God, are tasks to which this school
at the present moment appears to have especially
addressed itself. Hardly could it give a stronger

sign of that sterility in religion, to which, in spite of
all its benevolence and intelligence, it seems perpetually doomed.

VIII.

The objections most likely to make an untoward
impression on the reader of *Literature and Dogma* we
have now, we believe, noticed, and done our best to
remove. On others we will not linger, because they
can hardly occasion any real difficulty. The *Westminster* Reviewer complains of our talking of the *secret*
of Jesus, because, says the Reviewer, Jesus made no
secret of it himself. Neither did the Eternal make a
secret to Israel of righteousness, and yet Israel talks
of the secret of the Eternal. The truth which its
holder is supposed alone or in especial to have the
clue to and to deal in, men call his *secret*. Again, we
are told that we must not suppose an element of
genuine curativeness in the exorcising of unclean
spirits by Jesus, because the Jewish thaumaturgists
are represented exorcising them also. But what?
because there are charlatans who play upon the
nervous system for their own purposes, can there be
no doctor who plays upon it beneficently? Again,
we have said that it can be verified that Jesus is the
son of the Eternal that makes for righteousness, and
the *Westminster* Reviewer objects that "to say that
any man is the son of a natural law is absurd." But
the Bible never speaks of the Eternal as a natural
law, but always as if this power lived, and breathed,
and felt. Speaking as the Bible speaks, we say that

Jesus is verifiably the Son of God. Speaking as the
Westminster Reviewer speaks, and calling God a
natural law, we say that of this natural law Jesus is
verifiably the offspring or outcome. Finally, the
Quarterly Reviewer will not allow us to pronounce it
verifiable that righteousness is only possible by the
method of Jesus, because, says he, there was righteousness in the world before the Christian era. Really,
the Fourth Gospel answers him, where Jesus says :
Before Abraham was, I am.[1] But, perhaps, though
a *Quarterly* Reviewer, he has been dallying with the
Tübingen school, and pronounces the Fourth Gospel
a fancy-piece. Let us try him, then, with St. Augustine :—*Res ipsa, quæ nunc religio Christiana, nuncupatur
erat apud antiquos, nec defuit ab initio generis humani.*

We have just now appealed to the Fourth Gospel.
Professor Rauwenhoff lays down that the weakest
part of *Literature and Dogma* is its reliance on sayings
of Jesus from that Gospel. On his death-bed Baur
pleasantly remarked that to his Tübingen school, so
often reported vanquished, might with truth be
applied the words of St. Paul : *As dying, and behold
we live.* Well might Baur say so. He and his school
live, above all, in the strong and growing acceptance
of their criticism of the Fourth Gospel. Already
Liberal reviewers in this country begin to treat it as
certain. Discussions of it have hitherto not been
frequent in this country, but the vogue for such discussions will certainly increase. What we think of
this class of questions, and of its fundamental char-

[1] John viii. 58.

acter, we have said in *Literature and Dogma*. But to
return for a little to the subject, to treat it a little
more closely, may be well. Probably, too, the reader
of *Literature and Dogma* will expect us to make good
our free use, in that work, of the Fourth Gospel.
The method, the secret, and the sweet reasonableness
of Jesus are independent of the Fourth Gospel, but
from that Gospel they receive important illustration.

The question concerning the Fourth Gospel raises
the whole question concerning the Canon of the New
Testament, and, indeed, concerning the Canon of
Scripture generally. On this larger question also,
then, we cannot but touch ; we shall, however, particularly address ourselves to considering the Fourth
Gospel, and the criticisms which have been directed
against it. To invalidate it two tests are employed :
the test of external evidence, and the test of internal
evidence. We will, after saying what seems needful
on the general question of the Canon of Scripture,
proceed to take first the external evidence in the case
of the Fourth Gospel, the questions of dates and of
texts. But the internal evidence, the test of literary
criticism, is above all relied on as decisive by Baur
and his school. So we will, finally, try the Fourth
Gospel by that test too. *Cæsarem appellasti, ad
Cæsarem ibis.*

CHAPTER IV.

THE BIBLE-CANON.

We said in *Literature and Dogma*, that all our criticism of the Four Evangelists who report Jesus had this for its governing idea : *to make out what, in their report of Jesus, is Jesus, and what is the reporters.* We then went on to remark as follows :—" Now, this excludes as unessential much of the criticism which is bestowed on the New Testament. What it excludes is those questions as to the exact date, the real authorship, the first publication, the rank of priority of the Gospels, on which so much thought is by many bestowed ; questions which have a great attraction for critics, which are in themselves good to be entertained, which lead to much close and fruitful observations of the texts, and in which very high ingenuity may be shown and very great plausibility reached, but not more ; they cannot really be settled, the data are insufficient. And for our purpose they are not essential." And we concluded by saying :—" In short, to know accurately the history of our documents is impossible ; and even if it were possible, we should yet not know accurately what Jesus said and did ;

for *his reporters were incapable of rendering it, he was so much above them.*"

As to the character of the documents, however, we added this : " It must be remembered that of none of these recorders have we, probably, the very original record.   The record, when we first get it, has passed through at least half a century, or more, of oral tradition, and through more than one written account."

Nevertheless, we thought that in the Fourth Gospel we found, after all these deductions had been made as to the capacity of the Gospel-reporters and the quality of the Gospel documents, a special clue in one most important respect to the line really taken by Jesus in his teaching.   A Gospel-writer, having by nature his head full of the external evidence from miracles, would never, we said, have invented the insistence on internal evidence as what, above all, proves a doctrine.   " Wherever we find what enforces this evidence, or builds upon it, there we may be especially sure that we are on the trace of Jesus ; because turn or bias in this direction the disciples were more likely to omit from his discourse than to import into it, they were themselves so wholly pre-occupied with the evidence from miracles."   But we find in the Fourth Gospel a remarkable insistence upon the internal evidence for the doctrine promulgated by Jesus.   Here then we certainly come, we said, upon a trace, too little marked by the reporters in general, of the genuine teaching of Jesus ; and this gives a peculiar eminency and value to the Fourth Gospel.

All this is contested; some of it by one set of critics, some of it by another. Critics like the *Westminster* Reviewer will not allow that Jesus was over the heads of his reporters. The author of *Supernatural Religion*, far from thinking that the Fourth Gospel puts us in a special way on the trace of Jesus, declares that it "gives a portrait of Jesus totally unlike that of the Synoptics," contrasts "the dogmatic mysticism and artificial discourses of the one" with "the sublime morality and simple eloquence of the other," assigns, in short, the entire superiority to the Synoptics. On the other hand, the critics in the opposite camp,— critics of so-called orthodox views,—will by no means allow that in our Four Gospels we have not the very original record; or that they went through the period of incubation and of gradual rise into acceptance which we suppose. From the end of the first century of our era there was, according to these critics, a Canon of the New Testament, and our Four Gospels formed the Gospel-part of it.

But, above all, it is contested, and in the most practical way possible, that inquiries as to the exact date, the real authorship, the first publication, the rank of priority, and so forth, of our Four Gospels, can with any truth be called, as we have called them, unessential, or that the data are insufficient, as we have said they are, for ever really settling such questions. Whoever reads German will know that there exists a whole library of German theological works addressed to these questions; and that, far from being treated as questions which cannot really be settled,

they are in general settled in these works with the
greatest vigour and rigour.   Gradually these works are
getting known here, partly by translation, partly by
their influence upon English writers.   The author of
Supernatural Religion has nourished himself upon
them, and has thrown himself with signal energy,
and with very considerable success, into that course
of inquiry which these works pursue.   He occupies a
volume and a half with this line of inquiry, and he
has at any rate succeeded, one can see, in giving unbounded satisfaction to the Liberal world, both learned
and unlearned.   He huddles up into a page a declaration of adherence to "an infinitely wise and beneficent
Being," and to "the true and noble faith which is the
child of Reason;" and the claims of religion being
thus satisfied, with all the difficult and troublesome
questions which they open, he is free to devote his
volume and a half to a negative examination of the
current notions about the date and authorship of the
Bible-documents.   And so doing, and doing it with
much effectiveness, he is, we say, in the eyes of the
Liberal world, almost the ideal of what "an able
critic" on Biblical matters, "a profound critic," ought
to be.   Liberals say to one another, with an air of
thankful conviction : "Surely, Superstition is at last
doomed ; it can never survive this blow !"   Liberal
newspapers, Liberal reviews, Liberal philosophers, and
the scientific gentlemen in strong force besides (some
of the latter being inclined, however, to substitute
the word "Christianity" for the word "Superstition"), have with wonderful unanimity been moved

to blend their voices, ever since the book called
Supernatural Religion became known to the public, in
this new and strange kind of Hallelujah Chorus.

What, then, is the reader of *Literature and Dogma*
to think? That on these points, which we treated
as not admitting of complete settlement, one can, on
the contrary, attain full and absolute certainty?
That the Fourth Gospel, which we treated as affording
a special clue to the line of evidence insisted on by
Jesus, is, on the contrary, a guide utterly misleading?
And, finally, that the investigations which we treated
as unessential, are, on the contrary, all-important,
and that it behoves him to go eagerly into them?

In determining his answer to these questions, he
will do well to keep in mind what is the one object
we set before him in the present inquiry: *to enjoy the
Bible and to turn it to his benefit.* Whatever else he
may propose to himself in dealing with the Bible,
this remains his one proper object. In another order
of interest, the poetry of Homer supplies here a
useful illustration for us. Elaborate inquiries have
been raised as to the date, authorship, and mode of
composition of the Homeric poems. Some writers
have held, too, and have laboriously sought to prove,
that there is a hidden mystical sense running all
through them. All this sort of disquisition, or at
any rate some department of it, is nearly sure to
catch at one time or other the attention of the reader
of Homer, and to tempt and excite him. But, after
all, the proper object for the reader of the Homeric
poems remains this: to enjoy Homer, and to turn him

to his benefit. In dealing even with Homer, we say, this is found true, and very needful to be borne in mind ;—with an object where yet the main interest is properly intellectual. How much more does it hold true of the Bible ! where the main interest is properly not intellectual, but practical.

Therefore our reader has still his chief work with the Bible to do, after he has settled all questions about its mode of composition, if they can be settled. This makes it undesirable for him to spend too much time and labour on these questions, or indeed on any collateral questions whatever. And he will observe, moreover, that as to the rules with which he starts in setting himself to feel and apply the Bible, he is practically just in the same position when he has read and accepted our half-dozen lines about the composition of the Gospels, as when he has read the volume and a half devoted to it in *Supernatural Religion.* For the result is the same : that the record of the sayings and doings of Jesus, when we first get it, has passed through at least half a century, or more, of oral tradition, and through more than one written account. So, too, a man is practically in the same position when he has read and accepted our half-dozen pages about miracles, as when he has read the half volume in which the author of *Supernatural Religion* professes to establish a complete induction against them. For the result reached is in both cases the same : that miracles do not really happen. And we suppose our reader to be ready enough to admit what we say both of miracles and of the condition in

which the Gospel-record reaches us.   For our book is
addressed to those inclined to reject the Bible-testi-
mony, and to attribute to its documents and assertions
not too much authority, but too little.

When, however, our reader has accepted what we
say about the untrustworthiness of miracles and the
looseness of the Gospel-record, his real work has still
to begin.   Whereas when the author of *Supernatural
Religion* has demonstrated the same thing to him in
two volumes, his work is over.   Or, at most, he has
still to edify himself with the page saying how "from
Jewish mythology we rise to higher conceptions of an
infinitely wise and beneficent Being;" or perhaps, to
retire into the "one unassailable fortress" of the
Duke of Somerset.   With us at this stage, on the
contrary, his work only begins.   His work, with us,
is to learn to enjoy and turn to his benefit the Bible,
as the Word of the Eternal.   It would be inexcusable
in us, therefore, to give him more preliminary trouble
than we can help, by the elaborate establishment of
conclusions where he is with us already, or which he
is quite disposed to take from us on trust.

No : for the reader whom *Literature and Dogma*
has in view, learned discussions of the date, authorship, and mode of composition of this or that Bible-
document, — whether   complete   certainty   can   be
attained in them or whether it cannot,—are, as we
called them, unessential.   Even the question of the
trustworthiness of the Fourth Gospel is not an essential question for him.   For the value of the Fourth
Gospel, as we think, is that whereas Jesus was far

over the heads of all his reporters, he was in some
respects better comprehended by the author of this
Gospel than by the Synoptics; the line of internal
evidence which Jesus followed in pressing his doctrines is better marked. But still the all-important
thing to seize in Jesus is his method, and his secret,
and the element of mildness and sweet reasonableness
in which they both worked; and these are perfectly
well given in the Synoptics. In the Synoptics are
the great marking texts for all three. For the
method: "Cleanse the *inside* of the cup; what comes
from within, *that* defiles a man." For the secret:
"He that will save his life shall lose it; he that will
lose his life shall save it." For the sweet reasonableness and mildness: "Learn of me that I am mild and
lowly in heart, and ye shall find rest unto your souls."
So that if we lose the Fourth Gospel, we do not lose
these. All we lose is a little lifting up of the veil
with which the imperfection of the reporters, and
their proneness to demand miracles, to rely on
miracles, have overspread the real discourse and
doings of Jesus.

II.

Nevertheless, according to that buoyant and immortal sentence with which Aristotle begins his
Metaphysics, *All mankind naturally desire knowledge.*
When discussions about the Canon of the New Testament are so rife, the reader of *Literature and Dogma*
may well wish to know what he may most reasonably
think touching the origin and history of those docu-

ments to which he is so often referred by us. More particularly may he wish to know this about that wonderful document which has exercised such a potent fascination upon Christendom, the Fourth Gospel. Luther called it "the true head-Gospel:" it is hardly too much to say that for Christendom it has been so. The author of *Supernatural Religion* speaks contemptuously of its dogmatic, mysterious, and artificial discourses; but its chief opponents have spoken of it with more respect. Strauss is full of admiration of the Fourth Gospel for the artistic skill of its composition; Baur, for its spiritual beauty. The reader of *Literature and Dogma* cannot but be interested in getting as near as he can to the truth about such a document, the object of criticisms so diverse.

We will take him, then, by the same road which we travelled ourselves, when we sought to ascertain how stood the truth about the New Testament records, so far as it could be known. We shall suppose him to come to this inquiry as we did ourselves;—absolutely disinterested, with no fore-gone conclusion at the bottom of one's mind to start with, no secondary purpose of any kind to serve; but with the simple desire to see the thing, so far as this may be possible, as it really is. We ourselves had not, indeed, so much at stake in the inquiry as some people. For whenever the Gospels may have been written, and whether we have in them the very words of Matthew, Mark, Luke, and John, or not, we did not believe the reporters of Jesus capable, in either case, of rendering Jesus perfectly; he was too far above them.

In England the evidence as to the Canon of the Gospels ought to be well judged, if it be true, as Sir Henry Maine thinks, that the English law of evidence by its extreme strictness has formed English people to be good judges of evidence. Two things, however, must everywhere, if they are found present, impede men in judging questions of evidence well. One is, a strong bias existing, before we try the questions, to answer them in a certain manner. Of Biblical criticism with this bias we have abundance in England. In examining the evidence as to the literary history of the New Testament, this criticism does not, in fact, seek to see the thing as it really is, but it holds a brief for that view which is most convenient to the traditional theology current amongst us. We shall not blame this criticism. The position of the critic, the circumstances under which he writes, are perhaps such as to make his course inevitable. But his work, produced under such conditions, cannot truly serve men's need, cannot endure long; it is marked with death before it is born. Great learning it may have, or great ingenuity, or great eloquence; but the critic is all the time holding a brief, and these advantages are then, in fact, of use only to serve the side for which his brief is held. To be seriously useful, they should be employed solely to exhibit and recommend the truth of the things investigated, as this truth really is.

The other obstacle to a sound judgment of the

evidence respecting the Canon arises when people make too much of a business of such inquiries, give their whole life and thoughts too exclusively to them, and treat them as if they were of paramount importance. One can then hardly resist the temptation of establishing certainties where one has no right to certainty; of introducing into the arrangement of facts a system and symmetry of one's own, for which there are no sufficient data. How many a theory of great vigour and rigour has in Germany, in the Protestant faculties of theology, been due to this cause! A body of specialists is at work there, who take as the business of their lives a class of inquiries like the question about the Canon of the Gospels. They are eternally reading its literature, reading the theories of their colleagues about it; their personal reputation is made by emitting, on the much-canvassed subject, a new theory of their own. The want of variety and of balance in their life and occupations impairs the balance of their judgment in general. Their special subject intoxicates them. They are carried away by theorising; they affirm confidently where one cannot be sure; and, in short, prove by no means good and safe judges of the evidence before them.

In France and England people do not, certainly, in general err on the side of making too great a business of this particular speciality. In general we too much neglect it, and are in consequence either at the mercy of routine, or at the mercy of the first bold innovator. Of Biblical learning we have not enough.

Yet it remains true, and a truth never to be lost sight
of, that in the domain of religion, as in the domain
of poetry, the whole apparatus of learning is but
secondary, and that we always go wrong with our
learning when we suffer ourselves to forget this. The
reader of *Literature and Dogma* will allow, however,
that we did not there intrude any futile exhibition of
learning to draw off his attention from the one fixed
object of that work,—religion. We did not write for
a public of professors ; we did not write to interest
the learned and curious. We wrote to restore the
use and enjoyment of the Bible to plain people, who
might be in danger of losing it. We hardly subjoined a reference or put a note ; for we wished to
give nothing of this kind except what a plain reader,
busy with our main argument, would be likely to
look for and to use. Our reader will trust us, therefore, if we now take him into this subject of the
criticism of the Canon, not to bury him in it, not to
cozen him with theories of vigour and rigour, not to
hold a brief for either the Conservative side or the
Liberal, not to make certainties where there are none ;
but to try and put him in the way of forming a plain
judgment upon the plain facts of the case, so far as
they can be known.

Thus he will see the grounds for what we said in
Literature and Dogma about the Canon of the Gospels,
and about the Fourth Gospel's peculiar character,
without having himself to plunge into the voluminous
literature of the subject. In our search for a sure
standing-ground in the use of the Bible, we have had

to go through a great deal of this literature in our
time ; of how much of it may we not exclaim with
Themistocles : *Give me, not to remember, but to forget !*
If Goethe could say that all which was really worth
knowing in all the sciences he had ever studied would
go into one small envelope, how much more may one
say this of the harvest to be gathered from the literature now in question ! That may be no reason for
neglecting it, indeed ; light and adjustment often
come insensibly to us from labours of which the direct
positive result seems small. Nevertheless, in these
days of multifarious studies soliciting us let us keep
a wholesome dread, and let our reader share it with
us, of spending too much of our life and time over
the wrong ones. We have quoted in *Literature and
Dogma* the day's prayer given in a short sentence of
the Imitation : " *Utinam per unum diem bene simus
conversati in hoc mundo !* Would that for one single
day we may have lived in this world as we ought ! "
He who adds to that sentence this other from the
same book : "*Da mihi, Domine, scire quod sciendum est !*
Grant that the knowledge I get may be the knowledge that is worth having ! "—and sets the two
sentences together before him for his daily guidance,
will not have prayed amiss.

But let us come to the Canon. And as the New
Testament follows the Old and depends upon it, and
since about the Old Testament, too, we had in *Literature and Dogma* a great deal to say, our reader will
wish, perhaps, before going into the question of the
New Testament, to see brought together first, in the

shortest possible summary, what he may reasonably
think of the Canon of the Old.

III.

The law and the Prophets are often mentioned in
the New Testament.   But we also find there a threefold division of the Old Testament Scriptures : *Law,
Prophets, Psalms.*[1]   And the Greek translator of the
lost Hebrew book of the Wisdom of the Son of Sirach,
or, as we call it, Ecclesiasticus, who writes in the
latter half of the second century before Christ, speaks
of *the law, and the prophecies, and the rest of the books.*[2]
Here we have the Bible of the Old Testament Scriptures.   And, indeed, the writer calling himself Daniel,
—whose date is between the translator of the Book
of Ecclesiasticus, and this translator's grandfather,
who composed it,—in a passage wrongly translated
in our version, designates the body of Old Testament
Scriptures by a word answering to our very word
Bible.[3]   Can we trace, without coming down below
the Christian era to listen to late and untrustworthy
Jewish traditions, how this Bible came together?

We can.   In the second Book of the Maccabees,
dating probably from much the same time as our
Greek Ecclesiasticus, the writer, telling the Egyptian
Jews of the purification of the Temple at Jerusalem

---

[1] Luke xxiv. 44.   τὰ γεγραμμένα ἐν τῷ νόμῳ Μωυσέως καὶ
τοῖς προφήταις καὶ ψαλμοῖς.

[2] ὁ νόμος, καὶ αἱ προφητεῖαι, καὶ τὰ λοιπὰ τῶν βιβλίων.   Prologue to *Ecclesiasticus*, in the Septuagint.

[3] Daniel ix. 2.

after the Maccabean victories, and of the revival of
Jewish religion, says that Nehemiah, — who with
Ezra had accomplished the famous restoration of
Jewish religion three centuries before,—that Nehemiah, as was related in his writings and commentaries,
*founding a library, brought together in addition the things
concerning the kings and the prophets, and David's things,
and letters of kings about offerings.*[1] Offerings to the
Temple are here meant, such as those of King Seleucus
which the Maccabean historian mentions in his next
chapter.[2] At the rebuilding of the Temple, gifts of
this kind from friendly foreign kings had a peculiar
importance. The letters concerning them could not,
however, merit a permanent place in the Bible, and
they dropped out of it. But the other writings which
Nehemiah is said to have "brought together in addition" to the stock of already recognised Scriptures,
that is, to the Law, answer to that second instalment
of Scriptures, which did really, from Nehemiah's time
onwards, obtain authority at Jerusalem. They com-
prise the Books of Judges, Samuel, and Kings, for
the "things concerning the kings;" the Books of
Isaiah, Jeremiah, Ezekiel, and the twelve Minor Prophets, for the "prophets;" and the collection of the
Psalms,—called in general after the famous name of
the royal Psalmist David,—for "David's things."

But the Maccabean historian then proceeds :—" In
like manner also Judas (Maccabeus) brought together

---

[1] καταβαλλόμενος βιβλιοθήκην, ἐπισυνήγαγε τὰ περὶ τῶν βασιλέων καὶ προφητῶν, καὶ τὰ τοῦ Δαυίδ, καὶ ἐπιστόλας βασιλέων περὶ
ἀναθημάτων.—2 *Maccabees* ii. 13.

[2] 2 *Maccabees* iii. 3.

in addition all the things that were lost by reason of the war we had, and they remain with us."[1] Now, this further addition to the stock of recognised Scriptures corresponds to the third instalment of Scriptures,—some of them of then recent date, like the Book of Daniel, others much older, like the Book of Job,—which was received and authorised at Jerusalem. It comprehended exactly the same books, and no more, that our Bibles add to the books said to have been "brought together" by Nehemiah, and to the Pentateuch and the Book of Joshua. But the order of the later books in the Hebrew Bible was by no means the same as it is in ours, and to this we shall return presently.

The Law itself, the Thora, the first of the three great divisions of the Hebrew Bible, whom shall we call as evidence for it? The founder of the second division, Nehemiah himself. He has told us how at Jerusalem, after the restoration, "the people gathered themselves together as one man into the street that was before the water-gate, and they spake unto Ezra the scribe to bring the book of the law of Moses; and Ezra the priest brought the law, and he read therein from the morning until mid-day, before the men and the women and those that could understand; also day by day, from the first day unto the last day, he read in the book of the law of God."[2] This book was Israel's history from its first beginning down to

---

[1] 2 *Maccabees* ii. 14. ὡσαύτως δὲ καὶ Ἰούδας τὰ διαπεπτωκότα διὰ τὸν πόλεμον τὸν γεγονότα ἡμῖν ἐπισυνήγαγε πάντα, καὶ ἔστιν παρ' ἡμῖν.   [2] Nehemiah viii. 1, 2, 3, 18.

the conquest of the Promised Land, as this history stands written in the Pentateuch and the Book of Joshua. To that collection many an old book had given up its treasures and then itself vanished for ever. Many voices were blended there; unknown voices, speaking out of the early dawn. In the strain there were many passages familiar as household words, yet the whole strain, in its continuity and connection, was to the mass of the people at that time new and affecting. "All the people wept when they heard the words of the law." [1] And the Levites, in stilling them, gave in one short sentence the secret of Israel's religion and of the religion of the Bible: "Mourn not, nor weep," they said; "*the joy of the Eternal is your strength.*" [2]

Now, this revival of religion in Jerusalem, under Ezra and Nehemiah, had had its counterpart in a former revival, two centuries earlier, under King Josiah. In Josiah's discovery of the book of the law, and his solemn publication of it to the people, we have the original consecration of a written historic record embodying the law; we have the nucleus of our existing Bible. In repairing the Temple, "Hilkiah the priest found a book of the law of the Lord by the hand of Moses. Then Hilkiah delivered the book to Shaphan; Shaphan the scribe told the king, saying: Hilkiah the priest hath given me a book. And Shaphan read it before the king. And it came to pass, when the king had heard the words of the law, that he rent his clothes. And the king went up

---

[1] Nehemiah viii. 9.　　[2] *Ib.* viii. 9, 10.

into the house of the Lord, and all the men of Judah, and the inhabitants of Jerusalem, and the priests and the Levites, and all the people great and small, and he read in their ears all the words of the book of the covenant that was found in the house of the Lord. And he caused all that were present in Jerusalem and Benjamin to stand to it." [1] Here we have, in all probability, Deuteronomy; as an edifying summary, from the point of view of the time then present, [2] of the chosen people's early history and of its covenant with God. Around Deuteronomy the rest of the Pentateuch and the story of Joshua's conquest gathered. Many old books of the Hebrew nation contributed, as we have said, their contents to them. Of some of the books we have still the names; but when once their substance had been secured for ever in the Thora, their function was at an end, and they perished. Among the devout Jews of the Captivity, severed from the Holy Land and the Temple services, this first instalment of the Bible, this "volume of the book" of which a Psalmist of the exile speaks, [3] became firmly established. It came back with them at the return, a consecrated authority; and from this book it was that Ezra read to the people.

[1] 2 Chronicles xxxiv. 14, 15, 18, 19, 30, 32.   See also 2 Kings xxii. xxiii.

[2] Chapters xxxi. and xxxii. of Deuteronomy, if we read them with attention, tell us the book's date. They belong to the revival under Josiah in the seventh century, nearly a hundred years after the ruin and captivity of the house of Israel, and with "the line of Samaria and the plummet of the house of Ahab" threatening also Jerusalem and the house of Judah.

[3] Psalm xl. 7.

Do we inquire for the original nucleus of the Thora itself, for the Law as in its earliest written form it existed, in the primitive times when writing was scarce and difficult, and documents were short, and readers were few? This also we can find. It was the "Book of the Law," consisting probably of the Decalogue, and of some other portions besides the Decalogue of what we now find in Exodus, "put in the side of the ark of the covenant of the Lord." [1] The "testimony" thus laid up before the Lord and guarded by the priests and Levites, was given to the kings at their accession and solemnly accepted by them. [2]

The arrangement of the Hebrew Bible corresponds with this its history and confirms it. Only we must add, that from each of the two earlier collections the last book was taken, and was employed to serve as an introducer to the collection which followed. Thus the Pentateuch, or five books of Moses, stood alone as the "Thora." This first great instalment of the Bible Samaria, as is well known, received from Jerusalem, but would receive nothing more. The Book of Joshua stood at the head of the second instalment of the Bible,—the eight books of Prophets, "Nebiim," as they were called. For, indeed, prophecy and the prophet were the force and glory of Israel's religion ; and the Books of Joshua, Judges, Samuel, and Kings, which we call historical, were at Jerusalem prized chiefly as the records of many a word and deed

[1] Deuteronomy xxxi. 26.
[2] 2 Kings xi. 12 ; Deut. xvii. 18.

of prophets anterior to the age of literary prophetic
compositions, and went by the name of *Earlier
Prophets*. Isaiah, Jeremiah, Ezekiel, and the Book
of the Minor Prophets, were called the four *Later
Prophets*.

The third division of the Bible had the name of
" Ketubim," translated by Jerome *Hagiographa*, but
simply meaning *Writings*, *Scriptures*. These are the
" remaining writings " mentioned by the translator of
Ecclesiasticus. They were nine in number, and the
twenty-two books of the now completed Canon thus
answered to the twenty-two letters of the Hebrew
alphabet. At their head was placed the last book
of the second formation of authorised Scriptures,—
" the things of David," the Psalms. This admirable
book with its double merits,—merit prophetic and
religious, and merit poetic and literary,—might well
serve to usher in and commend a series of mixed
character. Early works of the highest poetical value,
not hitherto included in the Canon, such as the Book
of Job, this series adopted and saved ; early works,
also, of the highest ethical value, such as the Book of
Proverbs. It adopted contemporary works, like the
Book of Daniel ;—works which reflected and powerfully engaged, as we can see by the prominence of the
Book of Daniel at the Christian era, the feelings of
the time. It adopted works, like the Book of Ezra,
which glorified Jerusalem, and deeply interested the
Temple-hierarchy whose sanction made the books
canonical. But in gravity and indispensableness for
the proper religion of the Old Testament, this late

instalment of "the remaining writings," cannot certainly, after we leave the Psalms, in general quite
rank with the two earlier instalments of Law and
Prophets. Simply to recite the last names in the
Hebrew Canon is to mark sufficiently this somewhat
inferior character of the final gleanings. The last
books in the Hebrew Bible are not, as in ours, the
Minor Prophets; they are Esther, Daniel, Ezra,
Nehemiah, and Chronicles.

During the two centuries between Judas Maccabeus and the fall of Jerusalem, materials for a
fourth instalment of Scriptures accumulated. In
the deep spiritual agitation of those times, religious
books which met the needs of the moment, and which
spoke a modern language easy to be read and to be
understood, were greatly in request. Particularly
was this the case among the Greek Jews, and at a
distance from Jerusalem. The hierarchy at Jerusalem
had its authorised list; but at Alexandria or in the
provinces additional Scriptures were freely read and
became popular. The additions to Daniel and Esther,
the Book of Baruch, the Book of Tobit, Wisdom,
Ecclesiasticus,—almost all the books which we find
in our Apocrypha,—were Scriptures of this class.
Into the Greek Bible, the Bible for the great world
and in the then universal language, they made good
their entrance. Other new Scriptures, which did not
make their way into the Greek Bible, we find elsewhere. The Æthiopian Bible preserved the Book of
Enoch. Some of these books were earlier than books
admitted to the Hebrew Canon. Some, like the

Book of Wisdom were very late, and existed in Greek only. But they answered to the wants of their time, and spoke its language. *Resurrection,* the great word of the New Testament, never appears in the canonical books of the Old; it appears in the Apocrypha. Many of these works were edifying and excellent. We can trace in the New Testament their popularity and their strong influence; indeed, the Book of Enoch is quoted in the New Testament as a genuine Scripture.[1] At the Christian era, then, these books were knocking, we may say, for admission into the Hebrew Canon. And, undoubtedly, if Christianity had not come when it did, and if the Jewish state had endured, the best of them would have been (and with good reason) admitted. But there came the end of the Jewish state, the destruction of Jerusalem; and the door was shut.

For the stronghold on Mount Moriah was now gone: the Bible of the ancient people remained the one stronghold of its religion. It is well known with what rigidity Rabbinism established itself in this stronghold. At first it even bethought itself of sacrificing what might seem weak points, like the Book of Ecclesiastes and the Song of Solomon. They were retained, however, and the worship of the letter of Scripture, which then set in with full force, was extended to them also. But it extended not to Scriptures outside the Hebrew Canon, as this Canon had been for the last time formally approved in the days of Judas Maccabeus. The enlarged Greek Bible was

---

[1] Epistle of Jude, verse 14.

the Bible of Christians, and Greek was the language of Christianity. Rabbinism now deplored the day when the Bible had been translated into Greek. It retranslated it into Greek in an anti-Christian sense; it sternly rejected the Greek additions; it mocked at the ignorant Christians who received them. But the Greek Bible, with all its books, had become dear to Christians, and were by the Christian Church preserved. Learned men, like Origen and St. Jerome, knew well the difference between the books of the Apocrypha and the books of the Hebrew Canon. But this difference was by the mass of Christians unregarded or unknown, and the Latin Bible inevitably reproduced the books of the Greek. The African Synods, at the end of the fourth century, mark the time when the distinction between the Apocrypha and the Hebrew Canon had become so generally obliterated in the West, that the books of both were stamped by the Church as having one and the same canonical authority.

At the Reformation, Protestantism reverted to the Hebrew Canon. But the influence of the Latin Vulgate, and of the Greek Bible, still shows itself in the order of the books. The Greek, and the Vulgate following it, had adopted, in place of the old and significant tripartite division into Law, Prophets, and Writings, a division into prose books and poetical books, the prophets being counted with the latter; and in arranging the books of each class, the order of date was followed.[1] This innovation our Bibles

---

[1] The *Maccabees* only, though a prose book of history, is in the Vulgate printed by itself at the end of the poetical books.

retain; and therefore our Old Testament ends with the last of the poetical books, Malachi, instead of ending with the last of the *Ketubim,* Chronicles.

IV.

Thus we have summarised, for the benefit of the reader of *Literature and Dogma,* the history of the Canon of that Old Testament to which we are so often sending him. The points in the history of the Canon of the New Testament require to be treated with more of detail, for our positions have here to be made good against objectors.

We know how the Scriptures of the Old Testament are appealed to in the New. They are appealed to as an authority established and recognised, just as the Bible is now appealed to by us. But when did the New Testament, in that form in which we possess it, come to be recognised as *Scripture* like the Old Testament? Clearly the documents composing it appeared at different times, and were not first published to the world as one authorised whole called the New Testament. Clearly there was a time when they had not acquired the authority they possessed afterwards; when people preferred, for instance, to any written narrative, the oral relations of eye-witnesses. One of the earliest and most important witnesses to the written narratives, Papias, is a distinct witness, at the same time, to this preference for oral relations. "I did not consider," he says, speaking in the first half of the second century after Christ,

about the year 140,—" I did not consider things from
books to be of so much good to me, as things from
the living and abiding voice." [1] And he goes on to
mention his communications with those who had
actually heard " the disciples of the. Lord." For
Papias, then, there was not yet a body of Scriptures
fully answering to our New Testament, and having
like authority with the Old ; if there had been, he
would hardly have spoken in this fashion. And no
man can point to any exact moment and manner in
which our body of New Testament Scriptures received
its authority. But we can point to a moment after
which we find our present New Testament Canon in
possession of undisputed authority in the Church of
the West, and before which we do not.

We have mentioned the African Synods. The
two Synods of Carthage,—the first of them held
in the year 397 of our era, the second in the
year 419,—deliver the Canon of the New Testament as we have it now. [2] All its books, and no
others, are *canonical ;* that is, they furnish the rule
of faith, they form a class by themselves, they are
authorised for public use. And so, as every one

---

[1] See Papias in Eusebii *Historia Ecclesiastica*, iii. 39. οὐ
γὰρ τὰ ἐκ τῶν βιβλίων τοσοῦτόν με ὠφελεῖν ὑπελάμβανον, ὅσον τὰ
παρὰ ζώσης φωνῆς καὶ μενούσης. The latter words are commonly
taken to mean merely the voice of living speakers, but they
almost certainly contain a reminiscence of 1 Peter i. 23, and of
Isaiah xl. 8, and mean speakers who had heard the voice of Jesus.

[2] The earlier Synod mentions the Epistle to the Hebrews
apart, though as Paul's ; the second Synod drops this distinction,
and speaks of Paul's " Fourteen Epistles." The New Testament
Canon of the two Synods is in other respects the same.

knows, they have continued. For the Eastern Church, a similar authoritative enunciation of our Canon of the New Testament is first found in the Festal Letter of St. Athanasius, of which the date is probably A.D. 365. But an absence of fixed consent as to certain books goes on showing itself amongst Greek Christians for long afterwards. Our present business, however, is with our own Western Christianity.

St. Jerome died in 420, the year after the second Synod of Carthage. His Biblical labours and learning are celebrated; he knew more about the Bible than any of his contemporaries. Cavillers he had, as have all men who bring new criticism to disturb old habits; but his orthodoxy was undoubted. His Biblical publications were undertaken at a Pope's request; and the first instalment of them, a corrected Latin version of the Four Gospels, appeared in the year 383 with a prefatory letter addressed to the Pope himself. This great churchman has left us his remarks on several of the works which the African Synods were presently to include in the Canon of the New Testament, and which have stood there ever since, possessing in the eyes of Christendom a like sacredness and authority with the rest of the Canon. In reading him, we are to bear in mind the character of the speaker. It is as if Dr. Pusey, with the reputation for learning and orthodoxy which we know him to have, and commissioned, besides, by the heads of the Anglican Church to revise the Bible, was speaking of the Canon. St. Jerome, then, says of the Epistle to the Hebrews: —" The custom of the Latin Christians does not re-

ceive it among the Canonical Scriptures." [1] Of the
Apocalypse he says :—" The Greek Churches use the
same freedom in regard to John's Apocalypse." [2] Of
the so-called Second Epistle of Peter he says :—" It
is denied by most to be his." [3] Of the Epistle of
James he says :—" It is asserted to have been brought
out by somebody else under his name." [4] Of the
Epistle of Jude he says :—" Inasmuch as the author
appeals to the Book of Enoch, which is apocryphal,
the Epistle is rejected by most." [5] Of the three
Epistles attributed to St. John, Jerome says :—" He
wrote one Epistle which is acknowledged by all
churches and scholars, but the remaining two are
asserted to be by John the Elder." [6]

Now, all Jerome's sympathies were with what was
orthodox, ecclesiastical, regular. The works on which
he has here been remarking seemed to him good and
edifying; they had been much used, and had inspired
attachment. The tendency in the Church was to
admit them to canonicity, as the African Synods presently did. Jerome wished them to be admitted.
He helped forward their admission by arguments in
its favour, some of them not a little strained. But

---

[1] " Latinorum consuetudo non recipit inter scripturas
canonicas."

[2] " Nec Græcorum quidem ecclesiæ Apocalypsin Joannis
eadem libertate suscipiunt."

[3] " Secunda a plerisque ejus esse negatur."

[4] " Ab alio quodam sub nomine ejus edita asseritur."

[5] " Quia de libro Enoch, qui apocryphus est, in ea assumit
testimonium, a plerisque rejicitur."

[6] " Reliquæ autem duæ Joannis presbyteri asseruntur."

what we want the reader to observe is the entire
upset which Jerome gives to our popular notion of
the Canon of the New Testament; to the notion of a
number of sacred books, just so many and no more,
all alike of the most indisputable authenticity, and
having equal authority from the very first. It is
true, they were about to get invested with this character, but through the authority of the Church, and
because,—while this authority was on the increase,—
learning and criticism, amidst the invasions and
miseries of the general break-up which was then be-
falling Europe, languished and died nearly out.
Already the African Synods, which may be said to
have first laid down authoritatively for our Western
Europe the Canon of the New Testament, imagined
that Wisdom and Ecclesiasticus were by Solomon,
although Wisdom was composed in Greek hardly half
a century before the Christian era. St. Augustine,
who died ten years after St. Jerome, was far too
accomplished a man not to know, although his studies
had not lain in this special direction, how, in general,
the Canon of the New Testament had arisen, and
how great was the difference between the evidence
for some books and for others. But the authority of
the Church was enough for him. In a sentence,
which for Paul would have been inconceivable, he
shows us how the idea of this authority had by his
time grown :—"*I receive the Gospel itself,*" he says,
"*only upon the authority of the Catholic Church.*"[1] The

---

[1] "Ego evangelio non crederem, nisi me catholicæ ecclesiæ
auctoritas commoveret."

Reformation arrived, and to Protestants the authority of the Church ceased to appear all-sufficient for establishing the canonicity of books of Scripture. Then grew up the notion that our actual New Testament intrinsically possessed this character of a Canon, the notion of its having from the first been one sure and sacred whole as it stands, a whole with all its parts equipollent; a kind of talisman, as we have elsewhere said, that had been handed to us straight out of heaven.

Therefore the other day, when there was published for the use of the young a Bible in which some parts of the Scriptures were taken and others left out, the Dean of Carlisle wrote an indignant letter in blame of this audacious attempt, as he thought it, to make distinctions in what was all alike the Word of God. To very many his blame will have seemed perfectly just. Nay, all that mechanical employment of Scripture texts which is so common in the religious world, and so unhesitating, is due to just such a notion of Scripture as the venerable Dean's. Yet how evidently is the notion false! Four hundred years after Christ we have the last representative of Biblical learning before the setting-in of mediæval ignorance,—we have the Dr. Pusey of his time, a great churchman, orthodox, learned, trusted,—declaring, without the least concealment, the essential difference in authority between some documents in our New Testament and others! For manifestly the difference in authority is great between a document like the so-called Second Epistle of Peter, *rejected by most*, and a document like the Epistle to the Romans, which every churchman accepted.

And the more we ascend to the times before
St. Jerome,—to the primitive times, as they are
called,—the more does this difference between the
documents now composing the Canon become visible.
Churchmen like Eusebius and Origen testify as clearly
as Jerome to the non-acceptance, in their time, of
books now in the Canon, and do not, as Jerome,
plead for their acceptance. So that really, when one
comes to look into the thing, the common notion
about the Canon is so plainly false, that to take it
for granted, as the Dean of Carlisle does, and to
found indignant denunciations upon it, will one day
be resented as an outrage upon common sense and
notorious facts. It is like the Bishop of Lincoln's
allegation that "episcopacy was an institution of God
Himself;" an allegation which might make one suppose that in Genesis, directly after God had said *Let
there be light* (or, perhaps, even before it), he had pronounced, *Let there be bishops.* There are plenty of
true reasons for the existence of bishops without
invoking false ones; and the time will come when
thus to invoke the false ones solemnly and authoritatively will shock public opinion.

As to the Canon of the New Testament, then, we
see that consent determined it; that after the beginning of the fifth century this consent may be regarded
as established in favour of the books of our actual
Canon; that before the fifth century it was not yet
fully established, and the most eminent doctors in
the Church did not hesitate to say so. Consent depended on the known or presumed authenticity of

books as proceeding from apostles or apostolic men, from the Apostles of Christ themselves or from their personal followers. Some books of our Canon had not this consent, even in Jerome's time : and of its not being certain in primitive times that these books are what they are now commonly said to be, we have thus the clearest evidence. If the Christian Church of the fourth century had believed it to be absolutely certain that the Johannine Apocalypse was by the Apostle John, or the second Petrine Epistle by the Apostle Peter, no churchman would have rejected them. Some books, then, in our New Testament Canon there plainly are of which the authenticity is doubtful.

We have given cases in which the want of consent is grave. It is grave when we find it in churchmen ; it has its weight even when it is found in heretics. Marcion rejected St. Paul's Epistles to Timothy and Titus, while he admitted the others. It is something against the genuineness of the Pastoral Epistles that a fervent admirer of St. Paul, in the first half of the second century, should not have received them. It is possible that Marcion may have rejected these epistles because they did not suit him. It is possible; but we know that he and his party complained of the adulteration of the rule of Christianity, and professed to revert to what was genuine ; it may be, therefore, that Marcion rejected the Pastoral Epistles because they really were not genuine. Or he may have not used the Pastoral Epistles because they were in his time not yet written. It is a case in which the in-

ternal evidence for or against the authenticity of the
documents in question becomes of peculiar importance. The Alogi, again, heretics of the second century, rejected the Fourth Gospel. The authenticity
of this Gospel, therefore, cannot be said to have such
a security in general consent as the authenticity of
the First Gospel, which not even heretics challenged.

Now to be indignant with those who, under such
circumstances, will not take for granted the authenticity of books in the New Testament Canon, is really
unreasonable. We have for the books in the Canon,
it is sometimes said, as good evidence as we have for
the history of Thucydides; why not require the history of Thucydides to prove its authenticity? This
will not bear a moment's examination. The history
of Thucydides tells us itself, in the most explicit way
possible, the name of its author, and what he was,
and what he designed in writing his work. Its
authenticity no one has challenged. To forge it
under the name of Thucydides no one had any interest. But not one of our Four Gospels says anywhere who its author was. Heretics challenged the
authenticity of the Fourth Gospel, and we have seen
how documents now in the Canon, which purport to
be by this or that Apostle, were gravely suspected in
the Church itself. St. Paul himself, in the Second
Epistle to the Thessalonians, warns his converts not
to let themselves be "troubled *by letter as from us,*"
thus indicating that forgery of this kind was practised
as to epistles. As to gospels and acts it was practised
too. Tertullian mentions a detected case of it,—

forged Acts of Paul, authorising a woman to baptize.
The practice of forgery and interpolation was notorious, and the temptation to it was great.   One
explicit witness is as good as twenty, and we will
again take for our witness a great churchman, the
ecclesiastical historian Eusebius, Bishop of Cæsarea,
who died in the year 340.   He says that scriptures
were current "put forth by the heretics in the name
of the Apostles, whether as containing the Gospels of
Peter and Thomas and Matthias, or those also of any
others besides these, or as containing the Acts of
Andrew and John and the other Apostles." [1]

The Gospels give us the sayings and doings of
Jesus himself, and are therefore of the highest
importance.   How far back can we certainly carry
the chain of established consent in favour of our four
canonical Gospels ?   Let us begin with St. Jerome,
whom we have already quoted, and from him let us
go backwards.   For St. Jerome our canonical four
are already established :—"Four Gospels whereof the
order is this : Matthew, Mark, Luke, John." [2]   That
was at the end of the fourth century.   In the earlier
part of the same century, for Eusebius likewise, whom
we have just now cited to show the existence of
spurious gospels, the canonicity of our four was

---

[1] Eusebius, *Hist. Eccles.* iii. 25, γραφὰς . . . ὀνόματι τῶν
ἀποστόλων πρὸς τῶν αἱρετικῶν προφερομένας, ἤτοι ὡς Πέτρου καὶ
Θωμᾶ καὶ Ματθία ἢ καί τινων παρὰ τούτους ἄλλων εὐαγγέλια
περιεχούσας, ἢ ὡς Ἀνδρέου Ἰωάννου καὶ τῶν ἄλλων ἀποστόλων
πράξεις.

[2] *Præfat. ad Damasum.*   "Quatuor Evangelia quorum ordo
est iste : Matthæus, Marcus, Lucas, Johannes."

established. Let us follow back the chain of great
churchmen to the third century and to Origen. He
died A.D. 254. For him, too, our four canonical
Gospels are "alone undisputed in the Church of God
upon earth." [1] Let us ascend to the second century.
Irenæus wrote in the last quarter of it, and no testimony to the Four Gospels of our Canon can be more
explicit than his. "Matthew it was who, among the
Hebrews, brought out in their own language a written
Gospel, when Peter and Paul were preaching in Rome,
and founding the Church. Then, after their depar-
ture, Mark, the disciple and interpreter of Peter, he
too delivered to us in writing what Peter preached;
and Luke, moreover, the follower of Paul, set down
in a book the Gospel preached by Paul. Then John,
the disciple of the Lord, who also lay on his breast,
John too published his Gospel, living at that time at
Ephesus, in Asia." [2] And for Irenæus this number of
four, which the Gospels exhibit, has something fixed,
necessary, and sacred, "like the four zones of our
world, and the four winds."

---

[1] Quoted by Eusebius, *Hist. Eccles.* vi. 25, τῶν τεσσάρων
εὐαγγελίων, ἃ καὶ μόνα ἀναντίρρητά ἐστιν ἐν τῇ ὑπὸ τὸν οὐρανὸν
ἐκκλησίᾳ τοῦ θεοῦ.

[2] Quoted by Eusebius, *Hist. Eccles.* v. 8. ὁ μὲν δὴ Ματθαῖος
ἐν τοῖς Ἑβραίοις τῇ ἰδίᾳ αὐτῶν διαλέκτῳ καὶ γραφὴν ἐξήνεγκεν
εὐαγγελίου, τοῦ Πέτρου καὶ τοῦ Παύλου ἐν Ῥώμῃ εὐαγγελιζομένων
καὶ θεμελιούντων τὴν ἐκκλησίαν. μετὰ δὲ τὴν τούτων ἔξοδον,
Μάρκος ὁ μαθητὴς καὶ ἑρμηνευτὴς Πέτρου, καὶ αὐτὸς τὰ ὑπὸ Πέτρου
κηρυσσόμενα ἐγγράφως ἡμῖν παραδέδωκε, καὶ Λουκᾶς δὲ, ὁ ἀκόλουθος
Παύλου, τὸ ὑπ' ἐκείνου κηρυσσόμενον εὐαγγέλιον ἐν βίβλῳ κατέθετο.
ἔπειτα Ἰωάννης ὁ μαθητὴς τοῦ κυρίου, ὁ καὶ ἐπὶ τὸ στῆθος αὐτοῦ
ἀναπεσών, καὶ αὐτὸς ἐξέδωκε τὸ εὐαγγέλιον, ἐν Ἐφέσῳ τῆς Ἀσίας
διατρίβων.

Here then, about the year 180 of our era, we have from a great churchman the most express testimony to the Four Gospels of our Canon. Higher than this we cannot find a great churchman who gives it us. Ignatius does not give it, nor Polycarp, nor Justin Martyr. But a famous fragment, discovered by Muratori, the Italian antiquary, in the monastery of Bobbio in North Italy, and published by him in the year 1740, carries us, perhaps, to an age a little higher than that of Irenæus. The manuscript containing this fragment is said to be of the eighth century, and is in barbarous Latin. The monastery at Bobbio was founded by St. Columban, and it has been alleged that the barbarisms in our fragment are due to the Irish monks who copied it from the original. Others have assigned to these barbarisms an African source; others, again, have supposed that the fragment is a translation of a Greek original, Greek having been the language of the Roman Church at the time when the author of the fragment lived. However this may be, the important matter is that the fragment,—called, from its finder and first publisher, the *Fragment of Muratori*, the *Canon of Muratori*,—gives us with tolerable nearness its own date. It says that the *Pastor* of Hermas, a work received as Scripture by many in the early Church, was written "*quite lately, in our own times*, while Pius, the brother of Hermas, was filling the episcopal chair in Rome." Pius died in the year 157 of our era. If we believe what the author of the fragment here tells us, we have only to ask ourselves, therefore, what "quite lately, in our own times"

means.   And the words can hardly, one must allow,
mean a time more than thirty years back from the
time of the person uttering them.   This would give
us the year 187 as the latest date possible for the
original of the fragment in question ; and as there is
no reason why we should put it at the latest date
possible, it seems fair to assign it to a time some ten
or twelve years, perhaps, before A.D. 187 ; that is, to
a date rather earlier than the date of the testimony
of Irenæus.

But the author of *Supernatural Religion* will not
allow the Canon of Muratori to be authentic, any
more than he will allow to be authentic two fragments of Claudius Apollinaris, Bishop of Hierapolis,
quoted in the Pascal Chronicle, which show that
Apollinaris, about the year 170 of our era, knew and
received the Fourth Gospel.   The author of *Supernatural Religion* has a theory that the Fourth Gospel,
and, indeed, all the canonical Gospels, were not recognised till a particular time.   This theory the
Canon of Muratori and the fragments of Apollinaris
do not suit ; so he rejects them.   There is really no
more serious reason to be given for his rejection of
them.   True, Eusebius gives a list of some works of
Apollinaris ; and the work on the Paschal controversy, from which the two fragments are taken, is
not among them.   But Eusebius expressly says that
there were other works of Apollinaris of which he
did not know the titles.   True, Greek was the language of the Roman Church in the second century ;
but must we think a document forged sooner than

admit that a single Roman Christian may have chanced to write in Latin, or that a document written in Greek may have got translated? No; the one real reason which the author of *Supernatural Religion* has for rejecting these three pieces of evidence is, that they do not suit his theory. And this leads us to say a word as to the difference between the practice which we impose on ourselves in dealing with evidence, and the practice followed by critics with a theory.

For we suppose the reader of *Literature and Dogma*, for a while suspicious of the Bible, but now convinced that (to use Butler's famous phrase with a slight alteration) *there is something in it*, nay, that there is a great deal in it,—we suppose him to find that there is a hot controversy about the age and authenticity of many of the chief documents of the New Testament, and to wish to know what to think about them. Soon he will perceive that the controversy is in general conducted by people who, in the first place, think that for every question which can be started the answer can be discovered, and who, in the second place, have a theory which all things must be made to suit. Evidence is dealt with in a fashion that no one would ever dream of who had not a theory to warp him. In the so-called Epistle of Barnabas, a work of the end of the first century, the words *many called, but few chosen*, are quoted with the formula *as it is written*,[1] implying that they are taken from Scripture. The Greek words are the very same that we

---

[1] ὡς γέγραπται.

find in St. Matthew, and no one without a theory to
warp him would doubt that the writer of the epistle
quotes, not, indeed, necessarily from our Gospel of
St. Matthew, but from a collection of sayings of
Jesus.   Dr. Volkmar, however, maintains that what
is here quoted as Scripture must be a passage of the
Apocrypha : *There be many created, but few shall be
saved.*[1]   Strauss applauds him, and says that "beyond
all doubt " this is so.   And why ?   Because, to cite a
third well-known critic, Dr. Zeller, " if in a work of
earlier date than the middle of the second century we
find a passage quoted as *Scripture*, we may be sure
that either the quotation is not from the New Testament, or else the work is not genuine ; because *Scripture* is not used for the New Testament till long after
the middle of the second century."   That is to say,
because the New Testament is not *generally* called
Scripture till after the middle of the second century,
that it should *occasionally* have been called so before
is impossible.   But the New Testament did not begin
in one day to be called Scripture by an Order in
Council.   There must have been a time when to have
it called so was comparatively rare ; a time, earlier
still, when it was exceedingly rare.   But at no time,
after the written sayings of Jesus were first published,
can it have been *impossible* for a Christian to call them
Scripture.

The innovating critics are certainly the most conspicuous offenders in this way, but the conservative
critics are not to be trusted either.   Neander rejects,

[1] 2 *Esdras* viii. 3.

like the author of *Supernatural Religion*, a fragment of
Apollinaris, and rejects it for the very same reason:
that it fails (though from a different cause) to suit
him. Bunsen (unaware that by the Epistle to the
Alexandrians, named in the Canon of Muratori and
stigmatised as apocryphal, the Epistle to the Hebrews
is probably meant) lays it down that " it is quite impossible this Epistle could have been omitted," and
supposes that " there is, in the middle of this barbarous translation or extract of the Greek original, a
chasm, or omission, respecting the Epistle to the
Hebrews." What may we not put in or leave out
when we take licence to proceed in this fashion ?

Sick of special pleading both on one side and on
the other, the reader of *Literature and Dogma*, after a
brief experience of the impugners of the Canon and
of its defenders, will probably feel that what he
earnestly desires, and what no one will indulge him
in, is simply to be permitted to have the fair facts of
the case, and to let them speak for themselves. Here
it is that we sympathise with him and wish to aid
him, because we had just the same earnest desire ourselves after a like experience. And we treat the
evidence about the Canon with a mind resolutely free
and straightforward, determined to reject nothing
because it does not suit us, and to proceed as we
should proceed in a literary inquiry where we were
wholly disinterested. In the first place, we confess
to ourselves that a great many questions may be
asked about the New Testament Canon to which it is
impossible to give an answer. In the second place,

we own that it is *something* in favour of a fact that it
has been asserted, and that tradition delivers it.
Men do not, we acknowledge, in general use language for the purpose of falsehood, but to communi-
cate a matter faithfully.   Of course, many things
may be said which we yet must decline to receive,
but we require substantial reasons for declining, and
not fantastic ones.   The second Petrine Epistle calls
itself St. Peter's.   But we find the strongest internal
evidence against its being his; we know that epistles
were forged, and we find that its being his was in the
early Church strongly disputed.   On the other hand,
a writer at the end of the first century quotes words
of Jesus as Scripture, and a writer towards the year
175 gives a list of works then received in the Catholic
Church as apostolical.   We see no strong natural
improbability in their having done so; there is no
external evidence against it, no suspicious circumstance.   And the criticism which, because it finds
what they say inconvenient, pronounces their words
spurious, interpolated, or with a drift quite other than
their plain apparent drift, we call fantastic.

So we receive the witness of the Fragment of
Muratori to the canonicity, about the year 175, of
our four canonical Gospels, and of those Gospels
only.[1]   We receive the witness of Claudius Apollinaris, a year or two earlier, to the same effect.   He

---

[1] The Fragment begins with a broken sentence relating to the
Second Gospel, and continues: *Tertio, evangelii librum secundum
Lucam.*   It gives St. John's Gospel as the fourth, and there can
be no room for doubt that it named Mark and Matthew before
coming to Luke.

denies that St. Matthew assigns the Last Supper and the Crucifixion to the days which the Judaising Christians supposed, and to which St. Matthew, it seems certain, does assign them ; but to make him do so, says Apollinaris, is to make "the Gospels be at variance." Whatever we may think of his criticism, let us own that most probably the Bishop of Hierapolis has here in his eye the three Synoptics and St. John.

But he is really our last witness. Ascending to the times before him, we find mention of *the gospel*, of *gospels*, of *memorabilia* [1] and *written accounts* [2] of Jesus by his Apostles and their followers. We find incidents given from the life of Jesus, sayings of Jesus quoted. But we look in vain in Justin Martyr, or Polycarp, or Ignatius, or Clement of Rome, either for an express recognition of the four canonical Gospels, such as we have given from Churchmen who lived later, or for a distinct mention of any one of them. No doubt, the mention of an Evangelist's name is unimportant, if his narrative is evidently quoted, and if we recognise, without hesitation, his form of expression. Eusebius quotes words about John baptizing in Ænon, near to Salim, and continues his quotation : "For John was not yet cast into prison." Whether Eusebius expressly mentioned the Fourth Gospel or not, we might be sure that here he was quoting from it. But the case is different with "sayings of the Lord." These may be quoted either from oral tradition or from some

---

[1] ἀπομνημονεύματα ἅ φημι ὑπὸ τῶν ἀποστόλων αὐτοῦ καὶ τῶν ἐκείνοις παρακολουθησάντων συντετάχθαι.   [2] συγγράμματα.

written source other than our canonical Gospels.
We have seen from Papias how strong was at first
the preference for oral tradition ; and we know that
of written sources of information there were others
besides our canonical Gospels.   Learned Churchmen
like Origen and Jerome still knew them well ; they
mention them, quote from them.   The Gospel of the
Hebrews or according to the Hebrews, the Gospel
according to the Ægyptians, the Gospel according to
the Twelve Apostles, are thus mentioned.   Again,
there were the writings of which we quoted some
way back a list from Eusebius.

The Gospel of the Hebrews was of great antiquity
and currency ; it was held to be the original of our
St. Matthew, and often confounded with it.   The
Ebionites are said indifferently to receive no Gospel
but that of the *Hebrews*, and to receive no Gospel but
that of *Matthew*.   Jerome found in Syria, and translated, an Aramaic version of this old Gospel of the
Hebrews, which he was at first disposed to think
identical with our St. Matthew ; afterwards, however,
he seems to have observed differences.   From this
Gospel are quoted incidents and sayings which we do
not find in the canonical Gospels, such as the light on
Jordan at Christ's baptism, already mentioned by us
in our first chapter ; the appearance of the Lord after
his resurrection to James, expressly recorded by Paul,
but not in our Gospels ; the words of Jesus to his
startled disciples after the *Handle me and see* of our
Gospels : "For I am not a bodiless Ghost." [1]   We

---

[1] οὐκ εἰμὶ δαιμόνιον ἀσώματον.

know that this Gospel of the Hebrews was used by
the first generation of Christian writers after the
apostolic age, by Ignatius, Justin Martyr, and Hegesippus.   From it, or from other old gospels attributed
to Peter or James, come other sayings and stories
strange to our Gospels, but in the earliest times
current as authentic.   Such a story is that of the
birth of Jesus in a cave, mentioned by Justin, and
familiar to Christian art; and such a saying is the
saying of Christ, *Be ye approved bankers*,[1] quoted in the
pseudo-Clementine Homilies and the Apostolic Con-
stitutions, quoted by the Church historians Eusebius
and Socrates, and by Clement of Alexandria, Origen,
Ambrose, and Jerome.

Well, then, how impossible, when the Epistle of
Barnabus simply applies the verse of the 110th
Psalm, *The Lord said unto my Lord*, as Jesus applied it,
or when it quotes simply as "Scripture" the words
Many called, but few chosen,—how impossible to affirm
certainly that it refers to our canonical Gospels, and
proves that by the end of the first century our
Gospel-Canon was established !   Yet this is what
Tischendorf does all through his book on the Canon.
Wherever he finds words in an early writer of which
the substance is in our canonical Gospels, he assumes
that from our canonical Gospels the writer took
them, and that our Canon must already have existed.
We will not speak of Tischendorf without remember-
ing the gratitude and respect which, by many of his

---

[1] γίνεσθε τραπεζῖται δόκιμοι, or γίνεσθε δόκιμοι τραπεζῖται.   In
Jerome's Latin : "Estote probati nummularii."

labours, he has merited. But his treatment of the
question proposed by him, *When were our Gospels composed?* is really, to any one who reads attentively and
with a fair mind, absurd. It is as absurd on the
apologetic side, as Dr. Volkmar's treatment of the
quotation in the Epistle of Barnabas, *Many called, but
few chosen,* is on the attacking side. Tischendorf
assumes that the Epistle of Barnabas, in applying the
110th Psalm and in quoting *Many called, but few
chosen,* must needs be referring to our canonical
Gospels. But the writer of the Epistle of Barnabas
gives no reference at all for his application of the
words of the 110th Psalm. For the words, *Many
called, but few chosen,* he refers simply to Scripture;
and he elsewhere calls, let us add, the apocryphal
Book of Enoch also *Scripture.* In applying the 110th
Psalm he may have been going upon oral tradition
merely. In quoting *Many called, but few chosen,* as
Scripture, he was certainly quoting some written
and accepted authority, but what we cannot possibly
say.

In the times with which we are now dealing there
is no quotation from any one of our Evangelists with
his name, such as in Irenæus and from his time
forward is usual. There is no quotation from the
narrative of any one of the Synoptics in which the
manner of relating or turn of phrase enables us to
recognise with certainty the author. Sayings and
doings of Jesus are quoted, but there is nothing to
prove that they are quoted from our Gospels. Moreover, almost always, however briefly they may be

quoted, they are not quoted quite as they stand in our Gospels. But it is supposed that they are quoted from memory, freely and loosely. The question then arises, is a *Canon* habitually and uniformly quoted in this way? If our Four Gospels had existed in the time of Clement of Rome or of Justin Martyr as the canonical four, of paramount authority and in the state in which we now have them, would these writers have uniformly quoted them in the loose fashion in which now, as is alleged, they do quote them?

Here we will give, for the benefit of the reader of *Literature and Dogma,*—who by this time is convinced, we hope, that we endeavour to let the facts about the Gospel-Canon fairly and simply speak for themselves,—we will give for his benefit a piece of experience which on ourselves had a decisive effect. The First Epistle attributed to Clement of Rome is, as every one knows, of high antiquity and authority. It probably dates from the end of the first century. Jerome tells us that it was publicly read in church as authorised Scripture. It is included in the Alexandrian manuscript of the New Testament, and one may say that it was within an inch of gaining, and not undeservedly, admission to our Canon. A good while ago, in reading this Epistle with the disputes about the Canon of the Gospels perplexing our mind, we came upon a quotation of the beginning of the fifty-first Psalm. We read on, and found that as much as the first sixteen verses, or nearly the whole Psalm, was quoted. The Bible of Clement of Rome was the Greek Bible, the version of the Seventy.

"Well then, here," said we to ourselves, " is a good
opportunity for verifying the mode of quoting the
canonical Scriptures which is followed by an early
Christian writer." So we took the Septuagint, and
went through the first sixteen verses of the fifty-
first Psalm. We found that Clement followed his
canonical original with an exactness which, after all
we had heard of the looseness with which these early
Christian writers quote Scripture, quite astonished
us. Five slight and unimportant variations were all
that we could find,—variations so slight as the omission
of an *and* in a place where it was not wanted. One
knows, from Origen and his labours of reformation,
into how unsure a state the text of the Greek Vulgate
had in the second century fallen ; so that this exactitude of Clement was the more surprising.

Now, shortly before we came upon the fifty-first
Psalm, we had remarked, in the thirteenth chapter
of Clement's Epistle, a cluster of sayings from the
Sermon on the Mount. We turned back with eager-
ness to them, and compared them with the like sayings in St. Matthew and in St. Luke.[1] Neither in
wording nor in order did the Epistle here correspond
with either of these Gospels; the difference was
marked, although in such short, notable sayings, there
seems so little room for it. We turned to a longer

---

[1] We give the passage from Clement, which the reader can
compare with the counterparts in Matthew and Luke for himself. ἐλεεῖτε ἵνα ἐλεηθῆτε· ἄφιετε ἵνα ἀφεθῇ ὑμῖν. ὡς ποιεῖτε,
οὕτω ποιηθήσεται ὑμῖν· ὡς δίδοτε, οὕτως δοθήσεται ὑμῖν· ὡς κρίνετε,
οὕτως κριθήσεται ὑμῖν. ὡς χρηστεύεσθε, οὕτως χρηστευθήσεται
ὑμῖν· ᾧ μέτρῳ μετρεῖτε, ἐν αὐτῷ μετρηθήσεται ὑμῖν.

cluster of quotations from the Sermon on the Mount
in Justin Martyr's first Apology. It was with Justin
Martyr precisely as with Clement; the wording and
order in what he quoted differed remarkably from
the wording and order of the corresponding sayings
in our Gospels. The famous sentence beginning,
Render to Cæsar, was quoted by Justin. Words so
famous might well have been expected to be current
in one form only, and their tallying in Justin with
our Gospels would not at all prove that Justin quoted
them from our Gospels. But even these words, as
he quotes them, run differently from the version in
our Gospels. So that these early writers could quote
canonical Scriptures correctly enough when they
were Scriptures of the Old Testament, but when they
were Scriptures of the New they quoted them in
quite another fashion.

We examined a number of other passages, and
found always the same result, except in one curious
particular. Certain prophetic passages of the Old
Testament were quoted, not as they stand in the
Septuagint, but exactly, or almost exactly, as they
stand in our Gospels; at least, the variations were
here as slight as those of Clement quoting from the
Greek the fifty-first Psalm. Thus Justin quotes the
passage from Micah, *And thou, Bethlehem*, etc., almost
exactly as it is given in St. Matthew, although in the
Septuagint it stands otherwise; and the passage from
Zechariah, *They shall look on him whom they pierced*, as
it is given in St. John, although in the Septuagint it
stands otherwise. But this one point of coincidence,

amid general variation, indicates only that passages
of prophecy where the Greek Bible did not well
bring out the reference to Christ, were early corrected
among Christians, so as to let the reference appear ;
and that the Messianic passages are given in this
corrected form both in our Gospels and in Justin.
For it is in these passages that a literal, or almost
literal, correspondence between them occurs, and in
no others.

This satisfied us, and we were henceforth convinced
that at the end of the first century, and nearly up to
the last quarter of the second century, there existed
beyond doubt a body of canonical Scripture for
Christian writers and that they quoted from it as
men would naturally quote from canonical Scriptures.
Often they quote it literally and unmistakably ; and
therefore their variations from it, though they are
sometimes greater, sometimes less, are yet no more
than what may be naturally explained as loose quoting,
quoting from memory. But this body of canonical
Scripture was the Old Testament. The variations
from our Gospels we found to be quite of another
character, and quite inexplicable in men quoting from
a Canon, only with some looseness occasionally. And
we felt sure, and so may the reader of *Literature and
Dogma* feel sure, that either no Canon of the Gospels,
in our present sense, then existed, or else our actual
Gospels did not compose that Canon.

However, the author of *Supernatural Religion*, who
has evidently a turn for inquiries of this kind, has
pursued the thing much further. He seems to have

looked out and brought together, to the best of his powers, every extant passage in which, between the year 70 and the year 170 of our era, a writer might be supposed to be quoting one of our Four Gospels. And it turns out that there is constantly the same sort of variation from our Gospels, a variation inexplicable in men quoting from a real Canon, and quite unlike what is found in men quoting from our Four Gospels later. It may be said that the Old Testament, too, is often quoted loosely. True ; but it is also quoted exactly ; and long passages of it are thus quoted. It would be nothing that our canonical Gospels were often quoted loosely, if long passages from them, or if passages, say, of even two or three verses, were sometimes quoted exactly. But from writers before Irenæus not one such passage of our canonical Gospels can be produced so quoted. And the author of *Supernatural Religion*, by bringing all the alleged quotations forward, has proved it.

This, we say, the author of *Supernatural Religion* has proved ; and here, at any rate, if not against miracles, he may claim to have been successful in establishing his complete induction. We call him a learned and exact writer from the diligence and accuracy with which he has conducted this investigation. He deserves the title, and we take the liberty to maintain it. His construing of Greek and Latin may leave something to be desired. His conception of the Bible and its religion seems to us quite inadequate. His rejection of evidence which does not suit his purpose makes him,—as it makes so many another

critic, besides him, both among those who attack
popular Christianity, and among those who defend it,
—an untrustworthy guide.   But this, which it is the
main object of his book to show : that there is no
evidencé of the establishment of our Four Gospels as
a Gospel-Canon, or even of their existence as they
now finally stand at all, before the last quarter of the
second century,—nay, that the great weight of evidence is against it,—he has shown, and in the most
minute and exhaustive detail.   We should say, with
unnecessary detail ; because a reader whose eyes and
mind were open would satisfy himself with much less.
But the mass of Englishmen enjoy pounding away at
details long after it ceases to be necessary.   What
they hate is having to face the new ideas which
await them when the detail-hunt is done with, and to
re-make and re-settle their minds.   Probably, for
producing an impression on the public, the style in
which the author of *Supernatural Religion* has done
his work is well chosen.   We attach too,—for reasons
which we shall give when we come to sum up the
case as to the New Testament Canon, after we have
dealt with the Fourth Gospel,—much less importance
to the point he seeks to prove, than he and perhaps
most people do.   But his point, we say, he has proved.
No fineness of accomplishment, no pursuit of the
author of *Supernatural Religion* into side-issues, no
discrediting of him in these, will avail to shake his
establishment of his main position, where the facts are
for him and he has collected them with pertinacious
industry and completeness.

The upshot of all this for the reader of *Literature and Dogma* is, that our original short sentence about the record of the life and words of Jesus holds good. *The record*, we said, *when we first get it, has passed through at least half a century, or more, of oral tradition, and through more than one written account.*

CHAPTER V.

THE FOURTH GOSPEL FROM WITHOUT.

SOMETIMES a youthful philosopher, provoked at our disrespect towards metaphysics, tells us that he has been reading Hegel, and would greatly like to have a word with us about *being*. Our impulse is to reply that he had much better have been reading Homer, and that about Homer we, at any rate, had much rather he should talk to us. That divine poet is always in season, always brings us something suited to our wants. And now, when we have finally, after making good our general description of the Gospel-records, to make good our special estimate of the Fourth Gospel, and when, approaching the closer consideration of this Gospel, we are confronted by the theorisings of ingenious professors about it and might well be overawed by their exceeding vigour and rigour, a saying of Homer comes to our mind and raises our courage, and emboldens us to scrutinise the vigorous and rigorous theorisings with coolness. Yet the saying is not at all a grand one. We are almost ashamed to quote it to readers who may have come fresh from the last number of the *North American*

Review, and from the great sentence there quoted as summing up Mr. Herbert Spencer's theory of evolution :—"Evolution is an integration of matter and concomitant dissipation of motion during which the matter passes from an indefinite incoherent homogeneity to a definite coherent heterogeneity, and during which the retained motion undergoes a parallel transformation." Homer's poor little saying comes not in such formidable shape. It is only this :—*Wide is the range of words ! words may make this way or that way.*[1]

But really, of nine-tenths of the theorising about the Gospels which comes to us from Germany, these few words of Homer give us just the right criticism. There stand the Gospel words. It is possible to put a certain construction upon them. Off starts the German professor whose theory this construction suits, and puts it. Presently he forgets that this was only a *possible* construction for the words to bear, and often, though a possible, not even a probable one. He assumes it to be the certain, necessary construction for the words. He treats it as such in all his arguments thenceforward ; and his theory is certain, because, forsooth, the construction certainly to be placed on the Gospel words proves it.

How many a vigorous and rigorous theory owes its force to this process ! The Third Gospel is the Gospel of Paulinism, composed with a view to exalt Paul's teaching and to disparage the older apostles. Where are the proofs ? The famous words to Peter,

---

[1] ἐπέων δὲ πολὺς νομὸς ἔνθα καὶ ἔνθα. *Iliad,* xx. 249.

Thou art Peter, and upon this rock will I build my church,
are not given in the Third Gospel.   Well, it is a possible inference from that omission, that the writer
meant to disparage Peter.   But it is not the necessary
inference, there is not even ground for saying that
it is the probable inference.   And yet, when Baur
says that the words "are completely ignored in the
Third Gospel because the writer could not possibly
recognise such a primacy of Peter," all he really has
to go upon is the supposed necessity of his inference.

In the same Gospel, Peter has been fishing all
night, and has caught nothing.   Jesus appears, and
at his command the net is once more let down, and
"they inclosed a great multitude of fishes, and the
net brake."   Here, says Dr. Volkmar, the writer
meant to contrast the barren result of preaching the
Gospel to the Jews with the fruitful result of preaching it to the Gentiles.   If we concede to Dr. Volkmar,
not that the writer certainly meant this, but that it
is a not absolutely impossible construction to put on
his words, we make him a very handsome admission.
Yet the absolute *certainty* of this sort of construction
is the proof for the universalist and anti-Petrine
character of the Third Gospel !

Finally, it is "an ingenious conjecture" of Dr.
Schwegler, that by the two crucified thieves, the one
converted, the other impenitent, the writer of the
Third Gospel intended to contrast Jew and Gentile,
the obstinate rejection of Christ by the former, the
glad acceptance of him by the latter.   No doubt this
may be called "an ingenious conjecture," but what

are we to think of the critic who confidently builds
upon it?

The Fourth Gospel, again, is an advance beyond
the Third; it is composed with "a profoundly calculated art," as the Gospel of Universalism in the highest
degree. How is this proved? It is proved because
in relating the miraculous draught of fishes,—a miracle
borrowed, we are told, from Luke, but placed by the
borrower after the Resurrection,—the author of the
Fourth Gospel declares that the net was not broken,
whereas Luke says that it was. What can be clearer?
The advanced Universalist means to indicate that the
multitudes of the heathen world may be brought in
to Christianity without any such disruption of the
Christian Church as to his faint-hearted predecessor
had seemed inevitable. The Third Gospel, again,
speaks of two boats engaged in fishing, the Fourth of
but one. What a progress, cries Strauss, is here!
The peaceable co-existence of a Jewish and a Gentile
Christianity no longer satisfies the religious consciousness; it will be satisfied with nothing less than a
Catholic Church, one and indivisible.

The Dutch are determined not to be beaten at this
sort of criticism by the Germans. For the Germans,
the artistic Universalist who composed the Fourth
Gospel is still a writer wishing to pass himself off as
the Pillar-Apostle John. For Dr. Scholten, in Hol-
land, this is insufficient. For him, the disciple whom
Jesus loved is an ideal figure representing the free
Christian consciousness of a later time; corresponding to none of the original narrow-minded Jewish

disciples, but in a designed contrast with them. This ideal figure it is who starts with Peter for the sepulchre and outruns him,—arrives first at his Lord. To be sure, Peter is the first to enter the sepulchre. What does that matter, when the ideal disciple, who enters after him, has the advantage over him that he "saw and believed?" And what is meant, again, by Jesus saying to Peter of this same disciple: "If I will that he tarry till I come, what is that to thee?" Any reference to John and to the advanced age to which he went on living? Not at all. Jesus means that the free spiritual Gospel of the idealising artist, his latest expounder, is the true one and shall stand; that it shall endure indestructible until his own coming again.

Now, if it were positively established on other grounds that the case is with the author of the Third Gospel, or with the author of the Fourth, just as these critics say, then we might have no such great difficulty, perhaps, in putting on the texts above quoted the construction proposed for them. But really it is only by placing this construction on the texts that the case as to their authors can be made out to be what these critics say. And when we are summoned to admit the construction as if it were the necessary, or even most probable one, we demur, and answer with the good Homer: *Wide is the range of words! words may make this way or that way.*

Sometimes the construction which is to prove the critic's theory has against it not only that it is but one possible construction out of many;—it has even

more against it than this. The Paulinian author of
the Third Gospel has for his great object, we are told,
to disparage the older apostles. See, says Baur, how
he relates the story of the raising of Jairus's daughter![1] If it were not his main object to disparage
the Twelve, how could he have made their three
eminent representatives, Peter, James, and John,
figure in a situation which seems expressly designed
to show them in an unfavourable light? "When
Jesus came to the house of Jairus," says Luke, "he
suffered no man to go in save Peter and James and
John, and the father and the mother of the maiden."
Now, Matthew does not mention this; and why?
Because he does not write with Luke's object. For
what follows? "And all wept and bewailed her;
but he said, Weep not, she is not dead but sleepeth.
And they laughed him to scorn, knowing that she was
dead. *And he put them all out.*"[2] Who are here,
asks Baur, the laughers at Jesus, that are put out by
him? "Evidently the three apostles are of the number; who consequently here, in spite of their having
been a considerable time in close intimacy with Jesus,
only give a new proof of their spiritual incapacity?"
And again: "That the three most trusted of the
disciples of Jesus behaved to him in such a way as
to occasion his ordering them to leave him, *is the main
point, which the whole representation of our Evangelist is
directed to bring out!*" Was ever anything so fantas-

---

[1] Baur, *Kritische Untersuchungen über die kanonischen Evangelien* (Tübingen, 1847), pp. 458 and 469.

[2] Luke viii. 51-54. Compare Matt. ix. 23-25.

tical? And to think that Baur should have found a
brother critic of the Gospels, "The Saxon *Anonymus*,"
more fantastical than himself, whom he has to take
seriously to task for his flights! In the first place,
there is nothing whatever to show that the laughers
in Luke's narrative, whom Jesus puts out, are his own
three apostles and the father and mother of the maiden.
It is far more likely that they are, as in St. Matthew,
"the people." But there is not only this against the
sense imposed by Baur on the passage. The all-
important words, *He put them all out*, are wanting in
the two oldest and best manuscripts of the New Testament![1] They have probably crept into the text
through a remembrance of corresponding words in
St. Matthew: "But when the people were put out."
And this is positively the evidence for "the main
point which the whole representation of our Evangelist is directed to bring out,"—the point that *the three
most trusted of the disciples of Jesus behaved to him in such
a way as to occasion his ordering them to leave him*. A
precious main point indeed!

The sort of reasoning which proves this to be the
Evangelist's main point is not reasoning at all, it is
mere playing at reasoning. But how much of Baur's
Biblical criticism is of this nature! We will try him
once more. "Pauline Universalism is recognisable
as the view which prevails throughout the Third
Gospel."[2] Well, Baur has told us this again and

---

[1] The Vatican and the Sinaitic.

[2] "Gibt sich der Paulinische Universalismus als die Grund-
anschauung des Evangelium zu erkennen."—Baur, *Geschichte der
christlichen Kirche*, vol. i. p. 74.

again; we want some real proof of it. He proceeds
to give his proof:—"Those declarations of Jesus in
the First Gospel which have a particularistic turn are
absent from the Third." Certainly this is important,
if true; is it true? See how Baur proves it:—"That
saying which is so characteristic of Matthew's Gospel,
—the saying about the fulfilment of the law and its
enduring validity,—Luke's Gospel has not. What
Matthew's Gospel says of the indestructibility of the
very smallest part of the law, Luke's Gospel says,[1]
according to the original reading, of the words of Jesus."
According to the original reading? Do, then, our
earliest manuscripts of the New Testament, or does
one of them, or does any manuscript, read "one tittle
of *my words,*" instead of "one tittle of *the law?*" Not
a manuscript, old or new, important or unimportant.
Only Marcion quotes Jesus as having said *one tittle of my
words;* Marcion, who is handed down to us as having
"mutilated" Luke, and whose profound antipathy to
Judaism and its law would just have led him to alter
such a sentence as this. Let us allow all possible
weight to Tertullian's admission that Marcion complained of the adulteration of the rule of Christianity,
and professed to revert to what was genuine. Still
there is nowhere a syllable to show that this *reverting*
consisted in a return to the original, genuine text of
Luke, whereas the common text and all the other
Gospels were adulterated. Not one syllable is there
to this effect; yet the most explicit assurance to this
effect would be requisite to make Baur's assertion

[1] Luke xvi. 17.

even plausible. As the evidence stands, his *according to the original reading* is monstrous.

To put one's finger on the fallaciousness of the criticism in these cases will make us suspect it in others. There are questions of literary criticism where positive proof is impossible; where the assertor appeals to critical tact, and not to formal evidence. Still, when we have found a man arbitrary and fantastic in those judgments where he professes to go by formal evidence, there is likelihood that he will be arbitrary and fantastic in those also where he professes to go by critical tact. "Mark was no epitomator," says Baur; "he was a man with a special turn for adding details of his own, in order to give the *rationale* of things, and to supply the logical explanation of them." What sort of example does Baur bring of this? "Mark," says Baur,[1] "prefixes to the words with which, in the other Synoptics, the story of the disciples taking the ears of corn concludes, *The Son of Man is Lord also of the Sabbath*, Mark prefixes to these words a proposition to give the reason for them : *The Sabbath was made for man, not man for the Sabbath.*[2] One would think that Mark's motive for inserting these words might be, that there was a tradition of their having been really spoken by Jesus, in whose manner they exactly are. But no, this is the very last explanation which ever occurs to a critic of the Tübingen School. All our Gospels are more or less *Tendenz-Schriften*, tendence-writings,—writings

[1] *Kritische Untersuchungen über die kanonischen Evangelien*, p. 554.   [2] Mark ii. 27, 28.

to serve an aim and bent of their several authors;
and a Tübingen critic is for ever on the look-out for
tendence in them. The words in Mark *cannot* be
authentic, says Baur, because they *must* be an addition inserted to give the rational explanation of the
words following them. But the ground for this *must*
is really not in any necessary law of criticism, but
only that it pleases Baur to say so. Mark's turn for
little circumstantial details is indeed curious; but it
is a thing to be noticed in passing, not to be pressed
to this extravagant extent.

It is just the same with Baur's proof of another
assertion: the assertion that the Sermon on the
Mount in the First Gospel is a work of "artistic
reflection," a body of sayings on different occasions,
grouped by the Evangelist "in one logically ordered
whole, to produce a certain calculated total-effect."
The proof of this is that the Sermon on the Mount
follows throughout "a methodical march from point
to point according to a determined idea." That is to
say, Baur determines an idea for the Sermon on the
Mount, and makes it follow that idea methodically.
But the idea, and the Sermon's conformity to it, are
neither of them given by the necessary laws of
criticism, they are not facts commending themselves
to every sound judgment. They are merely a construction which it is possible to put upon the words.
But *wide is the range of words!* Very likely there
may be in the Sermon on the Mount sayings belonging to more than one occasion; but very likely,
nevertheless, the Sermon may not at all be a work of

" artistic reflection," and not at all follow " a methodical march from point to point."

Evidence has three degrees of force : demonstration, probability, plausibility.   Now, the truth is,
that on very many questions like the above, which
German critics of the Bible raise and treat as if they
were matter for demonstration, demonstration cannot
really be reached at all.   The data are insufficient for
it.   Whether there was one original written Gospel,
a single *schriftliche Urevangelium*, or whether there
was a plurality of written sources, a *Mehrheit von
Quellen-Schriften*, — a favourite question with these
critics,—is a question where demonstration is wholly
out of our power.   Whether the co-existence in the
First Gospel of passages which "bear the stamp of
Jewish Particularism," and of passages which breathe
"another, freer spirit," is due, as Dr. Schwegler maintains, to an incorporation of new and later elements
with the original Gospel, is a question not really
admitting of demonstration one way or the other.
Whether the Second Gospel, as Dr. Hilgenfeld asserts
and Baur denies, is "an independent Petrine Gospel
representing the transition from the strict Judaic
Christianity of Matthew to the law-emancipated
Paulinism of Luke ; " whether, as Dr. Volkmar con-
tends, all our canonical Gospels are "pure tendence-
writings of the at first kept under, at last victorious
Pauline spirit," can never be settled to demonstration,
either in the affirmative or in the negative.   Whether,
as Baur and Strauss confidently declare, the substitu-
tion by Luke, in reporting a speech of Jesus, of

adikia for Matthew's *anomia*, of *unrighteousness* for
iniquity, "metamorphoses a Judaic outburst against
Paul into a Paulinian outburst against Judaic Christianity;" whether Luke's Sermon in the *Plain* is
meant to be opposed to the Sermon on the *Mount* of
Matthew, no one can ever prove, and no one can ever
disprove. The most that can be reached in these
questions is probability or plausibility; and plausibility,—such a display of ingenuity as makes people
clap their hands and cry *Well done !* but does not
seriously persuade them,—is not much worth a wise
man's ambitioning.

There remains probability. But it is not the
necessity of a certain construction for certain texts
which creates probability. It is absurd, as we have
seen, to take such a necessity for granted. The probability of the thesis that our Four Gospels are "pure
tendence-writings of the at first kept under, at last
victorious Pauline spirit," does not depend on the demonstrable certainty of inferences from any text or
texts in them. It depends on considerations drawn
from experience of human nature, and from acquaintance with the history of the human spirit, which
themselves guide our inference from these texts. And
what is the great help for interpreting aright the experience of human nature and the history of the
human spirit, for getting at the fact, for discovering
what is fact and what is not? Sound judgment and
common-sense, bred of much conversation with real
life and with practical affairs.

Now, "nowhere else in the world," declares, as we

have already seen, Sir Henry Maine, "is there the same respect for a fact as in England, unless the respect be of English origin." He attributes this to the habits of strictness formed by the English law of evidence ; but the English law of evidence is itself due, probably, to the practical character of the people. Faults this character has, and plenty of them. Much may be said against its indifference to learning and study, its neglect of organising research ; much may be said in praise of Germany's superiority in these respects. Yet, after all, shut a number of men up to make learning and study the business of their lives, and how many of them, for want of some discipline or other, seem to lose all balance of judgment ! Hear the amenities of organised research in Germany, hear Dr. Volkmar on Tischendorf :—of every sovereign in the world he has begged decorations ; in vain ! people would not treat him seriously. Renan, in his life of the Messiah Jesus, never once names the Messiah Tischendorf ! " Hear Tischendorf on Dr. Volkmar : —" The liedom which tramples under foot Church and science indifferently ! stuck full of lying and cheating ! " But indeed, for fear we should lose these flowers of learned compliment, Professor Max Müller, —who has a foot in both worlds, the English and the German, — transplants into an English review this criticism by Professor Steinthal on a rival :—" That horrible humbug ! that scolding flirt ! that tricky attorney ! whenever I read him, hollow vanity yawns in my face, arrogant vanity grins at me." And only the other day the newspapers brought us an address of Dr. Mommsen, in which the new Rector of the University of Berlin, with a charming crudity, gravely congratulated his countrymen on not being modest, and adjured them never to fall into that sad fault! These are the intemperances and extravagances which men versed in practical life feel to be absurd. One is not disposed to form great expectations of the balance of judgment in those who commit them. Yet what is literary and historical criticism but a series of most delicate judgments on the data given us by re-search,—judgments requiring great tact, moderation, and temper? These, however, are what the German professor who has his data from research, and makes his judgments on them, is so often without, not hav-ing enough of the discipline of practical life to give it to him. We speak of judgments, be it observed, not in the exact sciences, but in matters where we deal with the experience of human nature and with the history of the human spirit.

Goethe seems to have strongly felt how much the discipline of a great public life and of practical affairs had to do with intelligence. "What else is *cultur*," he asks, in a remarkable passage, "but a higher con-ception of political and military relations? Every-thing depends, for a nation, upon the art of bearing itself in the world, and of striking in when neces-sary."[1] And he adds in a more remarkable sentence

---

[1] "Was ist Cultur anderes als ein höherer Begriff von politi-schen und militarischen Verhältnissen? Auf die Kunst sich in der Welt zu betragen, und nach Erfordern dreinzuschlagen, kommt es bei den Nationen an."

still : " Whenever and wherever the French lay aside
their Philistinism, they stand far above us in critical
judgment, and in the comprehension of original works
of the human spirit." [1]   He means that in France the
practical life of a great nation quickened the judgment, and prevented fumbling and trifling.   And we
shall see what Germany does, now that she, too, has
" struck in " with signal effect, and has the practical
life of a great nation to correct and balance her
learning.   But hitherto her learning has lacked this
counter-weight.

II.

We have led the reader thus gradually to the consideration of German theories about the Fourth
Gospel, because these theories, coming to us without
our having any previous acquaintance with their
character and their authors, are likely at first, though
not in the long run, to make a powerful impression
here.   In the first place, they have great vigour and
rigour, and are confidently presented to us as certain,
demonstrated fact.   Now an Englishman has such a
respect for fact himself, that he can hardly imagine
grave people presenting him with anything as fact
when they have absolutely no right to do so whatever.   Then, in the next place, the theories are presented and vouched for by English importers; and
they seem to feel no misgivings about them.   But

[1] " So oft die Franzosen ihre Philisterei aufgeben und wo sie
es thun, stehen sie weit über uns im kritischen Urtheil und in
der Auffassung origineller Geisteswerke."

then the very last English people to have misgivings
about them would naturally be their importers, who
have taken the trouble to get them up, translate
them, and publish them.   Finally, there is a fashion
in these things; and no one can deny that the fashion
just now is in favour of theories denying all historical
validity to the Fourth Gospel.   One can see it by
the reviews and newspapers.   To reject the Fourth
Gospel bids fair even to become, like disestablish-
ment, or like marriage with a deceased wife's sister,
a regular article of our Liberal creed, asserting its
place in the programme of the future, compelling Mr.
Gladstone to think once, twice, and thrice about it,
and setting Sir William Harcourt to consider whether
it may not be possible for him to build a new Liberal
party of his own upon some safer basis.

Sooner or later, however, these theories will have
to confront the practical English sense of evidence,
the plain judgment as to what is proved matter of
fact and what is not.   So long as the traditional
notion about the Bible-documents was accepted in
this country, people allowed the conventional defences
of that notion to pass muster easily enough.   The
notion was thought certain in itself, was part of our
life.   That the conventional defences should be produced was very proper.   Whether or no they were
exactly right did not much matter ; they were produced in favour of what was a certainty already.   The
old notion about the Bible-documents has given way.
But the result is that no theories about them will any
longer be allowed by English people to pass muster

as easily as the old conventional defences did.   All
theories, the old and the new, will have to stand the
ordeal of the Englishman's strong and strict sense for
fact.   We are much mistaken if it does not turn out
that this ordeal makes great havoc among the vigorous and rigorous theories of German criticism concerning the Bible - documents.   The sense which
English people have for fact and for evidence will tell
them, that as to demonstration, in most of those cases
wherein our critics profess to supply it to us, *wide is
the range of words,* and demonstration is impossible.
As to probability, which in these cases is as much as
can be reached, we shall discover that the German
Biblical critics are in general not the likeliest people
to reach it, and that their theories do, in fact, attain
it very seldom.

Let us take the performance of the greatest and
most famous of these critics, — Ferdinand Christian
Baur,—upon the Fourth Gospel.   "It is Baur's imperishable glory," says Strauss, himself in some respects a rival of Baur, "to have succeeded in stripping
the Fourth Gospel of all historical authority."   Baur
has *proved*, it is said, that the Fourth Gospel was composed about the year 170 after Christ, in the heat of
a conflict between Jewish and anti-Jewish Christianity, and to help the anti-Jewish side.   It has a
direct dogmatic design from beginning to end.   With
a profoundly calculated art, it freely treats the Gospel-
story and Gospel-personages in the interests of this
design.   It develops the Logos-idea, and its Christ
is a dogma personified.   Its form is given by the

Gnostic conception of an antithesis of the principles of light and darkness,—an antithesis found both in the physical and in the moral world, and in the moral world exemplified by the contrast of Jewish unbelief with true faith. The author does not intend to deliver history, but to deliver his idea in the dress of history. No sayings of Jesus are authentic which are recorded in the Fourth Gospel only. The miracles of the Fourth Gospel are not, like those of the Synoptics, matter given by popular report and legend. They are all, with deliberate art, "made out of the carver's brain," to serve the carver's special purposes.

For example.[1] The first miracle in the Fourth Gospel, the change of water into wine, is invented by the artist to figure Jesus Christ's superiority over his precursor, and the transition and progress from the Baptist's preparatory stage to the epoch of Messianic activity and glory. The change of water into wine indicates this transition. Water is the Baptist's element ; Jesus Christ's element is the Holy Ghost. But in the First Gospel the antithesis to the Baptist's element is not called Holy Ghost only, it is also called fire. In the Fourth Gospel this antithesis is, by means of the Cana miracle, figured to us as wine. "Why," asks Baur, "should not the difference and superiority of Jesus Christ's element be indicated by wine as well as fire ? *Geist*, fire, wine, are all allied notions."

Then come Nicodemus in the third chapter, the

[1] For what follows, see *Kritische Untersuchungen über die kanonischen Evangelien*, pp. 114-184.

woman of Samaria in the fourth. They are created
by the artist to typify two opposite classes of
believers. Nicodemus, who holds merely to miracles,
is the representative of Judaism,—Judaism which
even in its belief is unbelieving. The woman of
Samaria represents the heathen world, susceptible of
a genuine faith in Christ. The same capacity for a
true faith is observable in the nobleman of Caper-
naum ; he must therefore be intended by the author
for a heathen, and not, as is commonly thought, for a
Jew.

We proceed, and come to the healing of the impotent man at the pool of Bethesda. Now the Jesus
of the Fourth Gospel is the principle of life *and* light
in contrast to the principle of death and darkness.
The healing of the impotent man is a miracle designed
to exhibit Jesus as the principle of life. Presently,
therefore, it is balanced by the miracle wrought on
the man born blind, in order that Jesus may be ex-
hibited as the principle of light. The reader sees
what an artistic composition he has before him in the
Fourth Gospel. As Baur says, this is indeed a work
where all is intention and conformity to plan ;
nothing mere history, but idea moulding history !
Everything in the work is strictly, to speak like the
artists, *motived*. To say that anything in the Fourth
Gospel is not strictly motived, "is as good," says
Baur, "as calling the Evangelist a very thoughtless
writer."

Here, then, we have a theory of genuine vigour
and rigour. Already we feel its power, when we read

in one of our daily newspapers that "the author of the Fourth Gospel stands clearly revealed as the partisan and propagandist of a dogma of transcendental theology."

Now Baur himself would have told us that the truth of his theory was certain, demonstrable. But we have seen what these critics call *demonstration*. That wine *may* figure the Holy Spirit is with them a proof that in the Cana miracle it *does*, and that the true account of that miracle is what we have seen. Demonstrably true Baur's theory of the Fourth Gospel is not, and cannot be; but is it probably true? To try this, let us, instead of imposing the theory upon the facts of the case and rejecting whatever facts do not suit it,—let us, in our plain English way, take the evidence fairly as it stands, and see to what conclusions it leads us about the Fourth Gospel.

III.

What is the earliest piece of evidence we can find concerning the composition of this Gospel? It is given us in the already-mentioned Canon of Muratori, dating, probably, from about the year 175 after Christ. This fragment says:—"The fourth of the Gospels is by the disciple John. He was being pressed by his fellow disciples and (fellow) bishops, and he said: 'Fast with me this day, and for three days; and whatsoever shall have been revealed to each one of us, let us relate it to the rest.' In the same night it was revealed to the Apostle Andrew that John should write the whole in his own name, and that all the rest should revise it."

This is the earliest tradition ; and in Clement of Alexandria, who died A.D. 220, we find[1] the same tradition indicated. "John last," says Clement, "aware that in the other Gospels were declared the things of flesh and blood, *being moved thereto by his acquaintances,* and being inspired by the Spirit, composed a spiritual Gospel." To the like effect Epiphanius, in the latter half of the fourth century, says that John wrote *last,* wrote *reluctantly,* wrote because he was *constrained* to write, wrote in Asia at the age of ninety.[2]

Such is the tradition: that the Fourth Gospel proceeded from the Apostle John ; that it was the last written, and that it was revised by the apostle's friends. The theory, on the other hand, says that the Gospel proceeds from a consummate artist unknown, who wrote it during or after the Paschal controversy in Asia Minor in the year 170, in order to develop the Logos-idea, and to serve other special purposes. Which are we to incline to, the theory or the tradition ?

Tradition may be false; yet it is at least something, as we have before remarked, in a thing's favour, that men have delivered it. But there may be reasons why we cannot believe it. Let us see, then, what

[1] In his *Hypotyposes,* quoted by Eusebius, *Hist. Eccles.* vi. 14 :—Τὸν μέντοι Ἰωάννην ἔσχατον, συνιδόντα ὅτι τὰ σωματικὰ ἐν τοῖς εὐαγγελίοις δεδήλωται, προτραπέντα ὑπὸ τῶν γνωρίμων, πνεύματι θεοφορηθέντα, πνευματικὸν ποιῆσαι εὐαγγέλιον.

[2] See Epiphanii *Panarium, Hær.* LI. 12.

there is to make us disbelieve the tradition of Epiphanius, of Clement of Alexandria, and of the Fragment of Muratori.   There is the miraculous form of
the story, the machinery of dream and revelation;
that, we know at once, cannot be historical.   But it
is the form in which a matter of fact was nearly sure,
under the circumstances of the case, to have got
delivered; and the gist of the tradition,—the Fourth
Gospel's having its source in the Apostle John,—may
be matter of fact still.   What is there, then, against
St. John's authorship of the Fourth Gospel?

We shall not touch questions of language, where
the reader, in order to be able to decide for himself,
must know the Oriental languages, and where, if he
does not know them, he must take upon trust what
is said.   Our points shall be all such that an ordinary
reader of plain understanding can form an opinion on
them for himself.   And we shall not concern ourselves
with every point which may be raised, but shall be
content with what seems sufficient for the purpose in
view.

Now, a plain reader will certainly, when his attention is called to the matter, be struck with the
extraordinary way in which the writer of the Fourth
Gospel, whom we suppose a Jew, speaks of his brother
Jews.   We do not mean that he speaks of them with
blame and detestation; this we could quite understand.   But he speaks as if they and their usages
belonged to another race from himself,—to another
world.   The waterpots at Cana are set "after the
manner of *the purifying of the Jews;*" "there arose a

question between some of John's disciples *and a Jew
about purifying ;*" [1] "now *the Jews' Passover* was nigh
at hand ;" "they wound the body of Jesus in linen
clothes with spices, *as the manner of the Jews is to bury;*"
"there they laid Jesus, because of *the Preparation of
the Jews.*" No other Evangelist speaks in this manner.
It seems almost impossible to think that a Jew born
and bred,—a man like the Apostle John,—could ever
have come to speak so. Granted that he was settled
at Ephesus when he produced his Gospel, granted that
he wrote in Greek, wrote for Greeks ; still he could
never, surely, have brought himself to speak of the
Jews and of Jewish things in this fashion ! His lips
and his pen would have refused to form such strange
expressions, in whatever disposition he may have
written ; nature and habit would have been too much
for him. A Jew talking of *the Jews' Passover*, and of
a dispute of some of John's disciples *with a Jew about
purifying ?* It is like an Englishman writing of the
Derby as *the English people's Derby*, or talking of a
dispute between some of Mr. Cobden's disciples *and
an Englishman about free-trade.* An Englishman would
never speak so.

When once the reader's attention has been called
to this peculiarity in the Fourth Gospel, other things
will strike him which heighten it. The solemn and
mystical way in which John the Baptist is introduced:
"There was a man sent from God whose name was
John,"—how unlike the matter-of-fact, historical way
in which John the Baptist is introduced by Jewish

[1] The text followed is that of the Vatican manuscript.

writers who had probably seen him, like the writer of
the First Gospel, who at any rate were perfectly
familiar with him, knew all about him ! "In those
days came John the Baptist, preaching in the wilderness of Judæa." How much more is the Fourth
Gospel's way of speaking about John the Baptist the
way that would be used about a wonderful stranger,
an unknown ! Again : twice the Fourth Gospel
speaks of Caiaphas as "high-priest of that year," as
if the Jewish high-priesthood had been at that time
a yearly office, which it was not. It is a mistake a
foreigner might perfectly well have made, but hardly
a Jew. It is like talking of an American President
as "President of that year," as if the American
Presidency were a yearly office. An American could
never adopt, one thinks, such a way of speaking.
Again : the disciple who, at the high priest's palace,
brings Peter in, is called by the writer of the Fourth
Gospel "an acquaintance of the high priest." One
of the poor men who followed Jesus *an acquaintance*
of a grandee like Caiaphas ! A foreigner, not intimate
by his own experience with the persons and things of
Palestine, but seeing through a halo the disciples who
were with Jesus in the great tragedy, might naturally
have written so. But a Jew, a fisherman of Galilee,
who knew quite well the distance and difference between the humble people in the train of Jesus and
the rich, haughty, aristocratical priesthood at Jerusalem,—could it ever have occurred to *him* to commit
an exaggeration, which is like the exaggeration of
calling a London working-man, who is in the throng

round a police-court during an exciting inquiry and
has interest enough to get a friend in, "an acquaintance of the Secretary of State ?"

As the social distinctions of Palestine are confounded, so are its geographical distinctions.
"Bethany beyond Jordan"[1] is like "Willesden beyond Trent." A native could never have said it.
This is so manifest, indeed, that in the later manuscripts *Bethany* was changed into *Bethabara*, and so
it stands in our version. But the three earlier and
authoritative manuscripts all agree in *Bethany*, which
we may pronounce certainly, therefore, the original
reading. Nevertheless, the writer knew of the
Bethany near Jerusalem ; he makes it the scene
of the raising of Lazarus. But his Palestinian
geography is so vague, it has for him so little of the
reality and necessity which it would have for a
native, that when he wants a name for a locality he
takes the first village that comes into his remembrance, without troubling himself to think whether
it suits or no.

Finally,—and here, too, the plainest reader will
be able with a little reflection to follow us, although
to the reader of considerable literary experience the
truth of what we say will be most evident,—the lofty
strain of the prologue to the Gospel is nearly inconceivable as the Apostle John's. Neither form nor
matter can well have come from him. At least, to
suppose them his we must place ourselves in the
world of miracle,—in the world where one is trans-

[1] John i. 28.

ported from Bagdad to Cairo by clapping one's hands,
or in which one falls asleep, and wakes understanding
the language of birds and hearing the grass grow.
To this world we do not permit ourselves to have
recourse. But in the world of fact and experience it
is a phenomenon scarcely conceivable that a Galilean
fisherman, changing his country and his language
after fifty, should have compassed the ideas of the
introduction to the Fourth Gospel, and the style
which serves as organ to those ideas, and, indeed, to
the Gospel throughout. Paul was a highly educated
man, and yet Paul never compassed ideas and a style
of which the cast was Greek. The form in which the
Fourth Gospel presents its ideas is Greek,—a style
flowing, ratiocinative, articulated. The ideas of the
introduction are the ideas in which Gnosticism
worked, and undoubtedly there were Jewish Gnostics
as well as Greek. But the strange and disfigured
shape which the genuine Jewish mind, the mind of a
Jew with the sort of training of the Apostle John,
gave to Gnostic ideas when it worked among them,
is well shown in the fragments of the Book of Elxai.[1]
Not so are Gnostic ideas handled in the introduction
to the Fourth Gospel. They are there handled with
all the ease and breadth which we find in the masters
of Greek Gnosticism, in Valentinus or Basileides.

Well, then, the reader will say, the Tübingen
critics are right, and the tradition is wrong. The
Fourth Gospel has not its source in the Apostle John;

[1] See the fragments collected in Hilgenfeld's *Novum Testa-
mentum extra Canonem receptum*, vol. iii. pp. 153-167.

it is a fancy-piece by a Greek literary artist. But
stop ; let us look at the tradition a little more closely.
It speaks of a *revision* of what the Apostle John produced.   It speaks of a pressure put upon him, of his
being *moved by his friends* to give his recollections, and
of his friends having a hand in the work which stood
in John's name.   And if we turn to the Gospel itself,
we find things which remarkably suit with this
account of the matter.   We find things which seem
to show that the person who was the source of the
Fourth Gospel did not produce his work himself,
but that others produced it for him, and guarantee
what is said, and appeal to his authority.   They say :
" This is the disciple who testified these things and
who wrote these things : and *we know* that his testimony is true." [1]   They say again : " He who hath
seen, hath borne witness, and his witness is true : and
that man knoweth that he saith true, that ye may
believe." [2]   *That man knoweth that he saith true !*—
surely the actual composer of a work would never
refer to himself so strangely.   But if we suppose that
the editors of a work are speaking of the man who
supplied them with it, and who stands as their
authority for it, the expression is quite natural.

And then we shall find that all things adjust themselves.   In his old age, St. John, at Ephesus, has

---

[1] John xxi. 24.   οὗτός ἐστιν ὁ μαθητὴς ὁ καὶ μαρτυρῶν περὶ
τούτων καὶ ὁ γράψας ταῦτα, καὶ οἴδαμεν ὅτι ἀληθὴς αὐτοῦ ἡ μαρτυρία
ἐστίν.

[2] John xix. 35.   ὁ ἑωρακὼς μεμαρτύρηκεν, καὶ ἀληθινὴ αὐτοῦ
ἐστιν ἡ μαρτυρία · καὶ ἐκεῖνος οἶδεν, ὅτι ἀληθῆ λέγει, ἵνα καὶ ὑμεῖς
πιστεύητε.

logia, " sayings of the Lord," and has incidents in the
Lord's story, which have not been published in any
of the written accounts that were beginning at that
time to be handed about. The elders of Ephesus,
—whom tradition afterwards makes into apostles,
fellows with St. John,—move him to bestow his
treasure on the world. He gives his materials, and
the presbytery of Ephesus provide a redaction for
them and publish them. The redaction, with its
unity of tone, its flowingness and connectedness, is
by one single hand :—the hand of a man of literary
talent, a Greek Christian, whom the Church of
Ephesus found proper for such a task. A man of
literary talent, a man of soul also, a theologian. A
theological lecturer, perhaps, as in the Fourth Gospel
he so often shows himself,—a theological lecturer,
an earlier and a nameless Origen ; who in this one
short composition produced a work outweighing all
the folios of all the Fathers, but was content that his
name should be written only in the Book of Life.
And, indeed, what matters literary talent in these
cases ? Who would give a care to it ? The Gospel
is John's, because its whole value is in the *logia*, the
sayings of the Lord, which it saves ; and by John
these *logia* were furnished. But the redaction was
not John's, and could not be ; and at the beginning
of the second century, when the work appeared, many
there would be who knew well that John's the redaction was not. Therefore the Church of Ephesus,
which published the work, gave to it that solemn and
singular *imprimatur :* " He who hath seen hath borne

witness, and his witness is true ; *and that man knoweth that he saith true*, that ye may believe." The Asiatic public, to whom the document originally came, understood what this *imprimatur* meant, and were satisfied. The Fourth Gospel was received in that measure in which alone at that early time,—in the first quarter of the second century,—any Gospel could be received. It was read with love and respect ; but its letter did not and could not at once acquire the sacredness and fixity of the letter of canonical Scripture. For at least fifty years the Johannine Gospel remained, like our other three Gospels, liable to changes, interpolations, additions ; until at last, like them, towards the end of the second century, by ever increasing use and veneration, it passed into the settled state of Holy Scripture.

Now, this account of the matter explains a great deal of what puzzles us when we try to conceive the Fourth Gospel as having its source in the Apostle John. It explains the Greek philosophy and the Greek style. It explains the often inaccurate treatment of Palestinian geography, Palestinian usages, Jewish feelings and ideas. It explains the way in which the Jews are spoken of as strangers, and their festivals and ceremonies as things *of the Jews*. It explains, too, the unsure and arbitrary way in which incidents of the Gospel-story are arranged and handled. Apologists say that the first chapter bears the very stamp of a Palestinian Jew's authorship. Apologists will say anything ; they say that the Fourth Gospel must be St. John's, because it breathes the very spirit of the Apostle of Love, forgetting that our whole conception of St. John as the Apostle of Love comes from connecting him with this Gospel, and has no independent support from the testimony of writers earlier than Clement of Alexandria and Jerome, for whom the belief in the Johannine authorship was firmly established. In like manner, it is to set all serious ideas of criticism at defiance, to talk of the version of the calling of Peter in the first chapter, any more than the version of the clearing of the Temple in the second, as having the very stamp of a Palestinian Jew's authorship upon them. They have not. They have, on the contrary, the stamp of a foreigner's management of the incidents, scenes, and order of a Palestinian history.

The writer has new *logia*, or sayings of the Lord, at his disposal ; and he has some new incidents. But his treasure is his *logia ;* the important matter for him is to plant his *logia*. His new incidents are not, as Baur supposes, inventions of his own, any more than the incidents of the other three Evangelists ; but all his incidents stand looser in his mind, are more malleable, less impose themselves on him in a definite fashion than theirs. He is not so much at home amongst the incidents of his story ; but then they lend themselves all the better on that account to his main purpose, which is to plant his *logia*. He assigns to incidents an order or a locality which no Jew would have assigned to them. He makes Jews say things and feel things which they could never have said or felt ; but, meanwhile, his *logia* are

placed.   As we observed in *Literature and Dogma* :—
" The narrative,—so meagre, and skipping so unaccountably backwards and forwards between Galilee
and Jerusalem,—might well be thought, not indeed
invented, but a matter of infinitely little care and
attention to the writer of the Gospel ; a mere slight
framework, in which to set the doctrine and discourses
of Jesus."

Now there is nothing which the vigorous and
rigorous critics of Germany, and their English disciples like the author of *Supernatural Religion*, more
detest than the endeavour to make two parts in the
Fourth Gospel,—a part belonging to John, and a
part belonging to somebody else.   Either reject it
all, cries Strauss, or admit it all to be John's!   By
what mark, he adds, by what guide, except mere
caprice, is one to distinguish the hand of the Apostle
from the hand of the interpolator ?   No, aver these
critics ; the whole Gospel, without distinction, must
be abandoned to the demolishing sweep of inexorable
critical laws !

But that there went other hands as well as John's
to the making of the Fourth Gospel the tradition
itself indicates, and what we find in the Gospel seems
to confirm.   True, to determine what is John's and
what is not is a delicate question ; nay, it is a question
which we must sometimes be content to leave un-
determined.   Results of more vigour and rigour are
obtained by a theory which rejects the tradition, and
which lays down either that John wrote the whole, or
that the whole is a fancy-piece.   But that a theory

has superior vigour and rigour does not prove it to
be the right account how a thing happened. Things
do not generally happen with vigour and rigour.
That it is a very difficult and delicate operation to
separate the different elements in the Fourth Gospel
does not disprove that only by this operation can we
get at the truth. The truth has very often to be
got at under great difficulty.

No; but what makes the strength of those critics
who deride the hypothesis of there being two parts,
a Johannine part and another, in the Fourth Gospel,
is the strange use of this hypothesis by those who
have adopted it. The discourses they have almost
all assigned to John;—the discourses, and, from its
theological importance, the prologue also. The second
hand was introduced in order to account for difficulties
in the incidents and narrative. With the exception
of some bits in the narrative, the whole Gospel is,
for Schleiermacher, "the genuine biographical Gospel
of the eye-witness John." Far from admitting the
tradition which represents it as supplementing the
other three, Schleiermacher believed that it preceded
them all. Weisse regarded the prologue as the special
work of the Apostle. Ewald supposed that in the
discourses we have the words of Jesus transfigured
by "a glorified remembrance," after lying for a long
time in the Apostle John's mind. All this is, indeed,
open to attack. No difficulties raised by the narrative can be greater than the difficulty of supposing
the discourses of the Fourth Gospel to be St. John's
"glorified remembrance" of his Master's words, or

the prologue to be the special work of the Apostle, or the Gospel to be, in general, the record at first hand of pure personal experience (*lauter Selbsterlebtes*). The separation of elements is not to be made in this fashion. But, made as it should be, it will be found to resolve the difficulties of the case, not in a way demonstrably right indeed (for demonstration is here out of our reach), but in a way much more probably right than the theory of Baur.

IV.

Baur's theory, however, relies not only on its own internal certainty, but on external evidence. It alleges that there is proof against the existence of the Fourth Gospel during the first three-quarters of the second century. It is undeniably quoted, and as John's, by Theophilus, Bishop of Antioch,[1] who wrote in the year 180. This, it is said, is the earliest proof of its existence ; and it cannot have existed earlier.

But why? Let us put aside the Fragment of Muratori, of which the date and authority are disputed, and let us take facts which are undisputed. There is no doubt that Justin Martyr, in his first Apology, written probably in the year 147, says, speaking of Christian baptism and its necessity : "For Christ said, *Except ye be born again, ye shall not enter into the kingdom of heaven.* Now to all men it is manifest that it is impossible that they who are once born should enter into the wombs of them that bare

[1] *Ad Autolycum* ii. 22. The first and third verses of the first chapter are quoted, and as John's, and exactly.

them." [1] Every one will be reminded of the words
to Nicodemus in the Fourth Gospel : " Except a man
be born from above [2] he cannot see the kingdom of
God ; " and of the answer of Nicodemus : " How can
a man be born when he is old ? can he enter a second
time into his mother's womb and be born ? " Justin
does not quote the Fourth Gospel ; he never expressly
quotes any one of our Gospels. He does not quote
word for word in such a manner that we can at once
say positively : " He is quoting the passage in our
Gospel ! " But then he never does quote in such a
manner as to enable us to say this. All a candid yet
cautious reader will affirm is, that Justin here has in
his mind the same sayings as those given in the conversation between Jesus and Nicodemus in our Fourth
Gospel. He may have quoted from some other source.
Almost certainly, if he is quoting from our present
Fourth Gospel, this Gospel was not a canonical Scripture to him, or he would have quoted it more correctly.
But to no candid reader will it occur to think that
what Justin has here in his eye is not at all the conversation with Nicodemus about being born again

---

[1] καὶ γὰρ ὁ Χριστὸς εἶπεν, "Αν μὴ ἀναγεννηθῆτε, οὐ μὴ εἰσέλθητε
εἰς τὴν βασιλείαν τῶν οὐρανῶν. ὅτι γὲ καὶ ἀδύνατον εἰς τὰς μήτρας
τῶν τεκουσῶν τοὺς ἅπαξ γεννωμένους ἐμβῆναι, φανερὸν πᾶσίν
ἐστιν. Compare John iii. 3, 4.

[2] The word ἄνωθεν may quite well mean *again*. Origen,
referring in Greek to the famous story, *Domine, quo vadis ?
Vado Romam iterum crucifigi*, uses ἄνωθεν for *iterum :* ἄνωθεν
μέλλω σταυρωθῆναι. But ἄνωθεν cannot well mean *again* in one
place in a composition, and *from above* (" I am from above ")
in all other places. *Born from above*, however, is merely the
fuller description of being *born again*.

and its difficulties, but quite another matter, this
passage from the First Gospel : " Except ye be converted, and become as little children, ye shall not
enter into the kingdom of heaven."[1] This is what
critics of the Tübingen school advance, and we need
hardly say that the author of *Supernatural Religion*
follows suit. But to no plain reader would it ever
occur to advance it ; to no one except a professed
theological critic with a theory. If our Fourth
Gospel is to be a fancy-piece, and a fancy-piece not
composed before the year 170, sayings and incidents
peculiar to it must pass for inventions of its own,
cannot be real traditional sayings known and cited by
Justin long before. No ; but on the other hand, if
they *are* so known and cited, the Fourth Gospel
cannot well be a mere fancy-piece, and we lose a
vigorous and rigorous theory. If they are, and to
any unbiassed judgment they clearly are, then it is
probable, surely, that Justin, who used written
records, had in his eye, when he cited the sayings in
question, the only written record where we find them,
—the Fourth Gospel, only this Gospel not yet admitted to the honours of canonicity. But at any
rate, it is now certain that all sayings and incidents
not common to this Gospel with the Synoptics are
not to be set down as pure inventions.

But we can go back much farther than Justin.
Some twenty-five years ago there was published at
Oxford, under the title of Origen's *Philosophumena*, a
newly-discovered Greek work.   Origen's it is not ;

[1] Matt. xviii. 3.

but because, besides giving the *Philosophumena* or doctrines of heathen philosophy, from which all heresies are supposed to spring, the work purports also to be a *Refutation of all Heresies*, and because Hippolytus, Bishop of the Port of Rome in the early part of the third century, wrote a work with this title, of which the description in Photius well agrees with the so-called *Philosophumena*, Bunsen and others pronounced that here was certainly the missing work of Hippolytus. Against this we have the difficulty that the Paschal Chronicle, professing to cite textually in reference to the Quartodeciman controversy this work of Hippolytus, cites a passage which is not in our *Philosophumena*, although the Quartodeciman heresy is there refuted.[1] Bunsen is ready with the assertion that "This passage *must* have existed in our work," exactly as he was sure that in the Canon of Muratori the Epistle to the Hebrews *must* have been mentioned. But this is just the sort of assertion we will not allow ourselves to make; and we refrain, therefore, from pronouncing the *Philosophumena* to be certainly the *Refutation of all Heresies* by Hippolytus. Still the work is of the highest importance, and it gives its own date. The author was contemporary with Zephyrinus, and tells us of having had controversy with him. Zephyrinus was Bishop of Rome from the year 201 of our era to the year 219. To the heretics and heresies of the second century our author comes, therefore, very near in time, and his history of them is of extraordinary value.

[1] *Chronicon Paschale* (edition of Bonn), vol. i. p. 13.

In his account of the Gnostic philosopher Basileides, who flourished at Alexandria about the year
125 after Christ, he records the comments of Basileides on the sentence in Genesis, *Let there be light*,
and quotes as follows from Basileides, whose name he
has mentioned just before :—" This, says he (Basileides), is that which is spoken in the Gospels : *That
was the true light which lighteth every man that cometh
into the world.*" [1]   The words are quoted exactly as
they are given in the Fourth Gospel ; [2] and if we
cannot pronounce certainly that *logia* of Jesus are
quoted from one of our Gospels because they are to
be found there, yet no one will dispute that if we
find the reflections of one of our Evangelists quoted,
they must surely have been taken from that Evangelist. Therefore our Fourth Gospel, not necessarily
just as we have it now, not necessarily yet regarded
as canonical Scripture, but in recognisable shape, and
furnished with its remarkable prologue, already
existed in the year 125.

The Tübingen critics have an answer for this.
The writer of the *Philosophumena*, say they, mixes up
the deliverances of the founder of a school with those
of his followers,—what comes from Basileides or
Valentinus with what comes from disciples of their
school who lived long afterwards. The *he says* of the
quotation from the Fourth Gospel is really, therefore,
subjectless ; it does not mean Basileides in particular.

---

[1] *Philosophumena* vii. 22. We follow, for the passage in St.
John, the rendering of our version, although ἐρχόμενον probably
belongs to φῶς and not to ἄνθρωπον.   [2] John i. 9.

And of this *subjectless he says* the author of *Supernatural Religion*, following the German critics, makes a grand point. If Basileides is not meant, but only one of his school, then the quotation from the Fourth Gospel will not date from A.D. 125, but from some fifty years later, when no doubt the Gospel had appeared.

Now it is true that the author of the *Philosophumena* sometimes mixes up the opinions of the master of a school with those of his followers, so that it is difficult to distinguish between them. But if we take all doubtful cases of the kind and compare them with our present case, we shall find that it is not one of them. It is not true that here, where the name of Basileides has come just before, and where no mention of his son or of his disciples has intervened since, there is any such ambiguity as is found in other cases. It is not true that the author of the *Philosophumena* habitually wields the *subjectless he says* in the random manner alleged, with no other formula for quotation both from the master and from the followers. In general, he uses the formula *according to them* [1] when he quotes from the school, and the formula *he says* [2] when he gives the dicta of the master. And in this particular case he manifestly quotes the dicta of Basileides, and no one who had not a theory to serve would ever dream of doubting it. Basileides, therefore, about the year 125 of our era, had before him the Fourth Gospel. Schleiermacher talks wildly, no doubt, when in defiance of the tradition he claims for the Fourth Gospel a date earlier than that of the

---

[1] $\kappa\alpha\tau'$ $\alpha\vec{v}\tau\sigma\acute{v}s$.   [2] $\phi\eta\sigma\acute{\iota}$.

other three. But it is true that we happen to have
an earlier testimony to words which can be verified
as belonging certainly to the Fourth Gospel, than to
any words which can be verified as belonging certainly
to any one of the other three.

But this is not all the evidence afforded by the
Philosophumena. The first heresies described are those
of Oriental Gnostics, who preceded the Greek. The
line of heretics commences with the Naasseni and the
Peratæ, both of them " servants of the snake ; "—not
the Old Serpent, man's enemy, but " the Catholic
snake," the principle of true knowledge, who enables
his votaries to pass safely through the mutability and
corruption which comes of birth. The Naasseni are
the Ophites of Irenæus and Epiphanius. Their name
is taken from the Hebrew word for the Greek *ophis*,
a snake, and together with other Hebrew names in
the account of them indicates, what we might expect,
that as Jewish Christianity naturally preceded Greek
Christianity, so Jewish Gnosticism preceded Greek
Gnosticism. Moreover, the author of the *Philosophumena,* passing from this first batch of Gnostics to a
second, in which are Basileides and Valentinus, expressly calls this second batch of Gnostics *the subsequent ones.*[1] So we must take the Naasseni and the
Peratæ, whom the author of *Supernatural Religion*
dismisses in a line as " obscure sects towards the end
of the second century," we must take them as even
earlier than Basileides and the year 125.

---

[1] *Philos.* vi. 6. νυνὶ δὲ καὶ τῶν ἀκολούθων τὰς γνώμας οὐ
σιωπήσω.

These sects we find repeatedly using, in illustration of their doctrines, the Fourth Gospel. We do
not say that they use it as John's, or as canonical
Scripture. But they give sayings of Jesus which we
have in the Fourth Gospel and in no other, and they
give passages from the author's own prologue to the
Fourth Gospel. Both the Naasseni and the Peratæ
are quoted as using the opening verses of the prologue,
though with a punctuation for certain clauses which
is different from ours.[1] Both sects know of Jesus as
the door. "I am the door," one of them quotes him
as saying; the other, "I am the true gate."[2] The
Peratæ have the sentence, "As Moses lifted up the
serpent in the wilderness, even so must the Son of
Man be lifted up," with only one slight verbal change.[3]
With somewhat more of change they give the saying
to the woman of Samaria: "If thou hadst known,"
is their version, "who it is that asketh, thou wouldst
have asked of him and he would have given thee
living water springing up."[4] The Naasseni have,
without any alteration, the famous sentence to Nicodemus in the Fourth Gospel: "The Saviour hath
said, *That which is born of the flesh is flesh, and that
which is born of the spirit is spirit.*"[5]   Again, they

---

[1] ὃ γέγονεν is joined to ἐν αὐτῷ ζωή ἐστιν, not to οὐδὲ ἕν.
The Naasseni insert a δέ before γέγονεν. *Philos.* v. 8, 16.

[2] *Philos.* v. 8, 17.

[3] ὃν τρόπον καθὼς. *Philos.* v. 16 ; compare John iii. 14.

[4] *Philos.* v. 9. εἴρηκεν ὁ σωτήρ, Εἰ ᾔδεις τίς ἐστιν ὁ αἰτῶν, σὺ
ἂν ᾔτησας παρ' αὐτοῦ καὶ ἔδωκεν ἄν σοι πιεῖν ζῶν ὕδωρ ἀλλόμενον.
Compare John iv. 10.

[5] *Philos* v 7   Compare John iii. 6.

attribute to Jesus these words : "Except ye drink
my blood, and eat my flesh, ye shall not enter into
the kingdom of heaven. Howbeit, even if ye do
drink of the cup which I drink of, whither I go,
thither ye cannot enter."[1] A mixture, one must
surely confess,—a mixture, with alterations, of the
same sayings that we find in the sixth and thirteenth
chapters of St. John, and in the twentieth chapter of
St. Matthew.

Any fair person accustomed to weigh evidence,
and not having a theory to warp him, will allow
that from all this we have good grounds for believing
two things. First, that in the opening quarter of the
second century the Fourth Gospel, in some form or
other, already existed and was used. We find nothing
about its being John's, it is not called Scripture, its
letter is not yet sacred. It is used in a way which
shows that oral tradition, and written narratives by
other hands, might still exercise pressure upon its
account of Jesus, might enlarge its contents, or otherwise modify them. But the Gospel in some form or
other existed. Secondly, we make out that Baur
and Strauss go counter to at least the external
evidence, when they declare that all sayings of Jesus
appearing in the Fourth Gospel, and not appearing in
one of the Synoptics also, are late inventions and
spurious. The external evidence, at any rate, is

[1] *Philos.* v. 8.   ἐὰν μὴ πίνητέ μου τὸ αἷμα καὶ φάγητέ μου τὴν
σάρκα, οὐ μὴ εἰσέλθητε εἰς τὴν βασιλείαν τῶν οὐρανῶν. ἀλλὰ κἂν
πίητε, φησί, τὸ ποτήριον ὃ ἐγὼ πίνω, ὅπου ἐγὼ ὑπάγω, ἐκεῖ ὑμεῖς
εἰσελθεῖν οὐ δύνασθε.   Compare John vi. 53 ; xiii. 33 ; and
Matt. xx. 22.

against this being so. And this is the point which
mainly interests the reader of *Literature and Dogma*,
for in that book we assured him that the special
value of the sayings of Jesus in the Fourth Gospel
is, that they explain Jesus and the line really taken
by him. This they cannot do if they are spurious;
and here, therefore, is the centre of interest for us
in all these questions about the Fourth Gospel.
Not whether or no John wrote it, is for us the
grand point, but whether or no Jesus said it.

And that the sayings in the Fourth Gospel, at
least the chief and most impressive of them, are
genuine *logia* of Jesus, the external evidence goes to
prove with a force, really, of which what we have
hitherto said quite fails to give an adequate notion.
The Epistle to the Hebrews,—which undoubtedly
existed at the end of the first century, for it is so
much used by Clement of Rome that he has been
conjectured to be its author,—has the Johannine
phrase, "The shepherd of the sheep."[1] Probably
the Fourth Gospel did not yet exist when the
Epistle to the Hebrews was written; but what the
use of the phrase in the Epistle to the Hebrews
proves is, that the phrase was early current, and
does not, therefore, come from an inventor late in
the second century. Other phrases, connected with
this one, have also the strongest confirmation of their
authenticity. We have already seen how the earliest
Jewish Gnostics were familiar with the saying: *I am
the door*. Hegesippus, in the middle of the second

[1] Hebrews xiii. 20.

century, relates that the Jews asked James the Just:
"What is the door of Jesus?"[1] and it requires a very
vigorous and rigorous theory to make a man suppose
that the Jews were here thinking of something in the
Old Testament, and not of the saying of the Lord: *I
am the door*. We have the testimony of the Canon of
Muratori, that Hermas, the author of the *Pastor*, was
brother to Pius, Bishop of Rome; and that he wrote
his *Pastor* at Rome, while his brother Pius was sitting
in the episcopal chair of the church of that city,[2]—
that is, between the year 141 and the year 157. In
the *Pastor* we find it written, that *the new gate* was
manifested in the last days, "in order that they
which shall be saved might enter into the kingdom
of God by it;" and it is added: "Now the gate is
the Son of God."[3] The pseudo-Clementine Homilies
cannot be accurately dated; but from their mode of
quoting New Testament sayings and incidents,—
which is that of Justin, and never alleges the name
of a Gospel-writer,—we know that the work must
have been written before 170 and the age of Irenæus.
In the third Homily, Jesus is quoted as saying: "I
am the gate of life; he that entereth by me entereth
into life."[4] Presently, after the saying, *Come unto me
all that travail*, another (a Johannine) saying of Jesus
is quoted: "My sheep hear my voice."[5] Irenæus

---

[1] Euseb. *Hist. Eccles.* ii. 23.

[2] "In urbe Roma Hermas conscripsit, sedente cathedra urbis
Romæ ecclesiæ Pio episcopo fratre ejus."

[3] Hermæ *Pastor, Similitudo* ix. 12.

[4] *Clementis Romani quæ feruntur Homiliæ, Hom.* iii. 52.

[5] *Clementis Romani quæ feruntur Homiliæ, Hom.* iii. 52.

relies upon the authority of certain "elders, disciples of the Apostles;" and he says that his elders taught that in the Messianic kingdom the saints should have different habitations in proportion to the fruit borne by them, and confirmed this by quoting the Lord's saying: "In my Father's house are many mansions."[1]

Finally, every one has heard of the dispute about the Epistles of Ignatius, martyred in the year 115. Of his seven Epistles, mentioned by Eusebius, there exist a longer and a shorter recension;—the longer recension amplifying things much in the same way in which the later manuscripts used for our version of the Gospels have amplified, in the sixth chapter of the Fourth Gospel, Peter's confession of faith into *Thou art that Christ the Son of the living God*, from the original *Thou art the holy one of God* preserved by the Vatican and Sinaitic manuscripts. But a still shorter Syriac recension of the Epistles of Ignatius was found by Mr. Cureton, and this recension, besides, gives only three of the seven Epistles mentioned by Eusebius. We will not enter into the question whether the Syriac three do really annul the Greek seven; for our purpose it is sufficient to take the Syriac three only. For even in these three we have more than once the Johannine expression, *the prince of this world*.[2] We have: "The bread of God I want, which is Christ's flesh, and his blood I want for drink, which is love incorruptible." [3] We agree that we are not compelled

---

[1] Irenæus, *Adv. Hœreses*, v. 36.

[2] Ignatius, *Ad Ephesios* xvi. ; *Ad Romanos*, at the end.

[3] *Ad Romanos* vii. ἄρτον θεοῦ θέλω, ὅς ἐστιν σὰρξ Χριστοῦ,

to suppose that Ignatius took these expressions and
ideas from the Fourth Gospel; but that *the prince of
this world*, and *the bread which I will give is my flesh*, of
the Fourth Gospel, are expressions and ideas of Jesus,
and not inventions of a Greek literary artist after the
year 170, the employment of these ideas and expressions by Ignatius does compel us to suppose.

Again, Baur maintained that it was impossible to
produce testimony outside the Fourth Gospel to a
legend of any single Fourth Gospel miracle not common to it with the Synoptics. Soon afterwards the
conclusion of the pseudo-Clementine Homilies was
discovered; and in the nineteenth Homily, speaking
of sins of ignorance, the author says : "Our Master
being asked concerning the man afflicted from his
birth and who was restored to sight by him, whether
this man sinned or his parents, that he was born blind,
made answer : 'Neither this man sinned nor his
parents, but that the power of God should be made
manifest through him.'" [1] The miracle is clearly the
one recorded in the Fourth Gospel, and in the answer
of Jesus there is hardly the slightest verbal difference.

We may say, indeed, if we like, that the pseudo-
Clementine Homilies were composed in the third or
fourth century. We may say that not one word of
Ignatius is genuine, that Irenæus did not mean to

καὶ τὸ αἷμα αὐτοῦ θέλω πόμα, ὅ ἐστιν ἀγάπη ἄφθαρτος. The Greek
recensions, both the longer and the shorter, after θέλω add ἄρτον
οὐράνιον, ἄρτον ζωῆς.

[1] *Hom.* xix. 22 (Dressel's edition). οὔτε οὗτός τι ἥμαρτεν, οὔτε
οἱ γονεῖς αὐτοῦ, ἀλλ᾽ ἵνα δι᾽ αὐτοῦ φανερωθῇ ἡ δύναμις τοῦ θεοῦ.
Compare John ix. 2, 3.

quote his elders, or that he misquoted them ; we may
say that the author of the Epistle to the Hebrews
stumbled by chance on the expression *the great shepherd of the sheep ;* that Hermas, author of the *Pastor*,
was not brother to Pius, Bishop of Rome, and did not
write the *Pastor* during his brother's episcopate. All
this we may say if we like, and may bring many ingenious reasons to support it. But no plain man,
taking facts fairly, would ever say so ;—only some
professor with a theory to establish, a theory of vigour
and rigour.

But if the Johannine sayings are in great part
genuine, then a plain man will surely be disposed to
accept the tradition that the Fourth Gospel is supple-
mentary to the others, and that in John it had its
source. The sayings form a class distinct from the
sayings of the Synoptics. They must have come
from some one who had been with Jesus, and who
spoke with authority. Tradition says that they came
from John at Ephesus ; and the form of the Johannine
Gospel suits well enough, as we have seen, with this
tradition. To be sure, we have the famous argument
that the Fourth Gospel cannot have existed in the
time of Papias, between the years 130 and 140 of
our era, or Papias would have made mention of it ;
and if Papias had made mention of it, Eusebius,
from whom we get our knowledge of Papias,
would have quoted the mention. Eusebius declares,
says the author of *Supernatural Religion*, that he " will
carefully intimate " every early testimony to the
Christian Scriptures, both to the Scriptures received

and to the Scriptures disputed. But in the first place,
the words used by Eusebius do not mean : *I shall carefully intimate.*[1] They mean : *I shall be glad to indicate;
I shall think it an advantage to indicate.* And to suppose
that to even as much as is here promised Eusebius
would closely stick, because he had promised it, is to
know Eusebius very ill. Never, perhaps, was there
any writer who told us so much that was interesting,
and told it in so loose a fashion and with so little
stringency of method, as the good Bishop of Cæsarea.
In the second place, it is quite certain that another
Gospel, the Third, existed in some shape in the time
of Papias, for Marcion about the year 140 used it.
And yet on the subject of the Third Gospel, as well
as the Fourth, Papias as quoted by Eusebius is wholly
silent.

But then, again, there is the vigorous and rigorous theory of Professor Scholten that John never was
at Ephesus at all. If he had been, Papias and Hegesippus must have mentioned it; if they had mentioned
it, Irenæus and Eusebius must have quoted them to
that effect.[2] As if the very notoriety of John's resi-
dence at Ephesus would not have dispensed Irenæus
and Eusebius from adducing formal testimony to it,
and made them refer to it just in the way they do !
Here, again, we may be sure that no one, judging
evidence in a plain fashion, would ever have arrived

---

[1] See Eusebius, *Hist. Eccles.* iii. 3.   προΰργου ποιήσομαι ὑπο-
σημήνασθαι.

[2] See Dr. Scholten's treatise in the German translation, *Der
Apostel Johannes in Kleinasien* (Berlin 1872), pp. 24, 36.

at Dr. Scholten's conclusion; above all, no one of Dr. Scholten's great learning and ability. It is just an hypothesis for a man professorially bound to accomplish a feat of ingenuity, what the French call a *tour de force;*—to produce a new theory of vigour and rigour. We gladly make Professor Lightfoot a present of such foreign theories to put along with our home-grown theory of the One Primeval Language. The only distinction to be drawn, perhaps, is, that whereas the foreign theories, German or Dutch, come from having too much criticism, from an hypertrophy, as the doctors might say, of the critical organ; our British-born theory comes rather from not having criticism enough, from an absence of the critical organ altogether.

And now, in conclusion, for the internal evidence as to the Fourth Gospel.

CHAPTER VI.

THE FOURTH GOSPEL FROM WITHIN.

To any fair judge of evidence, the external evidence
is in favour of the belief that the Fourth Gospel had
its source in the Apostle John. But what is relied
on, as above all fatal to this belief, is the internal
evidence. The internal evidence is supposed to lead
us with overpowering force to the conclusion that the
Fourth Gospel is a fancy-piece by a Gnostically disposed Greek Christian, a consummate literary artist,
seeking to develop the Logos-idea, to cry up Greek
Christianity and to decry Jewish, and taking for
the governing idea of his composition the antithesis
between light and darkness. Everything in the Fourth
Gospel, we are told, is profoundly calculated in this
sense. So many miracles, and in such a graduation,
as were proper to bring out fully the contrast between
light and darkness, life and death, Greek willingness
to believe and Jewish hardness of heart, so many
miracles, and no more, does the Fourth Gospel assign
to Jesus. The whole history of the Last Supper and
of the Crucifixion is subtly manipulated to serve the
author's design. Admirable as is his art, however, he

betrays himself by his Christ, whose unlikeness to the
Christ of the Synoptics is too glaring. His Christ
"is a mere doctor; morality has disappeared, and
dogma has taken its place; for the sublime and pregnant discourses of the Sea of Galilee and the Mount
of Olives, we have the arid mysticism of the Alexandrian schools." So that the art of our Greek
Gnostic is, after all, not art of the highest character,
because it does not manage to conceal itself. It
allows the Tübingen critics to find it out, and by finding it out to pull the whole of the Fourth Gospel to
pieces, and to ruin utterly its historical character.

Now here, again, in what these critics say of the
internal evidence offered by the Fourth Gospel, the
external evidence in some respects makes it hard for
a plain man to follow them. The Gnostic author,
they say, governed by his idea of the antithesis
between light and darkness, assigns to Jesus no more
miracles than just what are required to bring out this
antithesis. Therefore the last two verses of the twentieth chapter, which speak of the "many other signs
which are not written in this book," are spurious.
Like the whole twenty-first chapter which follows,
they are a later addition by some one ignorant of the
artist's true design. Well, but in the seventh chapter
we find the Jewish people asking:[1] "When the
Christ comes, will he do more miracles than this
man does?" and in the sixth chapter it is implied[2]
that the miracles of Jesus were, as the Synoptics represent them, numerous. Did the artist forget himself

[1] Verse 31.   [2] Verse 2.

in these places; or is it the Tübingen critics who
have forgotten to tell us that in these places, too, the
text is spurious? In the eleventh chapter we have a
like oversight on the part of somebody, either the
artist or (which one would hardly have thought likely)
his German interpreters. The chief priests and Pharisees are, by some mistake, allowed to say: "This
man doeth many miracles."[1] In the twelfth chapter
matters are even worse; it is there said that the Jews
would not believe in Jesus "though he had done so
many miracles before them."[2] No doubt this is
spurious, and in omitting to tell us so the critics fail
a little in vigour and rigour. But, on the whole,
what admiration must we feel for the vigour and
rigour which in spite of these external difficulties can
see so far into a millstone, and find such treasures of
internal evidence there, as to be able to produce a
theory of the Fourth Gospel like Baur's?

The internal evidence, then, is what the rejectors
of the Fourth Gospel confidently rely on. But to us
the internal evidence seems to point by no means to
a speculative genius, a consummate artist, giving to
Christianity a new form of his own, adopting a certain
number of sayings and doings of the real Jesus from
the Synoptics, but inventing for Jesus whatever he
did not thus adopt. Much more it seems to us to
point to a sincere Christian, a man of literary talent
certainly and a Greek, but not a consummate artist;
having traditions from John, having, above all, *logia*
from John, sayings of the Lord, and combining and

[1] Verse 47.   [2] Verse 37.

presenting his materials in the way natural to him. The Evangelist's literary procedure is that of a Greek of ability, well versed in the philosophical speculation of his time, and having the resources of Greek style and composition at his command. But when one hears of a consummate artist, an idealising inventor, when one hears of a gifted writer arranging his hero's life for effect, and freely making discourses for him, one thinks of Plato. Now, the writer of the Fourth Gospel is no Plato. The redaction and composition of this Gospel show literary skill, and indicate a trained Greek as their author not a fisherman of Galilee. But it may be said with certainty, that a literary artist, capable of inventing the most striking of the sayings of Jesus to Nicodemus or to the woman of Samaria, would have also made his composition as a whole more flawless, more artistically perfect, than the Fourth Gospel actually is. Judged from an artist's point of view, it has blots and awkwardnesses which a master of imaginative invention would never have suffered his work to exhibit. Let us illustrate this by examples, taking, as our rule is, no case which is not clear, and where the plain reader may not be expected, if he will only take the trouble to look carefully for himself at the passages we quote, to follow us without doubt or difficulty.

II.

Our Evangelist has, we say, to place and plant records of Jesus supplied to him by John. But he

has to place them without a personal recollection of
the speakers and scenes, and without a Jew's instinct
for what, with such speakers and scenes, was possible
and probable. He combines and connects, but his
connection is often only exterior and apparent, not
real.

For example. No artist of Plato's quality would
have been satisfied with the connection in the discourse of Jesus reported at the end of the fourth
chapter, from the thirty-fifth verse to the thirty-
eighth : "Say not ye, There are yet four months,
and then cometh harvest! behold, I say unto you,
Lift up your eyes, and look on the fields, that they
are white already to harvest ; and he that reapeth
receiveth wages, and gathereth fruit unto life eternal,
that he that soweth and he that reapeth may
rejoice together. *For herein is that saying true: One
soweth and another reapeth. I sent you to reap that
whereon ye have bestowed no labour; other men have
laboured, and ye are entered into their labours.*" Surely
there are here two parts, of which that one which
we have given in italics has a motive quite different from the motive of the other which precedes
it. The motive of the first is the ripeness of the
harvest and the guerdon of the reapers. The motive
of the second is the admission of the disciples to reap
what they had not sown. Both have all the character
of genuine sayings of Jesus, but there is no real
connection between them, only they coincide in pair-
ing a sower with a reaper. Jesus did not make
continuous speeches, jointed and articulated after the

Greek fashion. He uttered pregnant sentences, gnomic sayings; and two sets of such sayings, quite distinct from each other, which were among the Greek editor's store of *logia*, we have here. But to this editor the continuous and jointed form of Greek discourse seemed the natural one; and therefore, caught by the verbal coincidence, he blends the two sets of sayings into one, and claps a *for* in between them to establish a connection. It is a matter of no great importance. The two *logia* of Jesus are safely there, and the real relation between them was sure to be brought out by time and scrutiny. It is only of importance as a gauge of the Evangelist's artistic faculty. A consummate artist, inventing for Jesus, could not have been satisfied with such a merely seeming and verbal connection.

More striking is the artistic failure at the beginning of the tenth chapter. We will remark, that on any supposition of a consummate artist and of perfect motiving, the mode of introducing all the lovely group of sayings about "the good shepherd" and "the door" is quite unaccountable. But let that pass, and let us look at the sayings themselves. Who can doubt that here, again, we have two separate sets of *logia* of Jesus :—one set which have *I am the good shepherd* for their centre, and another set which have for their centre *I am the door ;* and that our Evangelist has thrown the two together and confused them? Beautiful as are the sayings even when thus mixed up together, they are far more beautiful when disentangled. But the Evangelist had a doorkeeper

and a door and sheep in his first parable; and he
had another parable, in which was a "door of the
sheep." Catching again at an apparent connection,
he could not resist joining the two parables together,
and making one serve as the explanation of the
other.

To explain the first parable, and to go on all fours
with it, the second ought to run as follows: "I am
the door of the sheep. All that *climb up some other
way* are thieves and robbers; but the sheep *do not
hear* them. I am the door; by me if any man enter,
he is the shepherd of the sheep." The words in italics
must be substituted for the words now in the text of
our Gospel;[1] and Jesus must stand, not as the door
of salvation in general, but as the door by which to
enter is the sign of the true teacher. There can
be no doubt, however, that the words now in the text
are right, and that what is wrong is the connection
imposed on them. The seventh and ninth verses are
a *logion* quite distinct from what precedes and follows,
and ought to be entirely separated from it. Their
logion is: "I am the door of the sheep. I am the
door: by me if a man enter he shall be saved, and
shall go in and out and find pasture." The eighth
verse belongs to the first parable, the parable of the
shepherd; not to the parable of the door. It should
follow the fifth verse, and be followed by the tenth.

---

[1] See John x. 8, 9. Instead of ἦλθον πρὸ ἐμοῦ we must read
ἀναβαίνουσιν ἀλλαχόθεν, instead of ἤκουσαν we must read
ἀκούουσιν, and ποιμήν ἐστιν τῶν προβάτων instead of σωθήσεται
καὶ εἰσελεύσεται καὶ ἐξελεύσεται καὶ νομὴν εὑρήσει.

Jesus says of the sheep : " A stranger will they not follow, but will flee from him, for they know not the voice of strangers.   All that ever came before me are thieves and robbers, but the sheep did not hear them.   The thief cometh not but to steal and to kill and to destroy ; I am come that they might have life, and that they might have it more abundantly.   I am the good shepherd."

Piecing his *logia* together, seeking always a connection between them, the Evangelist did not see that he was here injuring his treasures by mixing them. But what are we to think of a consummate artist, inventing freely, and capable of producing, by free invention, such things as the most admirable of the sayings attributed to Jesus in the Fourth Gospel ;— what are we to think of such an artist, combining in cold blood his invented sayings of Jesus so ill, that any one with eyes in his head can detect a better combination for them ?

The reader, probably, will follow us without much difficulty here.   But certainly he will have no difficulty in following us if we take the last words of the fourteenth chapter, *Arise, let us go hence,* and assert that no consummate artist, no Plato, would ever have given us that.   Beyond all manner of doubt, Jesus never said in one connection : "As the Father gave me commandment, even so I do ; arise, let us go hence; I am the true vine, and my Father is the husbandman," and so on, without the least sign of rising or going away, but with the discourse continuing throughout three more chapters.   How the

Evangelist could have come to make him say it, is the question. Probably, with the commencement of the fifteenth chapter the writer passed to a fresh set of notes, containing another set of sayings of Jesus; and he marked the transition by inserting between the end of one set and the beginning of the next the words : " Arise, let us go hence." They were traditional words of Jesus, as we see from the " Rise, let us be going," [1] of St. Matthew; and the composer of the Fourth Gospel may have thought they would come in serviceably at this point. What he thought, we can only conjecture; but that no man freely inventing, not arranging and combining, and above all that no consummate artist, would ever have dreamed of placing those words at that point, we may affirm with the utmost confidence. Certainly there needed an imaginative intellect not less fine than Plato's to invent for Jesus such a saying as : " The hour cometh and now is, when the true worshippers shall worship the Father in spirit and in truth." But conceive a Plato ordering the march of his composition thus : "Arise, let us go hence ; I am the true vine, and my Father is the husbandman ! "

To the same category of defects of composition, inexplicable on the theory of a consummate artist freely inventing, but quite intelligible if we suppose a literary arranger sometimes embarrassed in dealing with his materials, for which he has the profoundest reverence, belong those curious jolts in the narrative which are occasioned, as we believe, by the author

[1] Matt. xxvi. 46.

having John's very words in his memory, and being
determined to preserve them. Such a jolt occurs in
introducing the dialogue with the woman of Samaria.
"Jesus, tired with his journey, sat *thus*[1] by the
well." Thus? how? There has not been a word to
tell us, and the expression as it stands is incongruous.
But the writer, probably, had in his mind John's own
words : "Jesus, tired with his journey, sat, *as I have
been telling you*, by the well;" and he could not for-
bear using them. The same formula appears in two
other places, and in both it probably is a relic of
John's own narrative. "He, lying *as I am telling you*
on Jesus' breast, saith unto him : Lord, who is it?"[2]
And again : "After these things, Jesus manifested
himself again to his disciples at the Sea of Tiberias ;
and he manifested himself *as I am going to tell you.*"[3]
In these two cases to preserve John's words does not
create any awkwardness ; but the writer still preserves them even when it does.

He preserves them, again, without duly adjusting
the context to them, in the forty-fourth verse of the
fourth chapter. "After the two days he departed
thence into Galilee. *For Jesus himself testified that a
prophet hath no honour in his own country.*" That was
a reason for staying away from Galilee, not for going
there. But the writer has John's words about the
testimony of Jesus in his mind, and hastens to give
them without preparing their way by saying: "And
this he did, notwithstanding his own testimony."
The embarrassed sentences about the return to Caper-

---

[1] οὕτως. John iv. 6.   [2] John xiii. 25.   [3] John xxi. 1.

naum, in the sixth chapter, owe their embarrassment, not improbably, to the same cause: to John's words sticking in the writer's memory, and not being properly fused by him with his own narrative.

In like manner, who can read without a shock of surprise, in the relation of the feeding of the five thousand among the hills beyond the Sea of Galilee, that abrupt and motiveless sentence: "Now the passover, the feast of the Jews, was nigh?"[1] The most fanciful and far-fetched explanations are offered. But who would not prefer the simple and natural explanation, that the words are a relic of John's original narrative which had been brought in by him to date his story; that they were fast lodged in our Evangelist's memory, and that he was loath to lose them? They are a little touch of detail, just like: "These things he said in the treasury as he taught in the temple;" or like: "It was then the feast of dedication at Jerusalem; it was winter, and Jesus walked in the temple in Solomon's porch."[2] They are exactly the expressions which a man telling a story would be likely to use; but our author preserves them in his regular composition, whether they suit the context or no. And an author such as we suppose our Evangelist to be was likely enough to do this; but a consummate artist, freely following his invention, does not do things thus negligently.

[1] John vi. 4.   [2] John viii. 20; x. 22.

III.

These are grounds for the improbability of Baur's theory which suggest themselves from a defectiveness of artistic construction in the Fourth Gospel. Other grounds of improbability are suggested by defects of philosophical grasp. It is alleged that our Evangelist improves on the Jesus of the Synoptics, invents his profoundest things for him. But it can be made as clear as light, to any unbiassed and attentive reader, that this wonderful inventor does not always himself fully understand the very things he is supposed to be inventing, obscures them by unintelligent comment on them. One instance of this we have given in *Literature and Dogma.* Jesus says: "If any man thirst, let him come unto me and drink." [1] Then, with a reminiscence of a passage in the Second Isaiah he adds: "He that believeth in me, as the Scripture saith, there shall flow out of his belly rivers of living water." Who can doubt that Jesus here meant to say that the believer's faith,—the faith of the follower of Christ,—should be an eternal source of refreshment? But the Evangelist proceeds to comment on the saying of Jesus, and to give what is, in his view, the proper explanation of it. And the explanation he gives is as follows: "But this spake he of the Spirit (*Pneuma*) which they that believe on him should receive ; for the Holy Spirit was not yet given, because Jesus was not yet glorified." Nothing can

[1] John vii. 37-39. Compare Isaiah lviii. 11.

be more natural than that a Christian of the first or second century should wish to date all comforts of the Spirit from after the famous effusion of *Pneuma* subsequent to Christ's death. But surely the true sense of this saying of Jesus is clear; and it is clear, too, that it is a narrowing and marring of his words to put our Evangelist's mechanical construction upon them. The reporter who puts it fails to grasp the words fully, deals with them unintelligently. And how incredible that a writer should fail to seize rightly the clear sense of a saying invented by himself!

Again, take a like case from the eighteenth chapter. Jesus had said of his disciples: "None of them is lost but the son of perdition." [1] Then comes the arrest, and the speech of Jesus to the band which arrested him: "I have told you that I am he; if therefore ye seek me, let these go their way." [2] He gives up himself, but puts his disciples out of danger. His speech is just what we might have expected; but instantly our Evangelist adds that he made it "*in order that the saying might be fulfilled which he spake: Of them whom Thou hast given me have I lost none.*" Can anything be more clear than that the two sayings have nothing at all to do with one another, and that it is a mechanical and narrowing application of the first-mentioned saying which makes it lead up to the second? In the first, eternal salvation is the theme; in the second, safety from a passing danger. And could the free and profound inventor of the first say-

[1] John xvii. 12.   [2] John xviii. 5-9.

ing have been so caught by the surfaces of things, as
to make it the mere prophecy of the second ?

Jesus over the heads of all his reporters !—this idea is
for us our constant guide in reading the Gospels.   It
is, we are convinced, the only safe one.   But the
Tübingen professors reverse the idea, and say that in
the Fourth Gospel it is the reporter who is over the
head of Jesus.   In the concluding chapters of this
Gospel the philosophical author, they say, so frames
the discourse of Jesus that his resurrection is presented "as an internal phenomenon continually being
accomplished in the believer's consciousness."   No
doubt this view of the resurrection is indicated in the
Fourth Gospel, as it is indicated also by St. Paul.
But the question is, does it come from Jesus himself,
or was it invented by the more spiritual among his
followers to give a profounder sense to the physical
miracle of his resurrection ?   We confine ourselves at
present to the Fourth Gospel, and we say : "True,
the resurrection of Christ is there suggested as a
phenomenon accomplishing itself in the believer's consciousness.   The idea is a profound one ; it needed a
great spirit to conceive it.   If the author of the
Fourth Gospel conceived it, we may allow that he
carries the significance of the resurrection higher than
the Synoptics carry it; higher than the Jesus of the
Synoptics visibly carries it.   But if he is the author
of this idea, he will present it firmly and clearly.   If
he presents it confusedly, then he probably got the
idea from Jesus, and did not quite understand it."
How in fact, does he present it ?

All through the discourses of Jesus in the Fourth
Gospel, the attentive reader may perceive that there
are certain fundamental themes which serve as *nuclei*
or centres, appearing repeatedly and in several connections, with a form sometimes shorter, sometimes
more expanded. It is of great importance to a right
understanding of the Fourth Gospel that we should
discover in such cases the primitive theme, the
original *logion* of Jesus. Now this, or at least the
nearest approach to it, will in general be given by
the theme in its shorter and less expanded form.
Very likely Jesus may himself have used a theme on
several occasions, and himself have sometimes given
to it a more expanded form ; still, from the theme in
its simplest and shortest form, we probably get our
best clue to what was said by Jesus.

Two such primitive themes in the long discourse
of Jesus before his arrest are these :—*I go to the
Father,*[1] and : *I go away, and come again to you.*[2] Let
us add to these two a third : *A little while and ye see
me not, and again a little while, and ye shall see me.*[3]
These three sayings appear and reappear, they come
in different connections, they take forms somewhat
varying. But they are primitive themes ; they give
us probably the nearest approach possible to the
words actually uttered by Jesus.

[1] ὑπάγω πρὸς τὸν πατέρα, John xvi. 17. This is probably
the primitive theme ; we have also : ὑπάγω πρὸς τὸν πέμψαντά
με (vii. 33, and xvi. 5); πρὸς τὸν πατέρα μου ὑπάγω (xvi. 10);
ἀφίημι τὸν κόσμον καὶ πορεύομαι πρὸς τὸν πατέρα (xvi. 28).

[2] ὑπάγω καὶ ἔρχομαι πρὸς ὑμᾶς. John xiv. 28.

[3] μικρόν, καὶ οὐ θεωρεῖτέ με, καὶ πάλιν μικρόν, καὶ ὄψεσθέ με.
John xvi. 17.

This, then, is what we have :—*I go to the Father. I go, and come again to you. A little while and ye see me not, and again a little while and ye shall see me.* Now it is alleged, and truly, that the Fourth Gospel suggests a view of the resurrection of Jesus as an internal phenomenon accomplishing itself in the believer's consciousness. The basis on which this allegation must rest is supplied by the three *logia* which we have quoted.

But the three *logia* lend themselves either to the announcement of a physical resurrection or to the announcement of a spiritual resurrection. Everything depends on their context and connection. And by piecing things together, by putting these *logia* in the front, by connecting them immediately with other *logia* given by our Evangelist, by dropping out things he inserts between, we can get at a resurrection announced by Jesus which is clearly spiritual. "I go to the Father; I go, and come again to you. A little while and ye see me not, and again a little while and ye shall see me. I will not leave you desolate, I will come to you. Yet a little while and the world seeth me no more; but ye see me, because I live and ye shall live." A disciple here asks how it is that they shall see him, and that the world shall not. Jesus answers : "If a man love me, he will keep my word; and my Father will love him, and we will come to him, and make our abode with him. Let not your heart be troubled, neither let it be afraid. I go away and come again to you."[1] And this

[1] John xvi. 10; xiv. 28; xvi. 16; xiv. 18, 19, 23, 27, 28.

resurrection of Jesus is connected by him with the
coming of the Paraclete, the Spirit of truth, the
new light, who should bring out in the hearts of the
disciples the real significance of Jesus and of what
he had said.[1]

Thus placed and connected, the primitive ἔρχομαι,
the *I come again* of Jesus, gives us, no doubt, the resurrection of Christ as "an internal phenomenon accomplishing itself in the believer's consciousness." It
gives it us as being this in Jesus Christ's own view
and prediction of it. The same idea is preserved for
us by the First Epistle of St. John, an Epistle which
cannot well have been written by our Evangelist, its
style is so unlike his. But the Epistle deals with
many of the ideas dealt with by our Gospel ; and it
presents the *abiding* in Jesus, and in his Father, as
the accomplishment of the promise of eternal life
made by Jesus to his followers.[2]

The idea is so fruitful and profound an one, that if
our Evangelist had ever fairly grasped it, still more
if he had conceived and invented it, he could hardly
have so dealt with it as to leave us in doubt whether
he himself entertained it or not. He could no more
do this than Paul could have left us in doubt whether
he himself entertained his great idea of the *necrosis*,—
of the dying and resurrection of Jesus accomplishing
themselves in this life in the believer's personal experience. The mind which, while fully accepting the
physical miracle of the resurrection, could yet discern
that the phenomenon, to be made fruitful, must have

[1] John xiv. 23-26.   [2] 1 John ii. 24, 25.

a moral and a spiritual significance given to it,—
such a mind would certainly have been impressed
deeply by such an idea, and have had it distinct and
firm. But our Evangelist so arranges his materials
as to make the reference of ἔρχομαι and ὄψεσθέ to a
spiritual resurrection very dubious, to overlay it with
other things, and to obscure it; while their reference
to a physical resurrection is brought out distinctly.
" In my Father's house are many mansions; if it were
not so, I would have told you. For I go to prepare
a place for you, and if I go, I will prepare a place for
you. I come again, and will take you unto myself,
that where I am ye may be also."[1] There can be
little doubt that the primitive theme of ἔρχομαι πρὸς
ὑμᾶς, *I come again unto you*, is here so used and connected as to make it point decisively to a physical
resurrection. And this key for the whole strain being
once given, the impression left by that other primitive
theme, μικρὸν καὶ ὄψεσθέ με, *a little while and ye shall
see me*, is in the main an impression to the same
effect. " A little while and ye see me not,
and again a little while and ye shall see me. Ye
shall weep and lament; ye shall be sorrowful, but
your sorrow shall be turned into joy. Ye have sorrow
now; but I will see you again, and your heart shall
rejoice, and your joy no man shall take from you."[2]
Here the whole wording and connection are such that
it seems clear the commentators have rightly interpreted the mind of the Evangelist, when they make

[1] John xiv. 2, 3. The text followed is that of the Vatican
manuscript. [2] John xvi. 19, 20, 22.

this passage, and the theme μικρὸν καὶ ὄψεσθέ με, a prophecy of the approaching physical resurrection of Jesus.

Must we then suppose that to a spiritual resurrection such sayings as the three primitive themes we have quoted do not really refer, but may be made to signify it only as a secondary and after meaning, brought in for purposes of edification, and originally hidden in them, perhaps, for those purposes? This, no doubt, will be the character assigned to the words both by official theology and by popular religion. To us, however, it seems certain that to a spiritual resurrection the words primarily and really point, and that our Evangelist has obscured their true scope. For him, as for Christendom long after him, Jesus Christ's physical resurrection stood, and could not but stand, a phenomenon fixed, immense, overpowering ; a central sun attracting everything to it. But experience slowly and inevitably reveals that phenomena of this kind do not actually happen. Romulus does not mount into heaven, Epimenides does not awake, Arthur does not return. Their adoring followers think they do, think they have promised it ;—but they do not, have not. We have, then, to account for the firm belief of the first Christians in the physical resurrection of Jesus, when this resurrection did not actually happen. We can only account for it from things really said by Jesus, which led them to expect it. That Jesus was a fanatic, expecting and foretelling his own physical resurrection, —deceived like his followers, but so filling them with his own belief that it prevailed and triumphed with them when he died,—is an explanation which the whole account we have of Jesus, read seriously, shows to be idle. His disciples were misled, therefore, by something Jesus did actually say, which had not really the sense that he should physically rise from the dead, but which was capable of lending itself to this sense, and which his disciples misunderstood and imagined to convey it.

And, indeed, they themselves tell us that this is what actually happened. Only, what was in truth *misunderstanding,* they call *understanding.* They themselves tell us that they unconsciously exercised a creative pressure, long after the time when they were going about with Jesus and hearing him, on sayings and doings of their Master. "When he was risen from the dead," they tell us, after recording one of his prophetic speeches, "*his disciples remembered that he had said this.*"[1] Even if one had not known beforehand that from the nature of the case it was impossible for the records of Jesus in our Gospels to have been notes taken down day by day, as by a Saint-Simon or a Boswell, here is an Evangelist himself telling us in so many words that they were not. "These things understood not his disciples at the first," he tells us again, after relating an incident which afforded a remarkable fulfilment of prophecy, "but when Jesus was glorified *then remembered they* that these things were written of him, and *that they had done these things unto him.*"[2] They recorded,

[1] John ii. 22.   [2] John xii. 16.

then, the sayings of Jesus about his resurrection
long after they had been uttered, and when the
belief in his physical resurrection was firmly fixed in
their minds.

But even after his death, " as yet," they tell us of
themselves, " they knew not the Scripture that he
must rise again from the dead." [1] This affords the
most irrefragable proof that the sayings of Jesus
about his resurrection cannot originally have been
just what our Gospels report ; that these sayings, as
they now come to us, must have been somewhat
moulded and accentuated by the belief in the resurrection.   If Jesus had simply said to the Twelve the
very words our Gospels report him to have said, the
Twelve could have been in no ignorance at all of
"the Scripture that he must rise again from the
dead," and in no doubt at all that they were to count
on his rising.   "He took unto him the Twelve, and
said unto them : Behold we go up to Jerusalem, and
all things that are written by the prophets concerning
the Son of Man shall be accomplished.   For he shall
be delivered unto the Gentiles, and shall be mocked
and spitefully entreated, and spitted on ; and they
shall scourge him, and put him to death ; and the
third day he shall rise again." [2]   It is in vain that
the Evangelist adds : "And they understood none of
these things, and this saying was hid from them,
neither knew they the things which were spoken." [3]
If Jesus had spoken merely as he is here reported, if
what he said had had no peculiar connection and sig-

[1] John xx. 9.   [2] Luke xviii. 31-33.   [3] Luke xviii. 34.

nificance given to it by something else which he also
said, if he had simply thus laid down in black and
white, as the phrase is, his death and resurrection as
going to happen, the disciples could not have helped
understanding him. It would have been quite impossible for them to make that astounding declaration,
which yet is evidently the plain truth, that even up
to the days which followed his death, "as yet they
knew not the Scripture that he must rise again from
the dead." Something was no doubt said by Jesus
not unlike what the Evangelist reports, something
which easily adapted itself to the character of a
simple and literal prophecy of the resurrection, when
that event had, as was believed, taken place. But
the precise speech put into the mouth of Jesus, that
speech and nothing more at all upon the subject, he
cannot have uttered.

The Third Gospel, which reports the speech just
quoted, is the Gospel which guides us to the discovery of what Jesus can have originally and actually
said about his rising again on the third day. He was
told that if he did not leave Jerusalem Herod would
put him to death. He made answer: "Go ye and
tell that fox, Behold, I cast out devils and I do cures
to-day and to-morrow, *and the third day I shall be
perfected.*" [1] Having for ever before his mind the
humble and suffering Servant of our fifty-third
chapter of Isaiah, and labouring for ever to substitute this in his disciples' minds as the Messias-ideal,

---

[1] τῇ τρίτῃ ἡμέρᾳ τελειοῦμαι. Luke xiii. 32. The text of the
Vatican manuscript is followed.

instead of the brilliant and triumphant Conqueror of
popular Jewish religion, Jesus here, beyond all doubt,
following the prophet,[1] spoke of his violent and
ignominious end as his perfection and victory. That
violent end he, as was natural, could plainly foresee
and often predicted. Here he predicts it in this
wise : "On the third day I shall be perfected."
What made him say : *On the third day ?* [2] We know
how he loved to possess himself of locutions of the
prophets and to use them. For instance, in that
well-known saying, "Take my yoke upon you, and
learn of me that I am mild and lowly in heart, and
ye shall find rest unto your souls," the concluding
phrase, *Ye shall find rest unto your souls*, is a reminiscence of Jeremiah.[3] And in like manner his phrase,
On the third day I shall be perfected, is a reminiscence
of the prophet Hosea. Amid the ruin of Israel, in
the eighth century before Christ, Hosea had said :
"Come and let us return unto the Eternal ; for he
hath torn and he will heal us ; *after two days will he
revive us, on the third day we shall rise again.*"[4] "We

---

[1] See Isaiah liii. 10, 11. "It pleased the Eternal to bruise
him, he hath put him to grief. When he hath made his soul an
offering for sin, he shall see his seed, he shall prolong his days,
and the pleasure of the Eternal shall prosper in his hand ; he
shall see of the travail of his soul and be satisfied."

[2] He talked, also, of his rising from the dead, without the
addition of the words *on the third day*, or *in three days*. See
Mark ix. 9, 10, where the disciples are represented as puzzled,
and as συνζητοῦντες τί ἐστιν τὸ ἐκ νεκρῶν ἀναστῆναι.

[3] Jeremiah vi. 16.

[4] Hosea vi. 1, 2. In the Greek Bible of the Seventy the
words are : ἐν τῇ ἡμέρᾳ τῇ τρίτῃ ἀναστησόμεθα, *on the third day*

shall be restored *presently*," Hosea means : and, " I
shall be perfected *presently*," is what Jesus means.

Here we lay our finger, almost certainly, upon the
veritable foundation for the belief that Jesus had
himself announced he would rise from the dead on
the third day. Let us seek to combine the scattered
logia, transposed, some of them to the time after his
death, which in a certain degree enable us, through
the cloud of his disciples' inadequate apprehension
and of legend and marvel, to follow the line of light
of the Divine Master.

The root of everything with Jesus is, as we just
now said, the effort, the eternal effort, to substitute
as the Messias-ideal in the mind of his followers the
Servant, mild and stricken, for the regal and venge-
ance-working Root of David. And he knew, that
the victory of this right Messias-ideal his own death,
and that only, could found. "O fools and slow of
heart at taking in all that the prophets have spoken !
must not the Messiah suffer these things, and enter
into his glory ? Behold, we go up to Jerusalem, and
the Son of Man shall be betrayed unto the chief
priests and scribes, and they shall deliver him to the
Gentiles to crucify. Nevertheless, I do cures to-day
and to-morrow; we must work the works of him that
sent me while it is day, the night cometh when no
man can work. I must walk to-day and to-morrow
and the day following, and the third day I shall be

we shall rise again. Compare this with the words in Luke : τῇ
τρίτῃ ἡμέρᾳ τελειοῦμαι ; and again, τῇ ἡμέρᾳ τῇ τρίτῃ ἀναστήσεται.
Luke xiii. 32, and xviii. 33.

perfected. All things written by the prophets for
the Son of Man shall be accomplished. He shall be
delivered to the Gentiles, and mocked and outraged
and spit upon; and they shall scourge him and put
him to death; and the third day he shall rise again.
Except a grain of corn fall and die, it abideth alone;
but if it die, it bringeth forth much fruit. As Moses
lifted up the serpent in the wilderness, so must the
Son of Man be lifted up; and I, if I be lifted up from
the earth, will draw all men unto me."[1]

Yes, *thus it was written that the Christ should suffer,
and* should *rise from the dead the third day.*[2] Inevitably the disciples materialised it all, wrested it all
into a prophesying of bodily reappearance and miracle.
And they did also with the words: "I go to the
Father; I go away and come again to you; a little
while and ye see me not, and again a little while and
ye shall see me." To these words the disciples gave
a turn, they placed them in a connection, to suit the
belief which alone, after the death of Jesus, could
reassure and console them;—the belief in his speedy
resuscitation and bodily reappearance on earth, his
temporary re-withdrawal and ascension into heaven,
to be followed soon by his triumphal bodily advent
to avenge and judge.

[1] Luke xxiv. 25, 26; Matt. xx. 18, 19; Luke xiii. 32; John
ix. 4 (in the Vatican manuscript); Luke xiii. 33, and xviii.
31-33; John iii. 14, xii. 24, and xii. 32. For *mocking*, see
Psalm xxii. 7; for *scourging* and *spitting*, see Isaiah l. 6. The
traits used by prophet and psalmist in delineating the stricken
Servant are to be conceived as always vividly present to the
mind of Jesus.

[2] Luke xxiv. 46. The Vatican manuscript is followed.

It could not but be so. *It was written that in his name should be preached to all nations repentance unto remission of sins;*[1] and only in this way could the work proceed. Only in this way, through profound misapprehension, through many crude hopes, under the stimulus of many illusions, could the method and secret, and something of the temper and sweet reason and balance of Jesus, be carried to the world. Only thus, through natural and national *extra-belief* reinforcing their real love to their Master and zeal to propagate his doctrine, could the weak arm of the disciples acquire energy enough to hold aloft the word of life, set up the kingdom of Christ, found the true Israel, and bring in everlasting righteousness.

But the promises and predictions of their Master were, nevertheless, not what they fancied. He had said : "Ye shall see me again, because I live and ye shall live ; if a man keep my saying he shall never see death. If ye love me and keep my words, I will come unto you and make my abode with you."[2] They construed this into : "Ye shall see me, because I will come again and take you unto myself to reign in the kingdom of the saints in the New Jerusalem."[3] The genuine promise of Jesus was the promise of a spiritual resurrection ; and this promise his disciples misapprehended, misconnected, and obscured. Only on this supposition is. even their own version of the history intelligible.

Far, therefore, from inventing the idea of the

---

[1] Luke xxiv. 47.   [2] John xiv. 19 ; viii. 51 ; xiv. 23.
[3] John xiv. 3 ; Matt. xix. 28.

resurrection as an internal phenomenon accomplishing itself in the believer's consciousness, the author
of the Fourth Gospel transmits the idea, indeed, but
obscures it.   He saved it for us, as in that second
harvest of the *logia* of Jesus he saves for us so much
which is precious.   He saved it from being lost, and
added it to the indications which survive for us of
the line truly taken by Jesus.   But from his very
mode of delivering it, we can see that he is not an
artist inventing it, but a reporter transmitting it
imperfectly.

IV.

Furthermore, Baur's theory of the artistic Greek
Christian inventing all things with a deep-laid design
to damage Jewish Christianity, and to exalt Christ's
divinity, is upset by the admission of things contrary
to the alleged design.   A free inventor, inventing with
the express aim of doing damage to Jewish Christianity,
would never have made Jesus say : "*Salvation is of the
Jews.*" [1]   A free inventor, inventing to impair the
credit of Peter and the original Apostles, would never
have made Peter enter the sepulchre first, or throw
himself into the sea, or receive the charge : *Feed my
sheep.*[2]   A free inventor, inventing from a zeal to
establish the dogma of Christ's personal divinity,
would never have made Jesus give the turn to his
calling himself *the Son of God* which is given in the
tenth chapter, when Jesus appeals to the authority of
the Old Testament for those being called *Gods* to

[1] John iv. 22.   [2] John xx. 6 ; xxi. 7, 16.

whom the word of God came, and asks why he, then,
may not call himself the Son of God?[1] "Why haggle
about words and definitions in these matters?" he in
fact asks ; " all you can say about them is approximate
merely." But the whole question of the dogma of
Christ's personal divinity is a question of words and
definitions in the very sphere where Jesus pronounced
such questions to be vain. All these things may be
ingeniously explained by Baur now that they stand
there in the Gospel, and challenge explanation from
him. But, had Baur's theory of the Fourth Gospel
been true, they would never have stood there for him
to explain.

Finally, the theory of the consummate artist
implies that the Fourth Gospel is a work proceeding
from the imaginative intellect. But we deny (and
here, too, the attentive reader will not, we think, find
it hard to follow us), we deny that the Fourth Gospel
has the character of a work proceeding from the
imaginative intellect. It has the character of a work
proceeding from the soul. It is profoundly and
solemnly religious. It is the work of a man who, we
grant, like all the reporters of Jesus, understood him
but imperfectly ; who gives us much which is not
Jesus, much which comes from himself and his time,
much which is addition and legend. But it is the
work of a man who gives us this seriously and in
good faith, and whose attitude of mind is not that of
a freely inventing artist. He is too much subjugated
by Jesus to feel free to deal with him in this fashion,

[1] John x. 34-36.

as a mouthpiece for his own purposes and his own ideas. He does sometimes attribute his own ideas to Jesus, but unconsciously ; and when he does, we can perceive that he is doing so. If he had attempted it consciously all through his Gospel, he would have produced something quite different from what we have, and we should easily have found him out. He would have given us a work where Jesus would have spoken, all through, as he now speaks from the sixteenth verse of the third chapter to the twenty-first, —a passage in which our theological lecturer evidently lectures us through the mouth of Jesus. For his mind did not hold itself so easily and independently towards Jesus,—no serious Christian's did or could,—as to suffer him to play freely with Jesus, to throw himself into his character, to use him as a vehicle for saying, but in character and with verisimilitude, whatever the user wanted to convey. Plato might do this with Socrates, but the author of the Fourth Gospel could not do it with Jesus. And the safe analogy to take, in considering what for our Evangelist in dealing with his subject could and did happen, is the analogy not of Plato but of Paul.

The old school of apologists was fond of urging that the Fourth Gospel could only have been the work of one of the original chief Apostles, it is so excellent. Baur had no difficulty in replying to this, that in Paul we have a Christian who had probably never even seen Jesus, who was certainly not one of the original chief Apostles ; and who yet is at least equal to any of them, and whose productions surpass theirs.   Why, therefore, may we not have, he argued, in the author of the Fourth Gospel a second gifted outsider like Paul, but whose name has remained unknown, because it was essential for his purpose that it should do so, and that his work should point mysteriously to the Apostle John as its author?

Certainly we, for our part, have no backwardness in admitting that outside of the primitive circle of the Apostles there might arise Christians, like Paul, capable of making invaluable contributions to the New Testament.   But we think that none of them could have done what Baur's theory supposes the author of the Fourth Gospel to have done.   St. Paul himself could not have done it.   The attitude of their minds towards Christianity and its Founder was too earnest and reverential to allow it.   When Paul quotes a *logion* like that exquisite *logion* quoted by him at Miletus, but not found in any one of our Evangelists, *It is more blessed to give than to receive*,[1] he is clearly quoting Jesus, as he says he is, not artistically inventing for Jesus, not original.   His manner when he is original we know, and it is quite different :—*I try not mine own self (for I am conscious of nothing to myself, yet am I not hereby justified), but he that trieth me is the Lord*.[2]   Imagine St. Paul sitting down to recommend the dogma of justification by faith, through means of a fancy Gospel composed of *logia* invented for Jesus, and suiting his character as *It is more blessed to give than to receive* suits his character !   Paul could not have done it; any sound

---

[1] Acts xx. 35.   [2] 1 Cor. iv. 3, 4.

critic will feel that he could not. So, too, with the
author of the Fourth Gospel. Where the *logia* are
suited to the character of Jesus, they come from
Jesus. Where they are not, there we have the theological lecturer merely expanding a theme given by
Jesus, developing or thinking that he develops it.
But he remains himself in doing so. To possess
himself as a dramatist of the personage of Jesus, to
fix his sentiments and his whole part for him, as
would be implied by inventing the fundamental
themes instead of merely developing them, he would
not have felt himself free.

The question for us will be, then : *Are* there fundamental themes discoverable in the Fourth Gospel, and
peculiar to it, which are quite according to the character of Jesus, and to his recognised habit of speech ?
Because, if there are, our Evangelist has not invented
them, but they must come from Jesus.

Now that there are *logia* peculiar to the Fourth
Gospel, which entirely suit the character and the
habit of Jesus as these are known to us from the
Synoptics, we can hardly conceive any one denying ;
except, indeed, he have a thesis to make good which
constrains him.   Let us bring forward a few of them :
" *My kingdom is not of this world.—In my Father's
house are many mansions.—The good shepherd giveth his
life for the sheep.—Other men laboured, and ye are entered
into their labours.—The night cometh, when no man can
work.—The servant abideth not in the house for ever, the
son abideth for ever.—A woman when she is in travail
hath sorrow because her hour is come ; but as soon as she*

*is delivered of the child she remembereth no more her
anguish, for joy that a man is born into the world.*"[1]
Except a man be, we say, in the clutches of some
tyrannous theory, we can hardly conceive his denying that these *logia* are as perfectly and naturally in
the character of Jesus as are the most characteristic
logia found in the Synoptics, such as : *Render Cæsar's
things to Cæsar, and God's things to God ; or, No man
having put his hand to the plough, and looking back, is
fit for the kingdom of God ; or, Foxes have holes and the
birds of the air have nests, but the Son of Man hath not
where to lay his head.*[2]

V.

Yet the Tübingen professors and our Liberal newspapers must surely have something to go upon, when
they declare that the Jesus of the Fourth Gospel
speaks quite differently from the Jesus of the Synoptics, and propound their theory of the Gnostic philosopher inventing, with profoundly calculated art, his
fancy Gospel.   No doubt they have.   Jesus never can
have delivered the long connected harangues, or entered into the formal development of his own nature
and dignity, or made the endless repetitions, which
are in the Fourth Gospel attributed to him.   All this
is so absolutely contrary to his manner, which we
know both from his sayings in the Synoptics and from
express testimony, that every rule of criticism bids us
suspect it.   The sayings in the Synoptics will be pre-

---

[1] John xiv. 2 ; x. 11 ; iv. 38 ; ix. 4 ; viii. 35 ; xvi. 21.
[2] Matt. xxii. 21 ; Luke ix. 62 ; Matt. viii. 20.

sent to every one's mind; two or three of them, indeed, characteristic specimens, we have just brought
forward. Justin's famous sentence has been again
and again quoted: "Short and concise are the sayings
that came from him, for he was no sophist, but his
word was power divine." [1] And equally express is
the following testimony, perhaps not so familiar,
given by the pseudo-Clementine Homilies: "His wont
was to make concise utterances touching the things of
concernment to the truth." [2] A better description of
the style of his sayings could hardly be given. They
were *concise utterances touching the things of concernment
to the truth.* The character of his parabolic and figured
teaching tells its own story, and needs no describing;
what distinguished his direct teaching was this its
gnomic or maxim-like character.

These gnomic sayings of Jesus the Evangelists had
to place in their narrative, and to provide for them a
setting and a connection. The Greek editor of the
Fourth Gospel provides this setting in a very different
style from the Synoptics, just because he is a Greek,
a man of literary skill and philosophical acquirements,
and with an intellect trained in the Greek fashion.
The gnomic form of teaching was not unknown in
Greek philosophy, but at the Christian era this form
was to Greek writers an archaic one. They had come
to dovetail their thoughts into each other, join their
sentences by articulations, and so frame their matter

---

[1] βραχεῖς δὲ καὶ σύντομοι παρ' αὐτοῦ λόγοι γεγόνασιν, οὐ γὰρ
σοφιστὴς ὑπῆρχεν, ἀλλὰ δύναμις θεοῦ ὁ λόγος αὐτοῦ ἦν.

[2] *Hom.* xvii. 6.   περὶ τῶν τῇ ἀληθείᾳ διαφερόντων συντόμως τὰς
ἀποφάσεις 'ποιεῖτο.

into one continuous discourse, just as we do now with ours; indeed it is from the Greeks that the world has learnt to do it. And in this Greek fashion the Fourth Gospel was composed.

The author of the First Gospel, on the other hand, was a Hebrew; and to a Semitic people the gnomic form, the delivering one's thought in detached sentences, was always natural. To the author of the First Gospel, therefore, this form was natural, as it was to Jesus himself. And there can be no doubt, that the *form* of the utterances of Jesus the First Gospel reproduces more faithfully than the Fourth. Still, it is incredible that the Sermon on the Mount, or the prediction in the twenty-fourth chapter of the final troubles and of the coming of the Son of Man, should have been spoken straight off by Jesus just as they are given in the First Gospel. No sane critic will maintain that they were. In both passages the Evangelist has had a number of *logia* to place, and has given to them, as well as he could, a setting and connection in accordance with their subject-matter, and with the occasion to which he knew them generally to belong. But he, for the most part, gives them their setting and connection simply by juxtaposing them; whereas the editor of the Fourth Gospel, having to give this setting and connection to his *logia*, gives it by articulating them. Therefore he changes the look of the *logia* which he reports more than either of the three Synoptics changes it. He less faithfully reproduces the fashion in which each separate *logion* was originally said by Jesus.

Furthermore, the editor of the Fourth Gospel had
to deal with a second harvest of *logia*, gathered from
John after the first harvest of sayings had been reaped,
and had made men eager for what might yet remain.
The mass of the first harvest was sure to consist of the
more simple and practical sayings of the Lord.   In
the nature of things it was probable that this should
be so ; from the character of the first reporters it was
certain that it would be so.   There remained a number of *logia* somewhat profounder and more obscure,
more over the heads of the disciples than the simple
logia, and therefore less interesting to them.   Of this
kind were sayings in which Jesus spoke of his relation
to the Father, and of life and death in the sense that
he loved to give to those words.   "*I came forth from
the Father.—The Father sent me.—My doctrine is not
mine, but his that sent me.—The Father is greater than I.
—I can of mine own self do nothing.—The Son can of
himself do nothing, but only what he seeth the Father doing.
—He that hateth me hateth my Father also.—I and the
Father are one.—He that believeth on me hath everlasting
life.—If a man keep my word he shall never see death.—
I am the resurrection and the life.*" [1]

That sayings of this kind were from the first known
and reported is proved by our finding in the First
Gospel such a *logion* as the following :—" All things
are delivered unto me by my Father, and no one
knoweth the Son but the Father, neither knoweth
any one the Father save the Son, and he to whom-

[1] John xvi. 27 ; xvii. 8, 18, 21, 23, 25 ; vii. 16 ; xiv. 28 ;
v. 30 ; v. 19 ; xv. 23 ; x. 30 ; vi. 47 ; viii. 51 ; xi. 25.

soever the Son will reveal him."[1] We need hardly
say that here the Tübingen professors smell *Tendenz*,
and affirm that a piece of Greek Gnosticism must
have got thrust into the Gospel of the old Jewish
Evangelist. But these solutions we do not permit
to ourselves ; and the *logion*, famous in the history of
the criticism of the New Testament text, is given by
two out of the three Synoptics,—by St. Luke[2] as
well as by St. Matthew. We receive it, therefore,
as giving clear proof of the existence of sayings of
the Lord on that class of subjects which the *logia* of
the Fourth Gospel touch so frequently, subjects such
as the relation of Jesus to the Father, and the like.
Indeed, we do not see how Jesus could have pursued
his design of transforming the popular ideal of the
Messiah, who was described by prophecy as the Son
of God, without touching on such subjects. And it
is in part to the prominence in the Fourth Gospel of
sayings on them that the tradition points, when it so
early distinguishes this as the *spiritual* Gospel.[3]

To the Greek editor of John's materials these *logia*
naturally assumed a transcendent interest and importance. He was plainly a man, as we have said,
of philosophical acquirements. True, religion was
uppermost with him, not speculation. The tone of
his prologue, though from Jesus such a performance
is inconceivable, is profoundly religious, penetrated
by the grace and truth of the religion of Jesus.
Whoever compares it with what remains to us of the

---

[1] Matt. xi. 27.   [2] Luke x. 22.
[3] πνευματικὸν εὐαγγέλιον. See Eusebius, *Hist. Eccles.* vi. 14.

great Greek Gnostics, of Basileides or Valentinus,
will feel that the difference between them and the
writer of the Fourth Gospel lies here : that while
they are above all men of speculative thought, he is
above all a man of religion. Still, in this world of
speculative thought he had lived, in this world of
ceaseless questions, as Tertullian says : " *Unde malum
et quare, et unde homo et quomodo, et unde Deus ?*—
whence and why is evil, and whence and how is man,
and whence is God ?" Such questions had in his
eyes an infinite interest and importance : sayings of
Jesus which bore upon them could not but rivet
and fascinate his mind. In his redaction of John's
materials we see that he cannot make too much of
such *logia.* He returns to them again and again, and
avails himself of every occasion for re-introducing
them.

Well, then, to charge the gnomic form of his
fundamental themes, the sayings of Jesus, and to
connect these into an articulated and flowing discourse, was a rule, as we have seen, of our Evangelist's
redaction, and of itself necessitated a considerable
change in his primitive data. A yet further change
was caused by affection for certain themes, leading
him to present these themes again and again, slightly
varied. Moreover, in his whole redaction, in his
presentment of sayings of Jesus as well as of incidents
in his life, he laboured, in spite of his superiority to
the Synoptics in literary skill and in philosophical
thought, under one disadvantage. He had the disadvantage of a foreigner who presents manners,

locutions, localities, not his own, but alien to him.
He could not be warned by that instinct which perpetually, on points of detail, keeps a native straight,
and makes him feel certain things to be improbable
and impossible.

We have seen that the internal evidence, to be
drawn from the Gospel itself, contradicts Baur's
theory of the consummate artist, at the end of the
second century, freely inventing it all.   But the
internal evidence suits very well with the supposition
of a Greek Christian editing a second harvest, for
which the materials were furnished by John, of
sayings and doings of the Lord, arranging them in
his own fashion, and giving to the *logia* an inter-
dependence and connection which originally they had
not; moreover, amplifying and repeating certain *logia*,
and making developments from them.   Now, the tradition gives us John, in Asia, supplying the materials
of this second harvest, but not himself editing them.
If another edited them in Asia, for the benefit of the
Asiatic Churches, this other was surely a Greek
Christian ; and if a Greek Christian edited them, he
was likely to proceed in the way alleged, and of
which the Gospel bears, surely, strong marks.

For according to all the rules, we will not say of
criticism, but of common sense,—according to all
rules of probability, and of speakers speaking in
character, and not violently and unaccountably
deserting it,—can anything be more incredible than
that Jesus should have actually spoken to Nicodemus,
or John the Baptist to a disciple, the latter part of

the speeches attributed to them in the third chapter of our Gospel? Let us take first the speech to Nicodemus. It is probable that the real end of the dialogue is to be found in the tenth verse: "Art thou Israel's teacher, and knowest not these things?" But our Evangelist had two other *logia* of Jesus: "We speak that we do know, and testify that we have seen, and ye receive not our testimony;"[1] and, "If I tell you earthly things and ye believe not, how shall ye believe if I tell you heavenly things?"[2] which admitted of being placed in this connection. So here he places them. This, we say, is probable; but what is certain is, that Jesus did not speak the verse which follows these two *logia*, the thirteenth: "And no man hath ascended up into heaven save he that came down from heaven, the Son of Man." That is a variation on a primitive theme of Jesus, *I am the bread that came down from Heaven*,[3] inserted here by our theological lecturer, because he knew it was a theme dwelt upon by Jesus and thought that he saw here a natural place for it. A genuine *logion* of Jesus follows, bearing every mark of being still quite or almost in its original form, but woven into this context by our lecturer, and owing its connection with what precedes simply to his conjunction *and:* "As Moses lifted up the serpent in the wilderness, so must the Son of Man be lifted up, that whosoever believeth on him may have everlasting life." Then enters the theological lecturer, and continues (one may almost say) lecturing in his own proper person

[1] John iii. 11.   [2] John iii. 12.   [3] John vi. 41.

till the end of the speech, from the sixteenth verse to
the twenty-first.   For who, that has studied the
sayings of Jesus well, can ever believe that Jesus
said : "For God so loved the world that he gave
his only-begotten Son, to the end that whosoever
believeth in him should have everlasting life," [1] and
the rest?   Our Evangelist does not, however, in
these verses, think he is inventing ; for he is going
all the time upon three primitive themes of Jesus :
*He that believeth on me hath everlasting life ; I came not
to judge the world, but to save the world ; I am come a
light into the world, that whosoever believeth on me should
not abide in darkness.*[2]   On these genuine *logia* he is
going, and he merely amplifies and repeats them ;
developing them, in his own judgment, naturally,
and as it was to be supposed Jesus himself did.

Let us now pass to the speech of John the Baptist,
at the end of the same chapter.   The real sayings
assigned to John the Baptist by our Evangelist's
tradition ended, one can hardly doubt, with the words :
"He must increase, but I must decrease."[3]   The rest,
down to the end of the thirty-sixth verse, is our
theological lecturer.   That criticism only which sees
no impossibility in Jesus having spoken the sixteenth
verse of this chapter will see no impossibility in John
the Baptist's having spoken the thirty-sixth.   But
again our Evangelist is not inventing, but developing.
He has certain genuine *logia* of Jesus as his basis, the
chief of them being that which we have already

---

[1] The text of the Vatican manuscript is followed.
[2] John xii. 47 ; vi. 47 ; xii. 46.   [3] John iii. 30.

quoted : " He that believeth on me hath everlasting
life." [1]   He has these *logia* with several variations of
phrase, indicating that they were used more than
once, in more connections than one, perhaps by more
than one speaker. The speech of John the Baptist
seems to him a connection eminently proper for them.
The Baptist's real words appear to him to imply their
adoption and addition ; it appears to him natural and
certain that the Baptist adopted and added them.
So we come to have John the Baptist saying : " He
that believeth on the Son hath everlasting life ; but
he that believeth not the Son hath not life, but the
wrath of God abideth on him." [2]

All that is said of " the dogmatic mysticism, and
artificial, prolix discourses " of the Fourth Gospel, all
the complaints of its substituting " for the sublime
and pregnant discourses of the Sea of Galilee and the
Mount of Olives the arid mysticism of the schools of
Alexandria," will be found, we think, so far as they
are just, to be best met by the supposition of a Greek
editor connecting, repeating, and amplifying themes
of Jesus ; not by the supposition of a consummate
artist inventing the whole Gospel.   The kernel of the
work, the fundamental themes of Jesus, we maintain
to be no "arid mysticism" at all, but to be in profound
unison with " the sublime and pregnant discourses of
the Sea of Galilee and the Mount of Olives."   And

---

[1] John vi. 47.   The true sense is given by Jesus in a *logion*
quoted v. 24 ; but the theme itself, in its most concise and
authentic form, is probably the verse at vi. 47, in the reading of
the Vatican manuscript, which omits *on me*, and has simply, ὁ
πιστεύων ἔχει ζωὴν αἰώνιον.   [2] John iii. 36.

we do not see who was capable of uttering them but
Jesus.   Unless our Evangelist invented them, we do
not see from whom he can have got them, except
from Jesus ; and, indeed, it is not even contended
that he got them from any one else.   But it is contended, in defiance of all the tradition, that he himself
invented them.   But to us it seems incredible, even
on grounds of literary criticism solely, that the man
who was such a consummate artist as to invent for
Jesus the first part of his conversation with Nicodemus should have followed it up by the second.
It seems incredible, again, that a dramatic genius
capable of inventing for John the Baptist : " He that
hath the bride is the bridegroom, but the friend of
the bridegroom, who standeth and heareth him, re-
joiceth greatly because of the bridegroom's voice ;
this my joy therefore is fulfilled," [1]—it seems incredible that such a genius should have finished the
Baptist's speech by making him say : " He that
believeth not the Son shall not see life, but the wrath
of God abideth on him." [2]   And the question, whether
this is incredible or no, we would cheerfully consent
to submit to the judgment of any competent tribunal ;
only the judges constituting the tribunal ought not
to be the professors of the theological faculties of
Germany, but Germans like Lessing, Herder, and
Goethe.

It is certain that what is theological lecture in the
speeches of Jesus comes not from him but from his
editor.   But a treasure of *logia* remains, which have

[1] John iii. 29.   [2] John iii. 36.

all the characters of genuine sayings of Jesus, and
which are invaluable as indicating the line really taken
by him. The *bread of life*, the *true vine*, the *good shepherd*, the *light of the world*, are all of them images from
the Old Testament, such as the hearers of Jesus were
familiar with and gladly heard, such as philosophers
like Philo were at that time copiously employing for
their allegorical theology, such as Jesus himself loved
naturally and used instinctively, and such as he could
and did make admirably helpful to his main design.
That design was, it cannot be too often repeated, to
change the popular Messias-ideal ; and what stroke
towards such an end could be at once more happy
and more characteristic of Jesus than when, for example, calling himself *the light of the world*,[1] he in a
moment identified for his followers his ideal of mildness and self-renouncement with the famous world-
light of Messianic prophecy : "It is a small thing
that thou shouldest be my servant to raise up the
tribes of Jacob, and to restore the preserved of Israel:
I will also give thee for *a light of the Gentiles, that my
salvation may be unto the ends of the earth ?*"[2]   Strokes
like these belong essentially to Jesus, and it is an unsound criticism which can think of assigning them to
our theological lecturer.

Many, too, of the objections brought against *logia*
of the Fourth Gospel are frivolous, and merely show
the bringer's want of imagination. It is objected
that Jesus cannot have said : "As Moses lifted up
the serpent in the wilderness, so shall the Son of

---

[1] John viii. 12.   [2] Isaiah xlix. 6.

Man be lifted up,"[1] because he could not have foreseen
the manner of his own death.   But he fixed on the
most miserable kind of death as his fitting and sure
climax; and Plato, following up a supposed sufferer
to his climax of misery, fixes, we shall find, upon the
very same :—"Finally," says he, "we will suppose
him *crucified*."[2]   It is objected that Jesus cannot
have said to his disciples things like : *He that eateth
me shall live by me*,[3] because the disciples were certain
to misunderstand them, and he would not have said
things they must misunderstand.   This is a most
extraordinary objection.   One can account for it
only by the strong reluctance of mankind to recognise
the gulf between every great spirit and themselves.
To this day, whoever reads a controversy about the
Real Presence, will find Christians,—and learned
Christians,—misapprehending the words of Jesus
about eating him, even after he himself has supplied
the plain explanation of them,[4] as totally as did the
Jews; will find the Christian theologians stumbling
and fumbling, just like the Jewish theologians, in
their gross, dark, narrow materialism.   Half of what
any great spirit says is sure to be misapprehended by
his hearers; much more than half of what Jesus said
was sure to be misapprehended by his disciples.   If
he talked to them at all, he could not but talk to
them as he did.   And if he talked to them as he did,
taking their language about God, the Messiah, bread
from heaven, life and death, and translating it into

[1] John iii. 14.   [2] Plato, *Gorgias*, cap. xxviii.
[3] John vi. 57.   [4] John vi. 63.

that of his higher ideal, they could not but misunderstand him. Yet he could not but talk to them, and
they could not but reap some benefit from it. What
Christianity has done up to this time is the measure
of the benefit which Jesus, even imperfectly apprehended, could produce ; and that benefit has been
something immense. But such are the necessary
conditions on which a great spirit speaks to those who
hear his word. They understand him imperfectly ;
nevertheless, they appropriate what they can of him,
and get helped along by it somehow.

Let us look closer at the very *logion*, the famous
logion, last quoted, and observe how in itself it is an
entirely probable saying of Jesus, and how its improbability all comes from its editor's treatment of it.
The *logion* is exactly what we call a primitive theme,
a nucleus. Our Evangelist composed, of course, his
sixth chapter with the institution of the Last Supper
full in his view, and with the words, *This is my body*,
This is my blood, ever present to his thoughts. But
he had anterior incidents and words to go upon. He
had a story from John, how the Jews, with the
multitude's faith in miracles and desire to get them
worked for its benefit, had required Jesus, as the
alleged "prophet like unto Moses," to feed them
miraculously as Moses did. Was it not written in
the Scriptures : "He gave them bread from heaven
to eat ?"[1] Our Evangelist, we say, had a tradition
from John of sayings and answers which this demand
of the Jews had called forth. Jesus had said :

[1] Ps lxxviii. 24.

"Labour not for the meat that perisheth, but for the meat that endureth unto everlasting life."[1] He had said : "Not Moses gave you the bread from heaven, but my Father giveth you the true bread from heaven."[2] "Give us then this bread,"[3] was the Jews' rejoinder. Jesus had answered : "He that believeth hath everlasting life; he that heareth my word, and believeth him that sent me, hath everlasting life. I am the bread of life ! I am the bread that came down from heaven ! He that cometh to me shall never hunger, and he that believeth on me shall never thirst ! Not as your fathers did eat manna in the wilderness and are dead ; he that eateth this bread shall live for ever."[4] The Jews, with their keen sensuousness, were familiar with the image of God's word as something to feed on, something good to eat and pleasant to taste. It is written in the Psalms : "How sweet are thy words unto my taste, yea, sweeter than honey unto my mouth !"[5] But they exclaimed, when Jesus called himself the bread from heaven : "Is not this Jesus the son of Joseph, whose father and mother we know ? how saith he that *I am come down from heaven ?* how can he give us his flesh to eat ?"[6] Then Jesus had answered : "As the living Father sent me, and I live by the Father, so he that eateth me, he also shall live by me."[7]

These we may take as the primitive themes out of which our Evangelist's sixth chapter is built up.

[1] John vi. 27.   [2] John vi. 32.   [3] John vi. 34.
[4] John vi. 41, 47 (compare v. 24), 48, 58, and 49.
[5] Ps. cxix. 103.   [6] John vi. 42, 52.   [7] John vi. 57.

Other genuine *logia* are worked into it. But they
are worked into it ; they are not its essential elements.
Most probably, too, the primitive themes were several
times reiterated by Jesus, not without some variation.
But we shall hardly err if we take the primitive
themes above given, as our nearest possible approach
to what Jesus and his interlocutors did actually say.
And this substratum being committed to our combining and amplifying Greek editor, how natural and
explicable becomes the apparition, in the chapter, of
those sayings which now stagger every serious critic !
It is almost inconceivable, if one thinks of it, that
Jesus should have actually said in the conversation
in question : "Except ye eat the flesh of the Son of
Man and drink his blood, ye have no life in your-
selves ; he that eateth my flesh and drinketh my
blood hath everlasting life, and I will raise him up
in the last day ; for my flesh is meat indeed, and my
blood is drink indeed."[1] But it is perfectly conceivable that he should have said, the image of the bread
from heaven being once started : *"I am the bread of
life ! he that eateth me shall live by me !"*[2] and that

[1] John vi. 53-55.

[2] John vi. 48, 57. For the current conception of the word
of God as a bread of life, see Jesus himself quoting Deuteronomy
(viii. 3) in Matt. iv. 4 : "Man shall not live by bread alone,
but by every word that proceedeth out of the mouth of God ; "
and see, too, Philo, in his *Sacrarum Legum Allegoriæ* (Mangey's
edit. vol. i. p. 120) : ὁρᾷς τῆς ψυχῆς τροφὴν οἵα ἐστίν ; λόγος θεοῦ
συνεχής, ἐοικὼς δρόσῳ, κ. τ. λ. Only it is to be observed, in
general, that while an allegorising theologian, such as Philo,
uses images of this kind like a pedant, Jesus uses them like a
poet.

our editor being such a man as we suppose, and
having the words of institution of the Last Supper
swaying his mind, should by his mode of combining,
reiterating and developing these primitive themes,
when he had them to place, have turned them into
such speeches of Jesus as now puzzle us.

For, again, it is almost inconceivable that Jesus
should have really said : "For the bread of God is
he *that cometh down from heaven*, and that giveth life
unto the world ;" or that he should have said : "*I
am come down from heaven*, not to do mine own will,
but the will of him that sent me."[1] But it is entirely
natural that our editor, having such primitive themes
of Jesus as : "I am the bread that came down from
heaven ! I am the bread of life ! I came not to do
mine own will, but the will of him that sent me !"[2]
should have combined them and developed them
in the way he does.   It is almost inconceivable that
after saying, "It is written in the prophets : *And
they shall be all taught of God !* Every one that heareth
and learneth from the Father cometh unto me,"—
Jesus should have subjoined the remark : "Not that
any man hath seen the Father, save he who is from
God ; he hath seen the Father."[3] An addition of
this kind is inconceivable from Jesus, because both
the matter and the manner of it are the clean opposite
of his.   But it was in entire conformity with our
theological lecturer's notion and style, after giving
the genuine *logia* of Jesus, to complete and guard

---

[1] John vi. 33, 38.   [2] John vi. 41, 48, 38.
[3] John vi. 45, 46.

the sense of them, as he fancied, by the amplifying clauses.

VI.

We might go through the Fourth Gospel chapter by chapter, and endeavour to assign to each and all of the *logia* in it their right character,—to determine what in them is probably Jesus, and what is the combining, repeating, and expanding Greek editor. But this would be foreign to our object. We seek, not to produce a complete work of ingenious criticism on the Bible, or on any one document in it, but to help readers, sick of popular and conventional theology, and resolved to take the Bible for nothing but what it really is,—to help such readers to see what the Bible really is, and how very much, seen as it really is, it concerns them. So we sought to show that the Old Testament is really a majestic homage to the grandeur of righteousness, or conduct, and a sublime witness to its necessity; while the New Testament, again, is really an incomparable elucidation by Jesus Christ of what righteousness in fact and in truth is. And there can be no question that books of which this is the real character do concern men vitally. So, again, we seek to show that of Jesus Christ's incomparable elucidation of what righteousness is, several main elements are really to be found in the Fourth Gospel. In that case it urgently concerns people to study the Fourth Gospel, instead of tossing it aside as a Gnostic forgery, crammed with "the arid mysticism of the schools of Alexandria."

But to lead men to study it, and to clear out of their way objections which might for ever prevent their studying it, is our aim ; when we have accomplished this, we have accomplished as much as we intend.

But to restore perfectly the Jesus of the Fourth Gospel, or indeed of any Gospel, is impossible. The data are insufficient, and the alteration, often important though perhaps verbally slight, which his sayings have undergone from the pressure of other minds upon them, is too considerable. Our restoration must frequently be conjectural, and we may be wrong in our conjectures. We do not pretend that we could establish as clear and certain our criticism of every passage, or nearly every passage, in the Fourth Gospel, supposing we were to go through it with our reader. And even if we could save him from one or two mistakes by not merely giving him the guiding ideas with which to read the Gospel for himself, but by going through it with him, our object is not to make as faultless a critic of him as possible, but to keep him in contact with a book which will do him good, and to make him study it for himself. If he thinks it spurious, he is not likely to study it ; but we try to show him that it is full of genuine things, and to give him the guiding ideas by which to account for the things that made the charge of spuriousness seem plausible, and by which to extricate the things that are genuine.

Nor let this be esteemed a slight assistance, or the abandoning him to uncertainty. What is uncertain, what a reader may frequently not determine right,

and what we might not determine right if we came
to help him, is the occasion on which each particular
saying was uttered and the connection to which it
belongs.　But the main doubt as to the Gospel's
genuineness arose from the occasion assigned and
the connection given by our *Evangelist* to his stock
of "Sayings of the Lord."　Now, we show that his
circumstances and literary procedure were such that
the occasion and connection imposed by him on his
logia are not to be trusted.　We may be tempted to
try and restore the right occasion and connection,
and in this work there must necessarily be some uncertainty.　But if we stop quite short of this, if we
simply set aside our Evangelist's combinations as
untrustworthy, then we leave to the *logia* of Jesus
in the Fourth Gospel,—those of them which are not
manifestly theological developments and exercita-
tions by our lecturer,—the character of maxim-like,
isolated sayings, complete in themselves.　Now, the
teaching of Jesus, as of the nation and race to which
he belonged, really had in general this character.
His deliverances were "concise utterances touching
the things of concernment to the truth."　And for
practical use among Christians it is in this way,—as
maxims, detached sayings,—that they are in fact
generally employed; and it is when they are employed in this way that their practical usefulness is
greatest.　As single sayings the mind ruminates
them, turns them over and over, feeds upon them.
For a critical curiosity, then, we may not yet have
done enough, when we have established that instead

of taking the sayings of Jesus in that connection wherein the Fourth Gospel places them, it is far safer to take them as detached sayings. But for the practical use of the contents of the Fourth Gospel we have by this means done very much.

Jesus, no doubt, did not in his discourse deliver sentences articulated in the Greek fashion one to another. He delivered sentences juxtaposed in the Semitic fashion one to another. Because in the Fourth Gospel his sentences are articulated in the Greek fashion, those sentences have been confidently pronounced not to be sayings of Jesus. But the *logion* of Jesus is there; and often, in order to get at it, we have only to drop the Greek editor's conjunctions. For instance; suppose we take the sayings which form the speech of Jesus at the end of the twelfth chapter, from the forty-fourth verse to the fiftieth. As a connected speech Jesus did not deliver those sayings; our Evangelist has made them into one speech for him. But drop the conjunctions and the connecting clauses, and there is not a *logion* there to offend, singly, even a jealous criticism; there is not one which does not show the characteristic and satisfying mark of Jesus.

Our great point, then, as to the Fourth Gospel is this: the Evangelist is a combiner, not an inventor. It is his forms of connecting and articulating which obscure the gnomic character of the sayings of the Lord in this Gospel; get rid of those forms, and the gnomic and genuine character reappears. Our Evangelist had a number of *logia* to plant. He did not,

he could not, know their true connection; and the
connection he imposes on them is not to be depended
upon. Often we, studying quietly his work as it
lies before us complete, can perceive a better connection for certain *logia* than that which he has
devised for them. Almost certainly, the last half
of the fourteenth verse and the first half of the
fifteenth, in the tenth chapter, have their right
place not where we now read them but in the
twenty-seventh verse of the same chapter. The
twenty-seventh verse should run : " My sheep hear
my voice, and I know them, and they know me, as
the Father knoweth me, and I know the Father ;
and they follow me." The thirtieth verse of the
same chapter ("I and the Father are one") has
almost certainly its right place, not where it stands,
but side by side with the *logion* in the fourteenth
chapter, "He that hath seen me hath seen the
Father,"[1] and in a similar connection. Almost certainly the fourteenth verse of the twentieth chapter,
"He that receiveth whomsoever I send receiveth me,
and he that receiveth me receiveth him that sent me,"
is misplaced where it stands, and should go with the
sixteenth verse of the fifteenth chapter, the eighteenth
verse of the seventeenth, and the twenty-first of the
twentieth,[2] and in a similar connection. Almost certainly the four verses from the twenty-second to the

---

[1] John xiv. 9.

[2] "I have appointed you that ye should go and bring forth
fruit, and that your fruit should remain." "As Thou sentest
me into the world, so send I them into the world." "As my
Father hath sent me, even so send I you."

twenty-fifth, in the fifteenth chapter, belong to a connection such as that in the eighth chapter, were said
to the Jews not to the Apostles, and are a mere un-
seasonable repetition, put by our Evangelist into the
mouth of Jesus speaking to his disciples, of things
which he had previously said to the Jews. But we
can never be absolutely sure of finding the real
original connection for any *logion* of this kind; the
safe thing is to distrust our Evangelist's connection,
and to take the *logia* singly. Even where they have
a dramatic propriety and beauty as joined together
by our Evangelist, it is often very questionable
whether Jesus thus joined them, whether we are
not more on the trace of Jesus when we take them
singly. Nothing can well be finer or more impressive than the speech formed by the series of *logia*[1]
attributed to Jesus after Andrew tells him of the
Greeks desiring to see him. But it is highly improbable that Jesus did actually thus deliver these
logia as a series, and in one speech, and on one
occasion; although we may grant every *logion* in the
series to be in itself authentic, and of the very highest
value.

Now, it is wonderful how the likelihood of our
having as the substance of the Fourth Gospel genuine
sayings of Jesus will be found to gain, and the un-
likelihood of it to dwindle, the moment we come to
disregard our Evangelist's combinations, and to sup-
press his repetitions and lecturings. Let us take the
series of chapters against which so much of objection

[1] John xii. 23-26.

has been brought, the series from the twelfth chapter
to the end of the seventeenth. They form almost
one continuous speech, and most certainly they were
not spoken as such. They contain, also, repetitions
which Jesus, to judge from everything that we know
of his manner, cannot have made, and some things
which he cannot have said at all. It is easy to see
this, and to reject the whole series of chapters as
unauthentic. But a little attention will show us a
number of primitive themes, or *nuclei*, on which our
Evangelist is operating; and that these themes,—to
judge, again, from everything that we know of the
manner of Jesus,—have all the marks of being
authentic. And we may with profit try to get back
to what Jesus can have actually said; only we must
be careful, in attempting this, to distinguish between
what is certain, and what can only be called probable.

For example. The governing word of our series
of chapters is certainly the word ὑπάγω, *I go away.*
And the chapters have their reason for existence,
certainly, in a development by Jesus of this governing word. And that development is: συμφέρει ἵνα
ἀπέλθω,[1]—*It is expedient that I depart.* And the form
of this development is certainly twofold at least:
συμφέρει ἐμοί, συμφέρει ὑμῖν,—*It is expedient for me, It
is expedient for you.* It is expedient for *me*, because I
go to the Father.[2] It is expedient for *you*, because
the Paraclete's coming to you depends on my going
from you.[3] This, we say, seems certain. And to us
it seems probable that there is also a third develop-

[1] John xvi. 7.   [2] John xiv. 28.   [3] John xvi. 7.

ment given by Jesus to his *I go away;* and that this
development is : συμφέρει τῷ κόσμῳ,—*It is expedient
for the world.* We find this third development in the
words of Jesus : "Ye shall weep and lament, but the
world shall rejoice; ye shall be sorrowful, but your
sorrow shall be turned into joy. A woman when she
is in travail hath sorrow, because her hour is come ;
but as soon as she is delivered of the child she remembereth no more her anguish, for joy that a man
is born into the world." [1] Combined as our Evangelist combines them, these words appear to mean, no
doubt, that the world, the wicked world, shall exult
in the sufferings and death of Jesus ; and so the commentators take them. But we cannot help thinking,
that, as Jesus spoke them, they were words to be
classed with the texts: " I am come a light into the
world, that whoso believeth on me should not abide
in darkness : " " A light to lighten the Gentiles ; "
"One flock, one shepherd." [2] We believe that they
really mean, not, *The world shall exult at my death,* but,
My death is good for the world as well as for you and me;
and that they are a third and admirable development
given to the ground-motive of our chapters, ὑπάγω.
This we believe ; and perhaps if we were in a professor's chair at Tübingen, we should say that we
could and did demonstrate it. But being what we
are, we say that it is not demonstrable, indeed, nor
yet with such overwhelming probability in its favour
as to seem certain ;—the evidence is not such as to
admit of its being either the one or the other. But

[1] John xvi. 20, 21.   [2] John xii. 46 ; Luke ii. 32 ; John x. 16.

we say that it is probable ; and that it has so much
to recommend it that we ourselves believe it.

That Jesus, however, uttered a great deal of what
is attributed to him in the series of chapters from the
twelfth to the seventeenth, that he gave the primitive
themes which are the basis of them, that the combination of the themes is the Evangelist's, and that
by the Evangelist Jesus is made to repeat himself
over and over again, to connect things as he never
connected them, and to say things which he never
said, we regard as so probable that it becomes certain.
For the primitive themes are in the characteristic
manner of Jesus, and we do not see from whom else
they can have proceeded. The combination, repetition, and development of the themes are in the characteristic manner of the Evangelist.

The governing word of the chapters under review
has been just now mentioned. In a former part of
our argument, we had occasion to single out one or
two of their primitive themes. Besides these, which
we showed to be the nucleus of sayings delivering
Jesus Christ's own real doctrine about his own resurrection, there is the parable of the heavenly house
with its many mansions, a parable which is the Evangelist's authentic nucleus for unauthentic combinations
and developments favourable to the popular doctrine
of the resurrection.[1] There is the parable of the vine
and the branches, illustrating that primitive theme of
Jesus : *Abide in me and I in you.*[2] There are the new

---

[1] John xiv. 2, 3 ; compared with xvi. 22, and xvii. 24.
[2] John xv. 4.

commandment; the promise of the Paraclete; the promise that the disciples' requests should be heard; the exhortation not to fear the world's hatred; the prayer for the disciples; the sayings of Jesus about his glory; the sayings about his relation to the Father. All of these have their primitive theme or themes; all of them are connected, introduced and reintroduced, and more or less developed by our Evangelist. Now, if the reader simply takes all the sayings belonging to each theme, and puts them together, he will do what is very conducive both to a right enjoyment of this series of chapters, and to a right criticism of them. On the one hand, he will bring out the beauty and significance of the genuine sayings of Jesus; on the other, he will bring out how much is evidently repetition, serving to introduce our Evangelist's developments. We should like our reader to distribute under the heads or themes indicated all the sayings for each theme, and then to judge them for himself. We will, however, taking one or two themes not hitherto touched by us, show him at least how true it is that by the process we recommend both objects are served : the right enjoyment of our Evangelist's materials, and the right criticism of them.

First, as to the enjoyment of what our Evangelist has, in these chapters, saved for us. We will simply put together the scattered *logia* about the new commandment, making the subject begin where it naturally does begin, with the sayings of Jesus after he has washed the disciples' feet at the Last Supper.

" Know ye what I have done unto you ? Ye call me
Master and Lord, and ye say well, for so I am. If I
then, your Master and Lord, have washed your feet,
ye also ought to wash one another's feet. For I have
given you an example that ye also should do as I
have done to you. Verily I say unto you, the
servant is not greater than his lord, neither is he that
is sent greater than he that sent him. A new commandment give I unto you, that ye love one another;
as I have loved you, that ye also love one another.
Hereby shall all men know that ye are my disciples,
if ye have love one to another. This is my commandment, that ye love one another as I have loved you.
Greater love hath no man than this, that a man lay
down his life for his friends. Ye are my friends, if
ye do that which I command you. Ye have not
chosen me, but I have chosen you. Henceforth I
call you not servants, for the servant knoweth not
what his lord doeth ; but I have called you friends,
for all things that I hear of my Father I make known
unto you. These things I command you, that ye
love one another." [1] All these sentences we may
take as genuine *logia*. Relieved from the separation
which the Evangelist, for the purposes of his long
discourse and its developments, inflicts on them,
simply put together again as by their subject they
belong together, how their effectiveness and impressiveness increases, how heightened is our enjoyment
of them!

And next, as to the right criticism of our Evange-

[1] John xiii. 12-16, 34, 35 ; xv. 12-17.

list's mode of procedure. Let us take another theme,
the primitive theme for all which is said about the
disciples' requests being granted, the words : " Whatsoever ye shall ask in my name, I will do it." [1] Let
us put with these words all the scattered repetitions
of this same theme, some of them with a little variation, others in words almost identical with the *logion*
we have quoted. When we see them all together, we
see that by all the repetitions nothing is really added,
either in the substance or in the form of expression,
to the primitive theme ;—nothing is gained. The
primitive theme, then, alone is from Jesus. The
repetitions are our Evangelist's, to enable Jesus to
make a long, connected speech, such as Jesus never
dealt in, such as is quite alien to his manner. Now,
it is argued that the *logia* proper to the Fourth Gospel
are all of them inventions, because they are unmean-
ingly and vainly repeated. But is the ineffective repetition, several times, of a *logion*, any reason why Jesus
should not have given it with effect once ?

The same with the sayings of Jesus about his glory.
It is argued that the frequent and earnest insistence
on his glory, particularly in the long prayer of the
seventeenth chapter, is not at all in the style of Jesus
and cannot be his. As the Evangelist presents and
develops it, we will own it cannot. But let us put
together all the sayings of Jesus about his glory, going
back for this purpose as far even as the eleventh
chapter, where is the first apparition of them, and we
shall be able to see, both what Jesus may probably

[1] John xiv. 13.

have said on the subject, and how the Evangelist has
probably dealt with it. First of all, we find a primitive theme entirely in the style of Jesus, in his
exclamation when he heard from Andrew and Philip
of the Gentiles, or, as our Evangelist calls them, the
Greeks, present at the last Passover that he kept and
desirous to see him : " The hour is come that the Son
of Man should be glorified !" [1] In all the Four Gospels there is not a saying of Jesus more safe to accept
than this, more perfectly in character. To Jesus,
these foreigners desiring to see him were the Gentiles,
the nations. The Messiah, of whom the Jews had
their minds full, he steadfastly identified, we know,
with the mild and stricken Servant of prophecy, "his
visage so marred more than any man, and his form
more than the sons of men," [2] and himself with this
Messiah. He knew that the victory of this Messiah
and of his cause could only come when he had " poured
out his soul unto death." [3] What was that victory ?
It was the foundation, and henceforth unconquerable
institution for the world at large, of the kingdom of
God, the reign of righteousness. " The Eternal will
cause righteousness and praise to spring forth before
all nations ; I will set my glory among the heathen ;
from the rising of the sun even unto the going down
of the same my name shall be great among the Gentiles." [4] But to bring in the reign of righteousness,
was to bring in the Eternal's glory ; and the Servant
who brought in this, founded his own by doing so.

[1] John xii. 23.   [2] Isaiah lii. 14.   [3] Isaiah liii. 12.
[4] Isaiah lxi. 11 ; Ezekiel xxxix. 21 ; Malachi i. 11.

We may conceive of many and various texts as contributing here.   Texts originally proper to the despised Servant, the Messias-ideal of Jesus : " So shall many nations exult in him ; kings shall shut their mouth before him." [1]   Texts originally proper to the renewed Israel : " The Gentiles shall see thy righteousness, and all kings thy glory." [2]   Texts originally proper to the righteous man in general : " Thou shall guide me with thy counsel, and afterwards receive me to glory." [3] Texts originally proper to the conquering Root of David, the Messias-ideal of the Jews : " His rest shall be glory." [4]   All these we may conceive as present and contributory in the mind of Jesus, when, seeing his death imminent, and hearing at the same time of the strangers desirous to see him, he said : "The hour is come that the Son of Man should be glorified !"

But once this primitive theme given, how natural that our Evangelist should harp upon it, recur to it, develop it !   The whole seventeenth chapter may be called a development of this theme, and of one other : *That they may be one as we are one !* [5]   It is as much in character for a disciple to love to prolong the theme of Christ's glory and dilate upon it, as it is little in character for Jesus himself to do so.   And the mode of development followed is just the mode tempting to a disciple,—Jew or Greek,—of Jesus, but never adopted or encouraged by Jesus himself.

---

[1] Isaiah lii. 15.   [2] Isaiah lxii. 2.
[3] Psalm lxxiii. 24.   [4] Isaiah xi. 10.
[5] ἵνα ὦσιν ἓν καθὼς ἡμεῖς.   See John xvii. 11, 21-23.

Jesus checked questions of theosophy. He contented himself with taking the conception of God as the Jews had it, and as the Old Testament delivered it, as the eternal and righteous Father; and with saying of himself: "I came forth from God," "God sent me." But questions of theosophy had and have, as we see by the history of Gnosticism, and, indeed, by the whole history of religion, an irresistible attraction for the human mind. Men asked themselves, as Tertullian says, *Unde Deus?*—and they loved to inquire, in like manner, precisely how was Jesus related to his Father who sent him. In a famous passage in the Book of Proverbs, Wisdom says of herself: "The Lord possessed me in the beginning of his way before his works of old; I was set up from everlasting. I was by him as one brought up with him, and I was daily his delight." [1] The Book of Wisdom, a late work, but for that very reason more likely to be popular, and of which in the Epistle to the Hebrews we can see the influence, added these striking traits: "Wisdom is the breath of the power of God, and a pure influence flowing from the glory of the Almighty. She is the brightness of the everlasting light, the unspotted mirror of the power of God, and the image of his goodness." [2] Eagerly did theosophy possess itself of these images, and spin its fancies by the help of two supposed personages, *Sophia* and *Logos*, the Wisdom and Word of God. Jesus spoke of himself as uttering

[1] Prov. viii. 22, 23, 30.

[2] *Wisdom* vii. 25, 26. Compare ἀπαύγασμα φωτὸς ἀϊδίου . . . καὶ εἰκὼν τῆς ἀγαθότητος αὐτοῦ, in this passage, with Heb. i. 3: ἀπαύγασμα τῆς δόξης καὶ χαρακτὴρ τῆς ὑποστάσεως αὐτοῦ.

the word of God; but that he called himself the
Logos, there is neither indication nor probability.
There is, however, some trace of his calling himself
the *wisdom* of God.   At least, a saying of the First
Gospel, "Wherefore, behold, *I* send unto you prophets
and wise men and scribes,"[1] is given in the Third
Gospel in the following different and remarkable form:
"Wherefore also *the wisdom of God* said, I will send
unto them prophets and apostles."[2]   It is possible
that we have here a trace of Jesus having really and
naturally, on at least one occasion, called himself "the
wisdom of God," and having to that extent seemed to
give countenance to the personifying lucubrations upon
these terms *Sophia* and *Logos*,—the Wisdom, Reason,
or Word, of God,—of both Jewish and Greek theosophy.   It is possible; possible that our Evangelist,
in developing what Jesus said of his glory, had thus
much to go upon,[3] as well as *logia* like "Before Abraham was, I am," and "I and the Father are one."[4]
At any rate, the glory of Jesus was made to accord
with that of the *Sophia* or *Logos* of theosophical speculation, and with the attributes assigned to them by
Scripture.   And so we have Jesus made to say: "And
now, Father, glorify thou me beside thine own self
with the glory which I had beside thee before the world

---

[1] Matt. xx. 34.   [2] Luke xi. 49.

[3] Perhaps, however, Jesus was simply referring to a well-known
phrase of prophecy: "I have sent unto you all my servants the
prophets, rising up early and sending them; but ye have not
inclined your ear nor hearkened unto me" (see Jeremiah xxxv.
15), and did not mean either *the Wisdom of God* or the *I* to stand
for himself.   [4] John viii. 58, and x. 30.

was."[1] We have him saying: "Father, that which thou
hast given me, I will that they also be with me where
I am, that they may see my glory which thou gavest
me because thou lovedst me before the foundation of
the world."[2]   These things are not at all in the
manner of Jesus.   Jesus, as we have said, never theo-
sophised.   Not thus did he employ Scripture, not
thus did he establish his divinity, not thus did he
conceive his glory.   But it is entirely in the manner
of our Evangelist.   And this is the good of putting
together everything which relates to a primitive theme;
because we then are enabled to perceive clearly, both
how simple and characteristic was the original nucleus
given by Jesus, and also how naturally the additions
to it which perplex us may have arisen from the
manipulation by the Evangelist of this given nucleus,
from his expansions and developments of it.

VII.

The seventeenth chapter is one where these expansions and developments appear to exceed considerably
in amount the original nucleus.   This is by no means
always the case in our Evangelist's report of the
sayings of Jesus.   But in his report of miracles, and
indeed in all reports of miracles, we may safely take
it that the additions exceed the original nucleus of
fact very largely.   We said in our first chapter, that
the suspension or diminution of hunger, when the

[1] John xvii. 5.
[2] John xvii. 24.   The Vatican manuscript is followed.

attention is absorbed and the interest excited, was quite basis enough for the story of the miraculous feeding of the thousands.   The answer has positively been hazarded, that no absorption or excitement could enable five thousand people to satisfy themselves upon five loaves and two fishes, and to leave twelve baskets full of fragments.   As if the details of a miraculous story had the sort of solidity which would warrant one in thus gravely arguing upon them ! as if any one who has come to distrust miracles trusts all the circumstances related for them and only distrusts the final result !   It is in the circumstances that the legend consists, that the creative power of the imagination shows itself active.   Granted that a starting-point and a hint of fact for the miracles related in our Gospels there has nearly always been, yet in nine cases out of ten we shall probably err if we imagine we can now seize even this hint of fact; it was so slight in the first instance, and has been so buried under the additions.

We have already remarked how perhaps the sole nucleus of solid fact for the miraculous incidents at Christ's baptism was that weird light on Jordan mentioned in the Apocryphal Gospels.   Sometimes the nucleus for a miracle was afforded, not improbably, by some saying of Jesus.   Perhaps this is the true way of accounting for the miracle of the raising of Lazarus.   The miracle of the raising of Lazarus has been the theme of endless disquisition; every detail of it has been canvassed with elaborate minuteness.   What part of the details is solid we shall never know. But it may safely be said, that, the human mind being what it is and stories of miracle arising as they do, the juxtaposition of one or two sayings of Jesus is sufficient, to an investigator willing to look at things simply, to account for the whole miracle. Let us try to effect this juxtaposition.

The crowning moment in the career of Jesus, as Jesus himself construed and connected his own career, had arrived,—the moment for " the Messiah to suffer and to enter into his glory." [1] *The hour is come that the Son of Man should be glorified !* [2] At this moment Jesus is told of the death of a faithful disciple and friend. He says to his followers : *Our friend Lazarus sleepeth ; I go to awake him.* [3] To the eye of Jesus, the kingdom of God, the reign of the saints, the introduction and triumph of everlasting righteousness,— that triumph in which re-live all the saints who are dead, and the saints who are yet alive live for evermore,—was at that moment beginning. The sisters of the departed are plunged in weeping and lamentation ; Jesus says to Martha : *Thy brother shall rise again.* [4] Not with the bodily resurrection which Martha and the popular religion of Palestine then expected, and which the popular religion of Christendom expects now ;—this materialism Jesus had to transform, as he had to transform the materialism of the Messias-ideal. Martha, however, imagines that Jesus is speaking of the resurrection in the sense of

---

[1] Luke xxiv. 26.   [2] John xii. 23 ; comp. xi. 4.
[3] John xi. 11.   [4] John xi. 23.

popular religion; but Jesus corrects her.   He corrected her; but his correction was a gleam of light
destined slowly to deepen, not of force at that time
to pierce the darkness.   His words were: *I am the
resurrection and the life; he who believeth on me, though
he die, shall live, and he who liveth and believeth on me
shall never die.*[1]   Out of that very *logion* which thus
points to a wholly new ideal of resurrection,—out of
that *logion*, passed from hearer to hearer, repeated,
brooded over, misapprehended,—grew up, not improbably, the story of the great miracle of resurrection according to the old ideal,—the miracle of the
raising of Lazarus.   That *logion*, with the saying to
Martha, *Thy brother shall rise again;* with the saying
to the disciples, *Our friend Lazarus sleepeth, I go to
awake him;* with some saying of Jesus about his
glory, such as, *The hour is come that the Son of Man
should be glorified!* were the materials out of which
was built up a miraculous tale exactly effacing the
truth which Jesus wished to convey.   *Sed nondum
est finis,* should always be our reflection in these cases.
"The end is not yet;"[2] the space and scale required
for working out the truths of the Bible are very
large.

The developing of miracle out of slight materials
is, however, common to our Evangelist with the
Synoptics.   Baur opposes these to our Evangelist in
such a fashion, that one is sometimes tempted to ask
whether he supposes, then, that the Synoptics are
historical.   They have, indeed, over our Evangelist

---

[1] John xi. 25, 26.   [2] Matt. xxiv. 6.

certain advantages already noticed; but historical
they are no more than he is. A creative pressure on
incidents they all alike exercise. A creative pressure,
too, on the sayings of Jesus, the Synoptics as well as
our Evangelist exercise, though in a different manner
from his. Nay, sometimes he is more historical than
the Synoptics. If we think of it seriously, for the
words spoken by Jesus during his agony in the
garden [1] the Synoptics could not possibly have had
evidence, since the only companions of Jesus were
asleep when the reported words were spoken. Their
real source, probably, the Fourth Gospel discovers to
us. This Gospel gives us two utterances of Jesus,
made, one of them shortly before his arrest, the other
at the moment of it. "Now is my soul troubled, and
what shall I say: Father save me from this hour?
But for this cause came I unto this hour." [2] And
again: "The cup which my Father hath given me,
shall I not drink it?" [3] We have here, probably, the
true original of the words assigned by the Synoptics
to the prayer of agony in the garden.

Where the Synoptics are more historical than our
Evangelist is in cases where knowledge of Jewish
localities and usages is required. When he varies
from them in such matters, however, it is because
this sort of knowledge is lacking to him, not because
he is warping facts to suit a design. Baur and his
Tübingen school are confident that the truth of their
theory about the Fourth Gospel is quite established

[1] Matt. xxvi. 39, 42.   [2] John xii. 27.
[3] John xviii. 11.

by our Evangelist's account of the Last Supper and
of the Crucifixion. Baur found design in the whole
of it : design to discountenance any observance of the
Passover Supper by Christians, design to identify the
Passover sacrifice with the death of Christ, design to
prove the ending of all things Jewish, the coming-in
of the reign of *Pneuma*, or spirit. But how slight are
his grounds when we examine them !

True, the Synoptics represent the Last Supper as
eaten on the day when the Passover was eaten. This
day was "the fourteenth day of the first month at
even,"[1]—the 14th of the Jewish month of Nisan; and
the Crucifixion they represent as taking place on the
day following, the 15th. True, the Fourth Gospel
represents the Crucifixion as happening on the very
same day on which the Passover was eaten,—on the
14th of Nisan, therefore, not on the 15th. On the
morning of the Crucifixion, the Jews, says our Evangelist, would not enter the Prætorium, "in order that
they might not be defiled, but might eat the Passover;"[2]—that Passover, which, according to the Synoptics, had been eaten the evening before ! The Last
Supper, then, must according to our Evangelist have
been eaten on the 13th of Nisan, not on the 14th; not
on the day appointed for eating the Jewish Passover.

There can be little doubt that the Synoptics, and
not our Evangelist, are right, although the growing
estrangement from things Jewish caused the Christian
Church to explain their testimony away, and to assign
the Crucifixion to the 14th of Nisan. *Christ did not*

[1] Exodus xii. 18.   [2] John xviii. 28.

eat the Paschal Lamb, he suffered as the Paschal Lamb,[1]
was the view which prevailed. In the latter half of
the second century, we find a keen controversy turning,
in fact, upon this,—whether the 14th of Nisan was
the day on which Jesus ate the Last Supper, as the
Passover Supper, with his disciples. The Asiatic
Churches contended that he did ; and Polycrates, the
aged Bishop of Ephesus, appealed[2] to the practice of
the Apostle John, who, he said, had always observed
the 14th as the day on which Jesus, keeping the
Passover Supper, had eaten his last meal with the
Twelve. But the Fourth Gospel puts this last meal
on the 13th. It cannot, then, argues Baur, have proceeded from St. John. It was written by one of the
anti-Jewish party, during the Paschal controversy, to
put a stop to the identification of the Last Supper
with the Jewish Passover.

It is certain that Rome, and the Christian Church
at large, adopted the view that the 14th was the day
of the Crucifixion, not of the Last Supper. There
was, however, for the Church one cause of doubt and
difficulty in the matter. How could it be that St.
John, the author of the Fourth Gospel, kept the 14th
as the day on which Jesus ate the Last Supper ?
This difficulty was got over by supposing that John,
having to do with a number of Jewish Christians, had
accepted, for the sake of peace, their identification of

[1] See *Paschal Chronicle* (edition of Bonn), vol. i. p. 12. οὐκ
ἔφαγεν τὸν νομικὸν ἀμνὸν ἐν ἐκείνῃ τῇ ἡμέρᾳ ὁ κύριος, ἀλλ' αὐτὸς
ἔπαθεν ὡς ἀληθὴς ἀμνός.

[2] In his letter to Victor and the Church of Rome, quoted by
Eusebius, *Hist. Eccles.* v. 24.

the Last Supper with the Passover, although he knew better all the time. In Bede's History, we find our English St. Wilfrid offering to doubters this explanation.[1]

Nothing can be more improbable than that St. John, knowing the observance of the 14th of Nisan as the day of the Last Supper to be an error, should nevertheless have countenanced the error by complying with it in his practice. The tradition that he kept the 14th may well be believed ; but then he must have kept it with the sincere conviction that it was the day of the Last Supper. And so, no doubt, it was. John, then, cannot have written the eighteenth chapter of the Fourth Gospel, cannot have put the Crucifixion on the day when the Passover Supper was to be eaten. This we freely concede to Baur. But does the chapter aim, as Baur imagines, at marking, and marking with a controversial and anti-Jewish intention, an error of the Synoptics about the respective days of the Last Supper and of the Crucifixion? Is this the reason why John, who shared the error of the Synoptics if it was an error, cannot have written the chapter? By no means. St. John cannot have written it for the same reason that he cannot have talked of *Bethany beyond Jordan,* or made the high-priesthood of Caiaphas a yearly office. He cannot have written it because he was a Jew, and exactitude about Jewish days and ceremonies came natural to him. Now, it is simply for want, as it seems to us, of this exactitude, that the Fourth Gospel

[1] Bede, *Hist. Eccles.* iii. 25.

varies from the Synoptics in dating the Last Supper
and the Crucifixion, not from any controversial
design.

John's Greek editor knew Jewish usages, and
liked to import them into his narrative. But he
knew them loosely, as a foreigner, and he sometimes
placed them incoherently. He is like Michelet en-
livening his account of things English with traits of
detail, and meaning to say that at a financial crisis in
London there was "consternation in Change Alley."
That would have been all very well. But Michelet
says, instead of Change Alley, *Alley Change*. Perhaps neither a Greek nor a Frenchman could ever
bring himself to learn with minute accuracy the details of any civilisation not his own. John's Greek
editor knew the Jewish scrupulosity, and that a Jew
in a state of defilement could not eat the Passover.
He takes the occasion of Jesus being carried before
Pilate to exhibit this piece of knowledge, and says
that the Jews could not enter the Prætorium with
Jesus, for fear they should be defiled and hindered
from eating the Passover. He does not observe that
he is thus contradicting the common tradition and
the Synoptics, who represent the Passover as being
eaten, not on the evening of the day of Christ's Crucifixion, but on the evening of the day before. Yet it
may surely be seen, except by people bent on finding
mountains in mole-hills, that he does not *mean* to
contradict the Synoptics ; for he calls the day of the
Crucifixion the Preparation Day,[1] as they do. The

[1] John xix. 31.

Preparation Day was the day intervening between the 14th of Nisan and the Sabbath. If Jesus was crucified on the 14th of Nisan, the day for eating the Passover, that day could not at the same time be the Preparation Day, the day subsequent to the day for eating the Passover, and coming between that day and the Sabbath.

The truth is, on these topics of Jewish doings and ceremonies, our Greek editor is rather in a haze. Thus he talks of putting *a sponge on hyssop* [1] where the Synoptics talk of putting *a sponge on a cane*.[2] Hyssop is the Hebrew name for a plant probably something like our marjoram, with a close, bunching head of flowers, which can serve for a mop or a sponge. To talk of putting a sponge on hyssop is, therefore, like talking of putting a sponge on sponge. But our Greek editor knew the connection of hyssop with "the blood of sprinkling," and did not clearly know what hyssop was; so he makes it do duty for the cane of the Synoptics. He has no profound dogmatic design to represent the death of Christ otherwise than as the Synoptics represented it; but his hold on Jewish details is less firm than theirs, and his use of Jewish details more capricious.

Again, the whole story of the soldier piercing the side of Jesus with his spear is said by Baur to be an invention of our Evangelist with the design of identifying Jesus with the Paschal Lamb (*a bone of him shall not be broken !*), and of mystically representing, by the

[1] John xix. 29.　　[2] Matt. xxvii. 48 ; Mark xv. 36.

effusion of water and blood, the apparition of the new
powers of *Logos* and *Pneuma.* No other Evangelist
mentions the incident, argues Baur. The quotation
from Exodus [1] shows what was in the writer's mind ;
and Apollinaris of Hierapolis, taking part in the
Paschal controversy soon after the year 170 of our
era, marks the figurative character of the incident,
identifies Christ with the Paschal Lamb slain on the
14th of Nisan, and the water and blood with *Logos*
and *Pneuma.*[2]

Now, the argument, that if an important thing in
the Fourth Gospel is not found in the Synoptics also,
it must be a mere invention of our Evangelist's, is
always pressed by Baur against our Evangelist only.
But why is it more incredible that the piercing of
Christ's side, though given in the Fourth Gospel alone,
should yet really have been matter of tradition, than
that the last words of Jesus : *Father, into thy hands I
commend my spirit,* which are in Luke only,[3] should
proceed, not from Luke's own invention, but from a
real tradition ! Nor has the quotation : *A bone of
him shall not be broken,*[4] in all probability the reference
alleged. Not Exodus or the Paschal Lamb is probably here in our Evangelist's mind, but one of the
Psalms on the preservation of the righteous : *Thou
keepest all his bones, so that not one of them is broken.*[5]
The form of the Greek verb corresponds with the

---

[1] Exod. xii. 46.

[2] ἡ ιδ' τὸ ἀληθινὸν τοῦ κυρίου πάσχα, says Apollinaris ; and
presently afterwards : ὁ ἐκχέας ἐκ τῆς πλευρᾶς αὐτοῦ τὰ δύο
πάλιν καθάρσια, ὕδωρ καὶ αἷμα, λόγον καὶ πνεῦμα.

[3] Luke xxiii. 46.   [4] John xix. 36.   [5] Psalm xxxiv. 20.

form in this passage from the Psalms,[1] not in the passage from Exodus; which latter passage runs: "Ye shall not break a bone thereof." Besides, the Evangelist is heaping together instances of the fulfilment of predictions made by Prophet and Psalmist, and to suppose him suddenly turning to the Law and its precepts is not natural.

It is most probable that the side-piercing, followed by the appearance of something thought to resemble blood and water, was really, like our Evangelist's incidents in general, given by tradition. As early as Justin's time, nay, as early as the date of the Apocalypse, the passage from Zechariah,[2] which in the Greek Bible was mis-translated to mean: *They shall turn their eyes towards me in exchange for their insulting,*[3] had been altered to its true meaning: *They shall look on whom they pierced,* as it stands in the Fourth Gospel.[4] This proves, it is true, nothing as to the antiquity of the Fourth Gospel. Passages of the Old Testament which had a Messianic sense were early, as we have said already, corrected to bring this sense out, if before they obscured it. But it proves the antiquity of some tradition of a piercing which the passage in Zechariah suited. If the piercing had been merely that of the hands and feet

---

[1] συντριβήσεται, and not συμτρίψετε. Some later manuscripts of the New Testament show the pressure to connect John xix. 36 with Exod. xii. 46, rather than with Ps. xxxiv. 20. See in Sabatier, *Bibliorum Sacrorum Latinæ Versiones Antiquæ,* his note on the verse in John. [2] Zechariah xii. 10.

[3] ἐπιβλέψονται πρός με ἀνθ' ὧν κατωρχήσαντο.

[4] John xix. 37. ὄψονται εἰς ὃν ἐξεκέντησαν.

by the nails, as given by one of the Messianic Psalms,
the Greek verb of that Psalm would probably have
been used for the prophecy of Zechariah also; now,
a different verb is taken.[1]

We do not at all deny that the identification of
Christ's sacrifice with the Paschal sacrifice was a conception entertained by our Evangelist, who speaks of
the Lamb of God that taketh away the sin of the world.[2]
It was a conception familiar also to Paul,[3] and a conception just and natural. What we deny is that it
has become with our Evangelist, any more than with
Paul, the nucleus of a theory for which he combines,
arranges, invents. In the Paschal controversy in the
latter part of the second century, the idea had become
a nucleus of this kind. There is no doubt as to what
Apollinaris makes our Evangelist's words mean, any
more than there is doubt as to what Baur makes our
Evangelist's words mean. But, if our Evangelist had
really meant what Apollinaris and Baur find in his
words, he would have expressed himself somewhat as
they do, he would have shown his intention as they
do. Now, he expresses himself so very differently.
Therefore we cannot credit him with the mystic
meaning and design they suppose for him. "The
14th is the true Passover of the Lord," says Apollinaris: "the great sacrifice, the Son of God in the
lamb's stead." Again: "His holy side was pierced,
and he shed back out of his side the two cleansers,

---

[1] ἐξεκέντησαν instead of ὤρυξαν. See, in the Greek Bible,
Psalm xxi. 16.

[2] John i. 29.   [3] See 1 Cor. v. 7.

water and blood, *word and spirit*."[1] There is no
uncertainty about the writer's intention, here; and
if our Evangelist had invented his Gospel to serve
the same intention, that intention would have been
as manifest. Probably, however, what the water
and blood figured to our Evangelist's mind was not
logos and *pneuma* at all, but,—as the First Johannine
Epistle indicates, and as Theophylact interpreted,[2]—
the union of the human and divine natures in Christ.
The water was a kind of celestial ichor, the blood was
the blood of mortal man.

VIII.

Tried fairly, then, and without a preconceived
theory to warp our criticism, the Fourth Gospel
comes out no fancy-piece, but a serious and invaluable document, full of incidents given by tradition
and of genuine "sayings of the Lord."

Sayings are not to be rejected as inventions too
easily. They are not to be rejected because they
seem strong and harsh, and we do not like them.
For example, there is the saying of Jesus to the
Jews about *their father the devil:* "He was a man-

---

[1] See the fragment of Apollinaris in Otto, *Corpus Apolo-
getarum Christianorum Sæculi Secundi*, vol. ix. p. 487; with
the notes in that work both to the fragments of Apollinaris
and to those of Melito of Sardis.

[2] In his Commentary on the Fourth Gospel. His words
are : τὸ μὲν αἷμα σύμβολον τοῦ εἶναι ἄνθρωπον τὸν σταυρωθέντα,
τὸ δὲ ὕδωρ ὑπὲρ ἄνθρωπον, τοῦ εἶναι θεόν.

slayer from the beginning." [1]   Its violence is objected
to.   But the Peratæ quote it in substance, and that
is an external testimony to its genuineness; the
invectives against the Scribes and Pharisees in the
Synoptics make it a not improbable saying in itself.

Neither are sayings to be rejected because they
are profound, and over their hearers' heads; as, for
example, the saying: "Before Abraham was, I am." [2]
Ever since man appeared upon earth, the clearing and
saving influences, which constitute the very being of
Jesus, have been present and at work amongst mankind; often they have been latent, but they have
been always there.   And always has this gentle and
healing virtue saved, and always has it been sacri-
ficed; therefore Jesus was well called by Apostle
and Seer, and well too might he have called himself:
The lamb slain from the foundation of the world. [3]   When
he said to the Jews, "Before Abraham was, I am,"
Jesus then did but pursue, as he pursued on so many
other occasions also, his lofty treatment of the themes
of life and immortality, while his hearers stuck fast
in their materialistic notions of them, and failed to
follow his real meaning.   In this there is nothing
strange or incredible.

Nor, finally, are sayings to be rejected because
they accommodate themselves to the materialism of
the disciples.   Only under these familiar figures of
a bodily resurrection and a visible judgment-assize,
of sitting on thrones to try the twelve tribes of Israel,

---

[1] John viii. 44.   [2] John viii. 58.
[3] Rev. xiii. 8; 1 Peter i. 19, 20.

of a heavenly Father's house with many mansions, could Jesus convey the ideas of happiness and recompense to these materialistically trained children of the new birth, whom yet to raise out of their materialism he for ever strove. If he was to say to them nothing but either what they could perfectly follow, or what they could not possibly misunderstand, he could not, as we have more than once said, have spoken to them at all. The only sayings we are called upon to reject are those which contradict the known manner and scope of Jesus, as his manner and scope are established for us by the mass of the evidence existing.

But we do not require our reader, even, to be so chary as we ourselves have been, about admitting sayings of the Fourth Gospel as genuine. If he finds himself disposed to receive as genuine some sayings of Jesus at which we hesitate, so be it. For we have sought merely to establish a minimum of what must be received, not a maximum; to show, that after the most free criticism has been fairly and strictly applied, and all deductions, to the very outside of what such a criticism can require, have been fully made, there is yet left an authentic residue comprising all the profoundest, most important, and most beautiful things in the Fourth Gospel.

We have found, however, in our study of the Fourth Gospel, nothing to shake our opinion about the canonical Gospels in general and their history, but everything to confirm it. For at least fifty years after its production the Fourth Gospel appears not to have been in the settled state of Holy Scripture.

There was a long period during which this Gospel yielded more easily to pressure, whether for altering its first contents or for interpolating additions to them, than it did afterwards.   And so with our other three Gospels also.

The rudiments of all four Gospels were probably in existence and current by the year 120 of our era, at the very latest.   As we accept the evidence of Basileides, to show that the Fourth Gospel in some shape or other already existed in the early part of the second century, so we accept the evidence of Marcion to show the same thing for the Third Gospel, and that of Papias for the Second and First.[1]   True, the description given by Papias does not accurately characterise our present Gospels either of Mark or Matthew.[2]   But the hypothesis of other works of theirs being meant is extremely improbable, while it is not at all improbable that between the first appearance of a Gospel and its admission to canonicity it should have undergone alterations.   The final admission of a Gospel to canonicity proves that it has long been in men's hands, and long been attributed to a venerable authority; that it has had time to gain their affections and to establish its superiority over competing accounts.   To suppose as the originals of our First and Second Gospels such collections by Matthew and Mark as are described by Papias; to

---

[1] See Eusebius, *Hist. Eccles.* iii. 39.

[2] Papias says of Matthew : τὰ λόγια συνεγράψατο.   Of Mark he says that he wrote, ἀκριβῶς, οὐ μέντοι τάξει, τὰ ὑπὸ τοῦ Χριστοῦ ἢ λεχθέντα ἢ πραχθέντα.   See the chapter of Eusebius just cited.

suppose as the original of our Third Gospel (which
in its prologue tells us itself that in its present form
it is not the work of an eye-witness but of a writer
with two stages, even, between him and the eye-
witnesses[1]) a work by the same hand from whence
proceed those records in the first person which crop
out in the Acts ; to suppose as the original of our
Fourth Gospel data furnished by John at Ephesus,—
is at once agreeable to what traditions we have, and
also the most natural way of accounting for the facts
which present themselves.

But to suppose that in our present Four Gospels
we have the original works as they at first stood,
that they were at their first birth formed into a
Canon and thereby protected from alteration, is contrary both to the direct evidence we have and to
probability.   The descriptions of Papias do not, as
we have said, at all well describe our present Gospels
of St. Matthew and St. Mark.   And we see that our
Gospels had gradually to establish themselves, because
before the time of Irenæus they are hardly ever
quoted as Scripture, but after his time constantly.
We know, too, that there were several other Gospels
besides these, and that works not in our present
Canon enjoyed such favour among Christians of the
second century that even Irenæus quotes the *Pastor*
of Hermas as "Scripture,"[2] and a so-called Gospel of

---

[1] The first stage is from the writer of our Third Gospel to
the πολλοί, whose διηγήσεις he criticises ; the second from these
πολλοί to the αὐτόπται, the original eye-witnesses.

[2] And in remarkable emphatic language : καλῶς οὖν εἶπεν ἡ

Peter was publicly read in Church with episcopal sanction.[1] We know, above all, that there is no instance,—not one,—before the age of Irenæus and the last quarter of the second century, of even two or three consecutive verses being anywhere quoted just as we now read them in our Gospels.

Nay, so little were our Gospels documents sacred from the very first against all change and interpolation, that the habit of interpolation went on along after the Canon was formed, and the difference between the received text and that of the earliest manuscripts shows it. If the Vatican and Sinaitic manuscripts of the Fourth Gospel contain neither the story of the woman taken in adultery nor the account of the angel troubling the water in the pool of Bethesda; if, where the later manuscripts which our received text follows make Peter say : " Thou art the Christ, the Son of the living God," the Vatican and Sinaitic make him say merely : " Thou art the holy one of God ; "[2] and if this sort of change could befall a Gospel-text between the fourth century and the tenth, while it was Holy Scripture beyond question ; how strong must have been the original bent to additions and interpolations, and how much more must

γραφὴ ἡ λέγουσα, κ. τ. λ. The words of Irenæus are quoted by Eusebius, *Hist. Eccles.* v. 8.

[1] The bishop was Serapio, Bishop of Antioch from A.D. 191 to 213; the church was that of Rhossus in Cilicia. Serapio discovered afterwards that there was Docetism in the gospel of which he had inadvertently permitted the public reading. See Eusebius, *Hist. Eccles.* vi. 12.

[2] John vi. 69.

the text have been exposed to them in its earlier and less closely watched period, when the settled stamp of Holy Scripture it as yet had not!

To suppose, therefore, that we have in our Gospels documents which can stand as the very original, strictly drawn up, strictly authenticated and strictly preserved depositions of eye-witnesses, is absurd. They arose not in the sort of world where depositions are taken, nor in the sort of world where manuscripts are guarded. They arose, and they passed many years, in the immense, underground, obscure, fluctuating world of the common people. Probably even neighbours and contemporaries never knew, or cared to know, quite accurately, the literary history of a document like one of our Gospels; and beyond question the knowledge, if it ever existed, was soon lost irrecoverably. The important inference to be drawn from this is, that the internal evidence must, in sayings and doings of Jesus which are given us in our Gospels, be considered with great care. Jesus was far over the heads of his reporters; he is not to be held responsible for their notions, or for all that they may make him do or say. And the way in which our Gospels arose and grew up was such, that pressure upon the stock of data furnished by the original eye-witnesses, and additions to this stock, and insertions, were extremely natural and extremely easy.[1]

---

[1] Nothing can be more vain, therefore, than attempts to *reconcile* our Four Gospels with one another, to make one exact, concordant and trustworthy history out of them. Griesbach,

In each of the chief Epistles of St. Paul, we have, much more indubitably than in any other New Testament documents, the real original production of the assumed author. Letters like his, with the strong stamp of the author's individuality, and following in general a continuous argument, lend themselves to additions and interpolations far less readily than works like the Gospels. We know, however, that forged epistles, covering themselves with the authority of apostolic names, were early current ; and here too, therefore, the internal evidence must have great weight. The exact literary history of our documents is irrecoverable ; and in the absence of it we cannot but have recourse to the test of internal evidence. But we ought, also, to resign ourselves to be ignorant of much, we ought to be sparing of vigorous and rigorous theories, to allow something to tradition, to dismiss the notion of sheer, designed forgery and imposture, to admit that for each and every Epistle, perhaps, in our Canon of the New Testament, there is something of a genuine basis.

Striking phrases from apostolic letters or addresses were likely to survive and float in men's memories

to whom the improvement of the New Testament text owes so much, has, in some remarks directed simply at the chronology of the Gospels, passed an excellent general criticism on all such attempts. He says : " Valde dubito, an ex Evangelistarum libellis harmonica componi possit narratio ; quid enim, si nullus Evangelistarum ordinem temporis accurate ubique secutus est ; et si sufficientia non adsunt indicia e quibus constare possit quisnam et quibusnam in locis a chronologico ordine recesserit ? Atque in hac me esse hæresi fateor."

though their context had been lost. Here was the
hint and at the same time the defence for an imitator,
speaking in an Apostle's name, and, as he imagined,
in that Apostle's sense. Everything is against the
genuineness of the Second Petrine Epistle as a whole.
But things like the phrase : "Give diligence to make
your calling and election sure," in the first chapter,[1]
and the passage beginning at the eighth verse of the
third chapter and ending with the words : "Nevertheless we, according to his promise, look for new
heavens and a new earth, wherein dwelleth righteousness," may well have been Peter's, and their incorporation would have, probably, quite served to justify
the Epistler both in his own eyes and in those of his
public.

It is easy to be too sweepingly negative in these
matters; easy, also, to think we can know more about
them, and more certainly, than we can. To us it
appears very rash to pronounce confidently against
the First Johannine Epistle being St. John's. Certainly there is the difficulty of a Galilean fisherman
learning to write Greek after the age of fifty ; but,
with this exception, almost all the difficulties are
absent which make it so hard to think that St. John
can have written the Fourth Gospel. The style is
not flowing and articulated ; the sentences come like
minute-guns as they would drop from a natural
Hebrew. The writer moves, indeed, amidst that
order of religious ideas which meets us in the Fourth
Gospel, and which was that of the Greek world

---

[1] 2 Peter i. 10.

wherein he found himself.   He moves amongst these
new ideas, however, not with the practised facility of
the Evangelist, but with something of helplessness,
although the depth and serene beauty of his spirit
give to all he says an infinite impressiveness and
charm.   Save one ambiguous expression of Eusebius,[1]
there is nothing to indicate that John's authorship of
the First Epistle was in the early Church ever ques-
tioned.   Papias used the Epistle,[2] and it may fairly
be inferred from what Epiphanius says[3] that even
the Alogi received it, although they rejected both the
Fourth Gospel and the Apocalypse.

Of the authorship of the Apocalypse, all we can
safely assert is what we learn from the book itself,—
that the author was named John, and wrote in Asia.
It was natural that this John in Asia, the recipient
of so weighty a revelation, should be identified with
the Apostle John, and as early as the middle of the
second century we find Justin Martyr thus identifying him.[4]   But there was so little sureness about the
matter, that for Eusebius, in the fourth century, the

---

[1] *Hist. Eccles.* vi. 14.   μηδὲ τὰς ἀντιλεγομένας παρελθών,
τὴν Ἰούδα λέγω καὶ τὰς λοιπὰς καθολικὰς ἐπιστολάς.   The word
λοιπάς is not certain, and even if it were, we could not be sure
from the sentence, Eusebius being the sort of writer he is, that
the First Johannine Epistle was disputed, or that Eusebius
meant to say that it was.

[2] *Hist. Eccles.* iii. 39.

[3] *Hær.* LI. xxxiv.   Epiphanius conjectures that the Alogi
must have rejected the Epistles because they rejected the Gospel
and the Apocalypse.   If they *had* rejected the First Epistle, he
would almost certainly have heard of it.

[4] *Dialogus cum Tryphone*, cap. 81.

Apocalypse was no more than a disputed and doubtful book of Scripture, which a Christian might receive
or not as he thought good. And to us it seems impossible to make out more than that the Apocalypse
was written by a John, but by what John there is
nothing to show.[1]

[1] M. Renan's confident conclusion that the author was the
Apostle John is one of the few points in his admirable criticism
of the Apocalypse where he fails to carry us with him. His
only serious argument is, that no one but an Apostle would
have ventured to speak so authoritatively. But surely the recipient of this grand revelation would, as such, have felt himself entitled to be authoritative to any extent in delivering it.

CONCLUSION.

THE Canon of the New Testament, then, is not what popular religion supposes; although, on the other hand, its documents are in some quarters the object of far too aggressive and sweeping negations. The most fruitful result to be gained from a sane criticism of the Canon is, that by satisfying oneself how the Gospel records grew up, one is enabled the better to account for much that puzzles us in their representation of Jesus,—of his words more especially. There were facilities for addition and interpolation, for adding touches to what the original accounts made Jesus do, for amplifying, above all, what they made Jesus say. Evidence such as apologists always imagine themselves to be using when they appeal to the Gospels,—the pure, first-hand, well-authenticated evidence of eye-witnesses,—our Gospels are not.

Such evidence is, indeed, remarkably wanting for the whole miraculous side in the doings recorded of Jesus. Sometimes we seem to be near getting such evidence, but it vanishes. Jerome tells us that Quadratus, in the second century, declared that there were yet living in his time persons who had beheld with their eyes Jesus raise the dead to life, and that he himself had seen them and spoken with them. It happens that the declaration of Quadratus is preserved by Eusebius, in whose History Jerome probably read it. Quadratus undoubtedly says that in his time there were yet alive those who had witnessed the raising of the dead by Jesus ; but the important addition which alone takes this statement out of the category of hearsay, and makes it personal evidence, —the addition that these alleged witnesses he himself had seen and known,— Quadratus does not make. The addition is merely a rhetorical flourish of Jerome's.[1]

No doubt this is so ; yet the importance of it all is greatly diminished by one consideration. *If we had the original reports of the eye-witnesses, we should still have reports not essentially differing, probably, from those which we now use.* Certain additions which improved a miraculous story as it grew, certain interpolations which belong to the ideas and circumstances of a later age, would be absent. But we should most likely not have a miracle the less, and we should certainly find a similar misapprehension of Jesus and of what he intended. The people who saw Jesus were as certain to seek for miracles, and to find them, as the people who lived a generation or two later, or as the people who resort to Lourdes or to La Salette now. And this preoccupation with miracles was sure to warp their understanding of Jesus, and their report

---

[1] See Eusebius, *Hist Eccles.* iv. 3 ; and Routh, *Reliquiæ Sacræ*, vol. i. pp. 71, 74. Routh quotes Jerome, and points out his exaggeration.

of his sayings and doings. The recurrence, so much talked of and recommended, to the Apostles, or to the first three centuries, for the pure rule of faith and the genuine doctrine of Jesus, is in truth therefore, however natural an expedient, an utterly futile one. There were indeed, as we have shown in *Literature and Dogma*, certain prominent points in the teaching of Jesus which his immediate followers had not yet lost sight of, and which fell more out of view afterwards. But the pure and genuine doctrine of Jesus neither his immediate followers, nor those whom they instructed, could possess ; so immured were they in the ideas of their time and in the belief of the miraculous, so immeasurably was Jesus above them.

II.

But our opponents say : " Everything turns upon the question whether miracles do or did really happen ; and you abstain from all attempt to prove their impossibility, you simply assume that they never happen." And this, which our opponents say, is true, and we have repeatedly admitted it. At the end of this investigation we admit it once more, and lay stress upon it. That miracles *cannot* happen we do not attempt to prove; the demonstration is too ambitious. That they *do not* happen, that what are called miracles are not what the believers in them fancy, but have a natural history of which we can follow the course, the slow action of experience, we say, more and more shows; and shows, too, that there is no exception to be made in favour of the Bible-miracles.

Epiphanius tells us, that at each anniversary of the miracle of Cana, the water of the springs of Cibyra in Caria and Gerasa in Arabia was changed into wine ; that he himself had drunk of the trans-formed water of Cibyra, and his brothers of that of Gerasa.[1] Fifty years ago, a plain Englishman would have had no difficulty in thinking that the Cana miracle was true, and the other two miracles were fables. He is now irresistibly led to class all these occurrences in one category as unsubstantial tales of marvel. Scales seem to drop from his eyes in regard to miracles ; and if he is still to hold fast his Chris-tianity, it must no longer depend upon them.

It was not to discredit miracles that *Literature and Dogma* was written, but because miracles are so widely and deeply discredited already. And it is lost labour, we repeat, to be arguing for or against them. Mankind did not originally accept miracles because it had formal proof of them, but because its imperfect experience inclined it to them. Nor will mankind now drop miracles because it has formal proof against them, but because its more complete experience detaches it from them. The final result was inevitable, as soon as ever miracles began to embarrass people, began to be relegated,—especially the greater miracles,—to a certain limited period long ago over. Irenæus says, that people in his time had arisen from the dead, "and abode with us a good

[1] Epiphanius, *Hær.* LI. xxx.

number of years." [1]   One of his commentators,
embarrassed by such stupendous miracles occurring
outside of the Bible, makes an attempt to explain
away this remarkable allegation ; but the most recent
editor of Irenæus points out, with truth, that the
attempt is vain.   Irenæus was as sure to want and to
find miracles as the Bible-writers were.   And sooner
or later mankind was sure to see how universally and
easily stories like this of Irenæus arose, and that they
arose with the Bible-writers just as they arose with
Irenæus, and are not a whit more solid coming from
them than from him.

A Catholic imagines that he gets over the difficulty
by believing, or professing to believe, the miracles of
Irenæus and Epiphanius, as well as those of the Bible-
writers.   But for him too, even for him, the *Time-
Spirit* is gradually becoming too strong.   As we may
say in general, that, although an educated Protestant
may manage to retain for his own lifetime the belief
in miracles in which he has been brought up, yet his
children will lose it ; so to an educated Catholic we
may say, putting the change only a little farther off,
that (unless some unforeseen deluge should overwhelm
European civilisation, leaving everything to be begun
anew) his grandchildren will lose it.   They will lose
it insensibly, as the eighteenth century saw the
gradual extinction, among the educated classes, of
that belief in witchcraft which in the century previous
a man like Sir Matthew Hale could affirm to have

---

[1] See Irenæus, *Adv. Hær.* lib. II. cap. xxxii. 4 ; with the
note on the passage in Stieren's edition.

the authority of Scripture and of the wisdom of all nations,—spoke of, in short, just as many religious people speak of miracles now. Witchcraft is but one department of the miraculous ; and it was comparatively easy, no doubt, to abandon one department, when men had all the rest of the region to fall back upon. Nevertheless the forces of experience, which have prevailed against witchcraft, will inevitably prevail also against miracles at large, and that by the mere progress of time.

The charge of presumption, and of setting oneself up above all the great men of past days, above " the wisdom of all nations," which is often brought against those who pronounce the old view of our religion to be untenable, springs out of a failure to perceive how little the abandonment of certain long-current beliefs depends upon a man's own will, or even upon his sum of powers, natural or acquired. Sir Matthew Hale was not inferior in force of mind to a modern Chief Justice because he believed in witchcraft. Nay, the more enlightened modern, who drops errors of his forefathers by help of that mass of experience which his forefathers aided in accumulating, may often be, according to the well-known saying, " a dwarf on the giant's shoulders." His merits may be small compared with those of the giant. Perhaps his only merit is, that he has had the good sense to get up on the giant's shoulders, instead of trotting contentedly along in his shadow. Yet even this, surely, is something.

III.

We have to renounce impossible attempts to
receive the legendary and miraculous matter of Scripture as grave historical and scientific fact. We have
to accustom ourselves to regard henceforth all this
part as poetry and legend. In the Old Testament,
as an immense poetry growing round and investing
an immortal truth, the "secret of the Eternal:"[1]
Righteousness is salvation. In the New, as an
immense poetry growing round and investing an
immortal truth, the secret of Jesus: *He that will
save his life shall lose it, he that will lose his life shall
save it.*

The best friends of mankind are those who can
lead it to feel animation and hope in presence of the
religious prospect thus profoundly transformed. The
way to effect this is by bringing men to see that our
religion, in this altered view of it, does but at last
become again that religion which Jesus Christ really
endeavoured to found, and of which the truth and
grandeur are indestructible. We should do Christians generally a great injustice, if we thought that
the entire force of their Christianity lay in the fascination and subjugation of their spirits by the miracles
which they suppose Jesus to have worked, or by the
materialistic promises of heaven which they suppose
him to have offered. Far more does the vital force
of their Christianity lie in the boundless confidence,

[1] Psalm xxv. 14.

consolation, and attachment, which the whole being and discourse of Jesus inspire. What Jesus then himself thought sufficient, Christians too may bring themselves to accept with good courage as enough for them. What Jesus himself dismissed as chimerical, Christians too may bring themselves to put aside without dismay.

The central aim of Jesus was to transform for every religious soul the popular Messias-ideal of his time, the ideal of happiness and salvation of the Jewish people ; to disengage religion, one may say, from the materialism of the Book of Daniel. Fifty years had not gone by after his death, when the Apocalypse replunged religion in this materialism ; where, indeed, it was from the first manifest that replunged, by the followers of Jesus, religion must be. It was replunged there, but with an addition of inestimable value and of incalculable working,—the figure and influence of Jesus. Slowly this influence emerges, transforms the turbid elements amid which it was thrown, brings back the imperishable ideal of its author. To the mind of Jesus, his own resurrection after a short sojourn in the grave was the victory of his cause after his death, and at the price of his death. His disciples materialised his resurrection ; and their version of the matter falls day by day to ruin. But no ruin or contradiction befalls the version of Jesus himself. He *has* risen, his cause has conquered ; the course of events continually attests his resurrection and victory. The manifest unsoundness of popular Christianity inclines at present many

persons to throw doubts on the truth and permanence
of Christianity in general.   Creeds are discredited,
religion is proclaimed to be in danger, the pious
quake, the world laughs.   Nevertheless *the prince of
this world is judged ;* [1] the victory of Jesus is won and
sure.   Conscience and self-renouncement, the method
and the secret of Jesus, are set up as a leaven in the
world, nevermore to cease working until the world is
leavened.   That this is so, that the resurrection and
re-emergent life of Jesus are in this sense undeniable,
and that in this sense Jesus himself predicted them,
may in time, surely, encourage Christians to lay hold
on this sense as Jesus did.

So, too, with the hope of immortality.   Our common materialistic notions about the resurrection of
the body and the world to come are, no doubt, natural
and attractive to ordinary human nature.   But they
are in direct conflict with the new and loftier conceptions of life and death which Jesus himself strove to
establish.   His secret, *He that will save his life shall
lose it, he that will lose his life shall save it,* is of universal
application.   It judges, not only the life to which
men cling here, but just as much the life we love to
promise ourselves in the New Jerusalem.   The immortality propounded by Jesus must be looked for
elsewhere than in the materialistic aspirations of our
popular religion.   *He lived in the eternal order, and the
eternal order never dies ;*—this, if we may try to for-
mulate in one sentence the result of the sayings of
Jesus about life and death, is the sense in which,

[1] John xvi. 11.

according to him, we can rightly conceive of the righteous man as immortal, and aspire to be immortal ourselves. And this conception we shall find to stand us in good stead when the popular materialistic version of our future life fails us. So that here again, too, the version which, unfamiliar and novel as it may now be to us, has the merit of standing fast and holding good while other versions break down, is at the same time the version of Jesus.

People talk scornfully of a "sublimated Christianity," as if the Christianity of Jesus Christ himself had been a materialistic fairy-tale like that of Messrs. Moody and Sankey. On the contrary, insensibly to lift us out of all this sort of materialism was Jesus Christ's perpetual endeavour. The parable of the king, who made a marriage for his son, ends with the episode of the guest who had not on a wedding garment, and was cast out.[1] And here, as usual, the Tübingen critics detect *tendence*. They see in the episode a deliberate invention of the Evangelist; a stroke of Jewish particularism, indemnifying itself for having had to relate that salvation was preached in the highways. We have disagreed often with the Tübingen critics, and we shall venture finally to disagree with them here. We receive the episode as genuine; but what did Jesus mean by it? Shall we not do well in thinking, that he, whose lucidity was so incomparable, and who indicated so much which was to be seized not by the present but by the future, here marked and meant to mark, although but inci-

[1] Matt. xxii. 1-14.

dentally and in passing, the profound, the utter insufficiency of popular religion ? Through the turbid
phase of popular religion his religion had to pass.
Good and bad it was to bear along with it ; the
gross and ignorant were to be swept in, by wholesale,
from the highways ; *the wedding was to be furnished
with guests.* On this wise must Christianity needs
develop itself, and the necessary law of its development was to be accepted. Vain to be too nice about
the unpreparedness of the guests in general, about
their inevitable misuse of the favours which they were
admitted to enjoy ! What could have been the end
of such a fastidious scrutiny ? To turn them all out
into the highways again ! But the king's design
was, that *the wedding should be furnished with guests.*
So the guests shall all stay and fall to ;—popular
Christianity is founded. But presently, almost as if
by accident, a guest even more unprepared and gross
than the common, a guest "not having on a wedding
garment," comes under the king's eye, and is ejected.
Only one is noted for decisive ejection ; but ah ! how
many of those guests are as really unapt to seize and
follow God's designs for them as he ! *Many are called,
few chosen.*

The conspicuous delinquent is sentenced to be
bound hand and foot, and taken away, and cast into
outer darkness. In the severity of this sentence,
Jesus marks how utterly those who are gathered to
his feast may fail to know him. The misapprehending
and materialising of his religion, the long and turbid
stage of popular Christianity, was, however, inevit-

able. But to give light and impulsion to future times, Jesus stamps this Christianity, even from the very moment of its birth, as, though inevitable, not worthy of its name ; as ignorant and transient, and requiring all who would be truly children of the kingdom to rise beyond it.

THE END OF VOL. VI.

Printed by R. & R. CLARK, *Edinburgh.*